BEHAVIORAL ECONOMY THEORY 2 EDITION

JOHN LOK

Copyright © John Lok
All Rights Reserved.

ISBN 979-888606027-0

This book has been published with all efforts taken to make the material error-free after the consent of the author. However, the author and the publisher do not assume and hereby disclaim any liability to any party for any loss, damage, or disruption caused by errors or omissions, whether such errors or omissions result from negligence, accident, or any other cause.

While every effort has been made to avoid any mistake or omission, this publication is being sold on the condition and understanding that neither the author nor the publishers or printers would be liable in any manner to any person by reason of any mistake or omission in this publication or for any action taken or omitted to be taken or advice rendered or accepted on the basis of this work. For any defect in printing or binding the publishers will be liable only to replace the defective copy by another copy of this work then available.

Contents

Foreword

Can apply economic theories to solve any social problems? In some market environments, whether economists can apply any kinds of economical theories to find the consumer behavioral cause and effect relationship and conclude the effect. Can property developers apply invisable hand (demand and supply theory) to explain or predict or solve house buyers renting or house purchase choice. Global houses demand may increase or decrease in any time. The month has many houses can sell easily, but it does not represent next month houses sale number can increase. What factors can influence house buyers' living need desires increase in long time? Why factors can influence house buyers' living need desires decrease in long time? How to apply behavioral economy thery in demand and supply view :demand (house buyer living demand) and supply (houses property developers sale number) to evaluate whether the year has how many house buyers hope to buy houses to live in the country's house market. I shall give reasons and evidences to support my idea. In behavioral economy view, I shall indiate how income factor, living environment factor, social policy factor, illness etc. different factors influence house buyers' demand desires in global housing market. I aims to prove whether house buyers' house purchase living desires will be influenced to change from unpredicted external environmental factor easily in behavioral economic view.

I shall indicate other economic theories to explain some business market behaviors, they may include: The demand and supply (invisible hand), Behavioral economy theory, The Classical Theory, Dependency theory, Colonialism and Neocolonialism Theory, Dependency Theory ,GAME THOERY, Keynesian Economics Theory ,Classical Economics Theory,New Keynesian Theory ,Political Economy,New Political Economy ,International Political Economy ,trickle-down theory, Solow Growth Model: Technology and Productivity,New Growth Theory (Romer & endogenous growth),Marxism theory Laissez-Faire THEORY Market socialism THEORY, Polluter Pays Principle .

Readers can evaluate whether economic theories can be applied to analyse any or some business market behaviors in our daily life really.

Prologue

Table of content

- New trade theory explains e-commerce brings China " one belt, one road strategy compatative advantage
- Competitive advantage applies to globalization e-commerce development brings China " one belt, one road strategy " advantages

CHAPTER ONE

How applying economy theories solve economic problems

Something Behavioral (e.g., Prospect Theory) applies to consumer choice making decision

What Is the Prospect Theory?

Prospect theory assumes that losses and gains are valued differently, and thus individuals make decisions based on perceived gains instead of perceived losses. Also known as the "loss-aversion" theory, the general concept is that if two choices are put before an individual, both equal, with one presented in terms of potential gains and the other in terms of possible losses, the former option will be chosen.

How the Prospect Theory Works

Prospect theory belongs to the behavioral economic subgroup, describing how individuals make a choice between probabilistic alternatives where risk is involved and the probability of different outcomes is unknown. This theory was formulated in 1979 and further developed in 1992 by Amos Tversky and Daniel Kahneman, deeming it more psychologically accurate of how decisions are made when compared to the expected utility theory.

The underlying explanation for an individual's behavior, under prospect theory, is that because the choices are independent and singular, the probability of a gain or a loss is reasonably assumed as being 50/50 instead of the probability that is actually presented. Essentially, the probability of a gain is generally perceived as greater. Although there is no difference in the actual gains or losses of a certain product, the prospect theory says investors will choose the product that offers the most perceived gains.

Tversky and Kahneman proposed that losses cause a greater emotional impact on an individual than does an equivalent amount of gain, so given choices presented two ways—with both offering the same result—an individual will pick the option offering perceived gains. For example, assume that the end result is receiving $25. One option is being given the straight $25. The other option is gaining $50 and losing $25. The utility of the $25 is exactly the same in both options. However, individuals are most likely to choose to receive straight cash because a single gain is generally observed as more favorable than initially having more cash and then suffering a loss.

Types of Prospect Theory

According to Tversky and Kahneman, the certainty effect is exhibited when people prefer certain outcomes and underweight outcomes that are only probable. The certainty effect leads to individuals avoiding risk when there is a prospect of a sure gain. It also contributes to individuals seeking risk when one of their options is a sure loss.

The isolation effect occurs when people have presented two options with the same outcome, but different routes to the outcome. In this case, people are likely to cancel out similar information to lighten the cognitive load, and their conclusions will vary depending on how the options are framed.

•The prospect theory says that investors value gains and losses differently, placing more weight on perceived gains versus perceived losses.

•An investor presented with a choice, both equal, will choose the one presented in terms of potential gains.

•The prospect theory is part of behavioral economics, suggesting investors chose perceived gains because losses cause a greater emotional impact.

•The certainty effect says individuals prefer certain outcomes over probable ones, while the isolation effect says individuals cancel out similar information when making a decision.

Prospect Theory Example

Consider an investor is given a pitch for the same mutual fund by two separate financial advisors. One advisor presents the fund to the investor, highlighting that it has an average return of 12% over the past three years. The other advisor tells the investor that the fund has had above-average returns in the past 10 years, but in recent years it has been declining. Prospect theory assumes that though the investor was presented with the exact same mutual fund, he is likely to buy the fund from the first advisor, who expressed the fund's rate of return as an overall gain instead of the advisor presenting the fund as having high returns and losses.

The economic problem – sometimes called the basic or central economic problem – asserts that an economy's finite resources are insufficient to satisfy all human wants and needs. Economics involves the study of how to allocate resources in conditions of scarcity However, viewing economics as the study of how society allocates resources can lead to conflation of normative economic planning and empirical study of how economic agents operate in these conditions.

In mainstream neoclassical economics, it is assumed that humans pursue their self-interest, and that the market mechanism best satisfies the various wants different individuals might have. These wants are often divided into individual wants (which depend on the individual's preferences and purchasing power parity) and collective wants (which are the wants of entire groups of people). Things such as food and clothing can be classified as either wants or needs, depending on what type and how often a good is requested.

However, economists have sometimes characterized "how" to produce as a "technological problem" of efficiency whereas the allocation of what is produced is an "economic problem". In a free market, the "how" of production and allocation of resources is distributed among economic agents. In a centrally planned economy, a principal decides how and what to produce on behalf of agents. Modern economies are often welfare capitalist with various regulations, which makes the economic system more equitable while retaining the distributed free market system. Due to human wants are unlimited, an infinite series of human wants remains continue with human life. Nobody can claim that all of his wants have been satisfied and he has no need to satisfy any further want. Everybody feels hunger at a time then other he needs water. Sometime one feels the desire of clothing then starts to feel the desire of having good conveyance. When all existing wants are satisfied then new wants starts to create in mind, so the series of wants remains continue till the last moment of life. So an economic problem arises because of existence of unlimited human wants.

- Problem of allocation of resources

The problem of allocation of resources arises due to the scarcity of resources, and refers to the question of which wants should be satisfied and which should be left unsatisfied. In other words, what to produce and how much to produce. More production of a good implies more resources required for the production of that good, and resources are scarce. These two facts together mean that, if a society decides to increase production of some good, it has to withdraw some resources from the production of other goods. In other words, more production of a desired commodity can be made possible only by reducing the quantity of resources used in the production of other goods.

The problem of allocation deals with the question of whether to produce capital goods or consumer goods. If the community decides to produce capital goods, resources must be withdrawn from the production of consumer goods. In the long run, however, [investment] in capital goods augments the production of consumer goods. Thus, both capital and consumer goods are important. The problem is determining the optimal production ratio between the two.

In fact, in our societies, resources are scarce and it is important to use them as efficiently as possible. Thus, it is essential to know if the production and distribution of national product made by an economy is maximally efficient. The production becomes efficient only if the productive resources are utilized in such a way that any reallocation does not produce more of one good without reducing the output of any other good. In other words, efficient distribution means that redistributing goods cannot make anyone better off without making someone else worse off. (See Pareto efficiency.) So, scientists will apply efficient distribution methods to help any countries to earn the absolute advantages when we buy and sell any kinds of products or food between ourselves countries, e.g. when US has good natural resource to grow any food, e.g. potato, wheat , vegetable, cotton , then US can export to sell to China, because China has no any farms to grow agriculture food to supply itself Chinese to eat. So, China must need to buy any agriculture food from US. Otherwise, China has cheap labor to supply to US any manufacturers to help them to manufacture their electronic products. SO, it has many US factories are built in China to let Chinese workers help them to produce their products because their wages are cheaper to compare US workers. So, comparative economic advantage will be choice to apply between US and China both countries. (Absolute advantage trade theory)

The inefficiencies of production and distribution exist in all types of economies. The welfare of the people can be increased if these inefficiencies are ruled out. Some cost must be incurred to remove these inefficiencies. If the cost of removing these inefficiencies of production and distribution is more than the gain, then it is not worthwhile to remove them.

● The problem of full employment of resources

In view of how to use available resources are fully utilized is an important one. A community should achieve maximum satisfaction by using the scarce resources in the best possible manner—not wasting resources or using them inefficiently. There are two types of employment of resources:

(1) Labour-intensive

(2) Capital-intensive

In capitalist economies, however, available resources are not fully used. In times of depression, many people want to work but can't find employment. It supposes that the scarce resources are not fully utilized in a capitalistic economy.

● The problem of economic growth

If productive capacity grows, an economy can produce progressively more goods, which raises the standard of living. The increase in productive capacity of an economy is called economic growth. There are various factors affecting economic growth. The problems of economic growth have been discussed by numerous growth models, including the Harrod-Domar model, the neoclassical growth models of Solow and Swan, and the Cambridge growth models of Kaldor and Joan Robinson. This part of the economic problem is studied in the economies of development.

● Needs and wants problems

Needs are things or material items of peoples need for survival, such as food, clothing, housing, and water. Everyone has a different needs and wants. Until the Industrial Revolution, the vast majority of the world's population struggled for access to basic human needs.

Wants are effective desires for a particular product, or for something that can only be obtained by working for it. While the fundamental needs of survival are key in the function of the economy, wants are the driving force that stimulates demand for goods and services. To curb the economic problem, economists must classify the nature and different wants of consumers, as well as prioritize wants and organize production to satisfy as many wants as possible.

● Five bases problems of economy

In our societies , in general, our societies will have these similar problems The following points highlight the five basic problems of an economy. The problems are: 1. What to Produce and in What Quantities? 2. How to Produce these Goods? 3. For whom is the Goods Produced? 4. How Efficiently are the Resources being utilized? 5. Is the Economy Growing?.

Problem 1:What to Produce and in What Quantities?

The first central problem of an economy is to decide what goods and services are to be produced and in what quantities. This involves allocation of scarce resources in relation to the composition of total output in the economy. Since resources are scarce, the society has to decide about the goods to be produced: wheat, cloth, roads, television, power, buildings, and so on. Once the nature of goods to be produced is decided, then their quantities are to be decided. How many tones of wheat, how many televisions, how many million of power, how many buildings, etc. Since the resources of the economy are scarce, the problem of the nature of goods and their quantities has to be decided on the basis of priorities or preferences of the society.

If the society gives priority to the production of more consumer goods now, it will have less in the future. A higher priority on capital goods implies less consumer goods now and more in the future. But since resources are scarce, if some goods are produced in larger quantities, some other goods will have to be produced in smaller quantities. Suppose the economy produces capital goods and consumer goods. In deciding the total output of the economy, the society has to choose that combination of capital goods and consumer goods which is in keeping with its resources.

Problem 2: How to Produce these Goods?

The next basic problem of an economy is to decide about the techniques or methods to be used in order to produce the required goods. This problem is primarily dependent upon the availability of resources within the economy. If land is available in abundance, it may have extensive cultivation. If land is scarce, intensive methods of cultivation may be used. If labour is in abundance, it may use labour- intensive techniques; while in the case of labour shortage, capital-intensive techniques may be used.

The technique to be used also depends upon the type and quantity of goods to be produced. For producing capital goods and large outputs, complicated and expensive machines and techniques are required. On the other hand, simple consumer goods and small outputs require small and less expensive machines and comparatively simple techniques.

Further, it has to be decided what goods and services are to be produced in the public sector and what goods and services in the private sector. But in choosing between different methods of production, those methods should be adopted which bring about an efficient allocation of resources and increase the overall productivity in the economy.

Problem 3. For whom is the Goods Produced?

The third basic problem to be decided is the allocation of goods among the members of the society. The allocation of basic consumer goods or necessities and luxuries comforts and among the household takes place on the basis of among the distribution of national income. Whosoever possesses the means to buy the goods may have then. A rich person may have a large share of the luxuries goods, and a poor person may have more quantities of the basic consumer goods he needs.

Problem 4: How Efficiently are the Resources being Utilised?

This is one of the important basic problems of an economy because having made the three earlier decisions, the society has to see whether the resources it owns are being utilized fully or not. In case the resources of the economy are lying idle, it has to find out ways and means to utilize them fully.

Problem 5: Is the Economy Growing?

The last and the most important problem is to find out whether the economy is growing through time or is it stagnant. If the economy is stagnant at any point inside the production possibility curve, it has to be moved on to the production possibility curve PP whereby the economy now produces larger quantities of consumer goods and capital goods. Economic growth takes place through a higher rate of capital formation which consists of replacing existing capital goods with new and more productive ones by adopting more efficient production techniques or through innovations.

All of these economy problems will be our societies often causes to anyone feels need to solve problems in order to achieve our societies can have enough resources to satisfy our every day living.

● The Consumer Problem

Consumer theory is concerned with how a rational consumer would make consumption decisions. What makes this problem worthy of separate study, apart from the general problem of choice theory, is its particular structure that allows us to derive economically meaningful results. The structure arises because the consumer's choice sets are assumed to be defined by certain prices and the consumer's income or wealth. The consumer's problem is to choose that is most preferred or, equivalently, that has the greatest utility.

The assumption of perfect information is built deeply into the formulation of this choice problem, just as it is in the underlying choice theory. Some alternative models treat the consumer as rational but uncertain about the products, for example how a particular food will taste or a how well a cleaning product will perform. Some goods may be experience goods which the consumer can best learn about by trying ("experiencing") the good. In that case, the consumer might want to buy some now and decide later whether to buy more. That situation would need a different formulation. Similarly, if the agent thinks that high price goods are more likely to perform in a satisfactory way, that, too, would suggest quite a different formulation. Agents are price-takers. The agent takes prices p as known, fixed and exogenous. This assumption excludes things like searching for better prices or bargaining for a discount.

Hence , it seems that economic problems and consumer problems are similar, I feel that it is possible , economists can attempt to apply any economic theories to solve some consumer problems in some situations. They can find the accurate solutions when they can apply the suitable economic theories to solve the suitable consumer or economic problems in our societies. I shall indicate that how economists can apply the suitable economic theories to attempt to solve some consumer problems in our societies as below:

Permanent Income / Life Cycle Hypothesis predicts consumer behaviors

What Is the Permanent Income Hypothesis?

The permanent income hypothesis is a theory of consumer spending stating that people will spend money at a level consistent with their expected long-term average income. The level of expected long-term income then becomes thought of as the level of "permanent" income that can be safely spent. A worker will save only if his or her current income is higher than the anticipated level of permanent income, in order to guard against future declines in income.

The permanent income hypothesis was formulated by the Nobel Prize-winning economist Milton Friedman in 1957. The hypothesis implies that changes in consumption behavior are not predictable because they are based on individual expectations. This has broad implications concerning

economic policy.
The permanent income hypothesis is a theory of consumer spending stating that people will spend money at a level consistent with their expected long-term average income.
Under this theory, even if economic policies are successful in increasing income in the economy, the policies may not kick off a multiplier effect from increased consumer spending. Rather, the theory predicts there will not be an uptick in consumer spending until workers reform expectations about their future incomes.
How the Permanent Income Hypothesis Works
For example, if a worker is aware that he or she is likely to receive an income bonus at the end of a particular pay period, it is plausible that said worker's spending in advance of that bonus may change in anticipation of the additional earnings. However, it is also possible that workers may choose to not increase their spending based solely on short-term windfall. They may instead make efforts to increase their savings, based on the expected boost in income.
Something similar can be said of individuals who are informed that they are to receive an inheritance. Their personal expenditures could change to take advantage of the anticipated influx of funds, but per this theory, they may maintain their current spending levels in order to save the supplemental assets. Or, they may seek to invest those supplemental funds in order to provide long-term growth of their money rather than spend it immediately on disposable products and services.
The liquidity of the individual can play a role in future income expectations. Individuals with no assets may already be in the habit of spending without regard to their income, current or future. Changes over time, however—through incremental salary raises or the assumption of new long-term jobs that bring higher, sustained pay—can lead to changes in permanent income. With their expectations elevated, employees may allow their expenditures to scale up in turn.
Hence, they are related. The life-cycle hypothesis contains two results: 1. The life-time consumption must equal to the life-time income, which produces Friedman's permanent consumption-income line. 2. The life-time income must be spread evenly over all years of the life, which produces the transitional consumption line.

Something Behavioral (e.g., Prospect Theory) applies to public transport service choice

What Is the Prospect Theory?

Prospect theory assumes that losses and gains are valued differently, and thus individuals make decisions based on perceived gains instead of perceived losses. Also known as the "loss-aversion" theory, the general concept is that if two choices are put before an individual, both equal, with one presented in terms of potential gains and the other in terms of possible losses, the former option will be chosen.

How the Prospect Theory Works

Prospect theory belongs to the behavioral economic subgroup, describing how individuals make a choice between probabilistic alternatives where risk is involved and the probability of different outcomes is unknown. This theory was formulated in 1979 and further developed in 1992 by Amos Tversky and Daniel Kahneman, deeming it more psychologically accurate of how decisions are made when compared to the expected utility theory.

The underlying explanation for an individual's behavior, under prospect theory, is that because the choices are independent and singular, the probability of a gain or a loss is reasonably assumed as being 50/50 instead of the probability that is actually presented. Essentially, the probability of a gain is generally perceived as greater. Although there is no difference in the actual gains or losses of a certain product, the prospect theory says investors will choose the product that offers the most perceived gains.

Tversky and Kahneman proposed that losses cause a greater emotional impact on an individual than does an equivalent amount of gain, so given choices presented two ways—with both offering the same result—an individual will pick the option offering perceived gains. For example, assume that the end result is receiving $25. One option is being given the straight $25. The other option is gaining $50 and losing $25. The utility of the $25 is exactly the same in both options. However, individuals are most likely to choose to receive straight cash because a single gain is generally observed as more favorable than initially having more cash and then suffering a loss.

Types of Prospect Theory

According to Tversky and Kahneman, the certainty effect is exhibited when people prefer certain outcomes and underweight outcomes that are only probable. The certainty effect leads to individuals avoiding risk when there is a prospect of a sure gain. It also contributes to individuals seeking risk when one of their options is a sure loss.

The isolation effect occurs when people have presented two options with the same outcome, but different routes to the outcome. In this case, people are likely to cancel out similar information to lighten the cognitive load, and their conclusions will vary depending on how the options are framed.

•The prospect theory says that investors value gains and losses differently, placing more weight on perceived gains versus perceived losses.

•An investor presented with a choice, both equal, will choose the one presented in terms of potential gains.

•The prospect theory is part of behavioral economics, suggesting investors chose perceived gains because losses cause a greater emotional impact.

•The certainty effect says individuals prefer certain outcomes over probable ones, while the isolation effect says individuals cancel out similar information when making a decision.

Prospect Theory Example

Consider an investor is given a pitch for the same mutual fund by two separate financial advisors. One advisor presents the fund to the investor, highlighting that it has an average return of 12% over the past three years. The other advisor tells the investor that the fund has had above-average returns in the past 10 years, but in recent years it has been declining. Prospect theory assumes that though the investor was presented with the exact same mutual fund, he is likely to buy the fund from the first advisor, who expressed the fund's rate of return as an overall gain instead of the advisor presenting the fund as having high returns and losses.

Demand And Supply Theory Solves Consumer Problems

What is economy rule predict consumer behaviour? Why and How does economist can apply economy rule to predict consumer behaviours? I shall explain the reasons as below:

Why does economic principle be the best to predict consumer behaviour. It may include these two reasons: The first focuses on the substantive domain of study, in this interpretation , economics is a social science devoted to understanding how the economy works. The second definition focuses on methods: economics is a way of doing social science, using particular tools. In this interpretation the discipline is associated with formal modelling and statistical analysis rather than particular hypotheses or theories about the economy. Therefore, economic methods can be applied to many other areas besides the economy, everything from decisions within the family to questions about political institutions.

● Demand and supply principle predict public transport tool passenger behaviour

Economists need to use the right economic ideas to predict consumer behaviour. So, Misuse the wrong economy ideas to predict consumer behaviours. It will do more wrong judgement to evaluate or predict why and how and when the country's consumer behaviours will change. It is every economist needs to consider issue. For example, the economy idea application of economic supply-demand principles to public transport. Different fares would give commuters with more-flexible hours the incentive to avoid peak travel times. They would allow passenger traffic to spread out over time, reducing the pressure on the public transport system when enabling even larger total passenger flow. IT aims to reduce traffic congestion, increased public-transport use, reduced car-bon emissions and cause air pollution and generated considerable revenue for the country's transport system. So, if the country can apply supply and demand economic principle to attempt to predict how many passengers number needs to catch transport tools to go to work or go to school or other activities. Then, it can predict how many bus, ferry, taxi, train, underground train, tram etc. different public transport tools to satisfy future public transport passengers' needs in society.

So, this demand and supply principle is the comparative best rule to predict any kinds of public transport passengers' road needs, when they need to either go to school, go to office, go to leisure or shopping etc. different kinds of activities. So, applying the demand and supply principle to predict road and sea public transport passengers can help the country to reduce air pollution when they feel that they can find any public transport tools to catch any time conveniently , then it can encourage them to reduce car purchase desire. When many people choose to catch public transport tools, then it will reduce many cars number on the road. Then, air pollution will reduce as well as any public transport tools' income will also increase as well as traffic jam will also reduce. When the country can evaluate how many people choose to catch bus or taxi or ferry or train or underground train, or tram or train etc. different kinds of public transport tools, then the country can predict the more accurate public transport tools number to every kind of public transport tool to satisfy their journey needs. e.g. whether underground train or train or tram need to decrease or increase the frequent times or number to catch the volume of passenger in busy or non-busy time; or whether bus company has need to increase how much buses to catch the city location passengers when they are living in the city. Moreover, supply and demand principle can help any public transport tools to explain why their passengers number reduces in the year, it may due to fare charge is unreasonable, feeling uncomfortable to sit on the seat or air condition is poor in the transport tool environment, or there are no more seats because many there are much time is full passenger and no seat vacancy to provide to them to sit .

So, supply and demand principle can help any kinds of public transport tools to find whether which is (are) the factor(S) can influence the current or last year passengers number reduce. Then, they can concentrate on improving their weaknesses to raise their service quality . So, supply and demand principle can also help they to evaluate whether what their weakness are in order to improve to increase passengers number. They can do questionnaires to enquiry their passengers' response to evaluate whether which areas of services that they feel unsatisfactory. So, the different kinds of service satisfactory feeling to the passengers number data will be the main source to help the kind of public transport tool to analyse and conclude the results more accurate, then they can make the more accurate judgement to improve the of service. For example, the questionnaires indicate that the many passengers feel the bus fare is reasonable, but many passengers feel they can not find any seats to sit easily. So, it implies that the bus firm ought buy more buses or enlarges bus size and increases more seats in the enlarged buses. Then, it does not reduce its fare but it needs to find solutions to let passengers can find seats to sit in every bus more easily. But, if the questionnaires indicate that there are many passengers feel its fare is higher or unreasonable to compare other kinds of public transportation tools. Hence, it can avoid to spend more expenditure to increase bus number to the city, if the city has many passengers , they still choose bus to catch, but they feel its fare is too higher to compare other kinds of public transport tool. Then, it only needs to reduce its fare , it ought help it to increase passengers number. Hence, demand and supply principle is the most suitable economic method to evaluate any kinds of public transport system passenger needs in any country nowadays.

Tragedy Of The Commons to energy shortage challenge

What is Tragedy Of The Commons?

Te tragedy of the commons is an economic problem in which every individual has an incentive to consume a resource at the expense of every other individual with no way to exclude anyone from consuming. It results in overconsumption, under investment, and ultimately depletion of the resource. As the demand for the resource overwhelms the supply, every individual who consumes an additional unit directly harms others who can no longer enjoy the benefits. Generally, the resource of interest is easily available to all individuals; the tragedy of the commons occurs when individuals neglect the well-being of society in the pursuit of personal gain.

•The tragedy of the commons is an economic problem that results in overconsumption, under investment, and ultimately depletion of a common-pool resource.

•For a tragedy of the commons to occur a resource must be scarce, rivalrous in consumption, and non-excludable.

•Solutions to the tragedy of the commons include the imposition of private property rights, government regulation, or the development of a collective action arrangement.

•Historical examples of tragedies of the commons include the collapse of the North Atlantic Cod fisheries and the extinction of the dodo bird.

Tragedy of the Commons

Understanding the Tragedy of the Commons

The commons is a very real economic issue where individuals tend to exploit shared resources so the demand greatly outweighs supply, and the resource becomes unavailable for the whole. Garrett Hardin, an evolutionary biologist by education, wrote a scientific paper titled "The Tragedy of the Commons" in the peer-reviewed journal Science in 1968. The paper addressed the growing concern of overpopulation, and Hardin used an example of grazing land take from early English economist William Forster Lloyd when describing the adverse effects of overpopulation.

Lloyd's example, grazing lands held as private property will see their use limited by the prudence of the land holder in order to preserve the value of the land and health of the herd. Grazing lands held in common will be oversaturated with cattle because the food the cattle consume is shared among all herdsmen. Hardin's point was if humans faced the same issue as in the example with herd animals, each person would act in his own self interest and consume as much of the commonly accessible scarce resource as possible, making the resource even harder to find.

Economics of Tragedy of the Commons

In economic terms, the tragedy of the commons may occur when an economic good is both rivalrous in consumption and non-excludable. These types of goods are called common-pool resource goods (as opposed to private goods, club goods, or public goods). A good that is rivalrous in consumption means that when someone consumes a unit of the good, then that unit is no longer available for others to consume; all consumers are rivals competing for the good, and each person's consumption subtracts from the total stock of the good available. Note that in order for a tragedy for the commons to occur the good must also be scarce, since a non-scarce good cannot be rivalrous in consumption; by definition there is always plenty to go around. A good that is non-excludable means that individual consumers are unable to prevent others from also consuming the good.

The combination of properties (scarcity, rivalry in consumption, and non-excludability) that creates the tragedy of the commons. Each consumer maximizes the value they get from the good by consuming as much as they can as fast as they can before others deplete the resource, and no-one has an incentive to reinvest in maintaining or reproducing the good since they can not prevent others from appropriating the value of the investment by consuming the product for themselves. The good becomes more and more scarce and may end up entirely depleted.

Overcoming the Tragedy of the Commons

critical aspect to understanding and overcoming of the tragedy of the commons is the role that institutional and technological factors play in the rivalry and excludability of a good. Human societies have evolved many varied methods of dividing up and enforcing exclusive rights to economic goods and natural resources, or punishing those who over consume common resources over the course of history.

The possible solution is top-down government regulation or direct control of a common-pool resource. Regulating consumption and use, or legally excluding some individuals, can reduce overconsumption and government investment in conservation and renewal of the resource can help prevent it's depletion. For example government regulation can set limits on how many cattle may be grazed on government lands or issue fish catch quotas. However, top-down government solutions tend to suffer from the well known rent-seeking, principal-agent, and knowledge problems that are inherent in economic central planning and politically driven processes.

In particular, collective action can be useful in situations where technical or natural physical challenges prevent convenient division of a common-pool resource in to small private parcels, by instead relying on measures to address the good's rivalry in consumption by regulating consumption. Often this also involves limiting access to the resource to only those who are parties to the collective action arrangement, effectively converting a common pool resource in to a kind of club good.

Hence, Tragedy Of The Commons to energy shortage challenge is sure, because our energy resource , e.g. oil, gas , coal, electricity naural resource will be used all in our earth when global population number is continue increasing, but natural resource will not be increased. So, energy need (demand) must be more than energy supply. How to solve this natural resource, energy shortage challenge. I believe that second energy resource or renew energy will to be invented in order to replace natural resource energy before all of natural energy is used in our earth.

SomethingBehavioral (e.g., Prospect Theory) applies to energy useful choice

● Supply and demand and price elasticities principle predict oil energy user behaviour

The another case is that demand and supply principle can predict oil buyer behaviour to find whether what factors can cause the oil buyer individual need reduces. For example , a rise in production costs increases market prices and reduces quantities demanded and supplied. Or when, energy cost rise, utility bills increases and households fid extra ways of saving heating and electricity. But, others are nor. For example, whether a tax is imposed on the producers or consumer of a commodity, say oil has nothing to do with who ends up paying for it. The tax might be administered on oil companies, but it might be consumers who really pay for it through higher prices at the pump. Or the extra cost might be imposed on consumers in the form of a sale tax, but the oil companies might be forces to absorb it through lower prices. It all depends on the " price elasticities" of demand and supply. With the addition of extra assumption, this model also generates rather strong implications about how well markets work. In particular, a competitive market economy is efficient in the sense that it is impossible to improve one person's well-being without reducing somebody.

Something Behavioral (e.g., Prospect Theory) applies to the two firms participate advertisement to promote

● Demand and supply principle can misuse to predict consumer behaviour when the two firms participate advertisement to promote their products in the same time

Why can demand and supply principle misuse to predict consumer behaviour when the two firms participate advertisement to promote their products in the same time ? I shall explain as below: Assume that two competing firms must decide whether to have a big advertising budget. Advertising would allow one firm to steal some of the other's customers. But when they both advertise, the effects on customer demand cancel out. The firms end up having spent money needlessly.

We might expect that neither firm would choose to spend much on advertising, but the model shows that this logic is off base. When the firms make their choices independently and they care only about their own profits, each one has an incentive to advertise, regardless of what the other firm does. When the other firm does not advertise, you can steal customers from it if you do advertise, when the other firm does advertise, you have to advertise to prevent loss of customers. So, these two firms end up in a bad equilibrium in which both have to waste resources. This market can not apply demand and supply principle to predict consumer behaviours because they depends advertisement to promote their products. If these two firms advertise their products in the same time. Then , it is not possible that if one firm increases it price and it will cause its customer number loss, due to its advertise can help it to attract customers to consider its product from television or radio or newspapers or magazine promotion channels. So, I suppose that these two firms decide to increase their price, when they advertise their products to let customers to know in the same time. They will not lose their customers or reduce their customers easily. Because their customers can be persuaded to choose to buy their products to compare other similar products in preference. So, their increasing price will not influence their customers number lose easily. It explains that demand and supply principle is not right to this case, so demand and supply principle can misuse to help them to predict consumer behaviours when they advertise their products in the same time. Also, demand and supply principle is not suitable to them to predict consumer behaviours when they advertise their products in the same time. They will do wrong prediction to their consumers purchase desire when they advertise their products in the same time.

ON conclusion, using these demand and supply and price elasticity techniques, economists derive specific prediction for how consumers choose which products to buy, how households save, how firms invest, how workers search for jobs, as well as for how these actions depend on the particulars. They can help them to predict job and consumption behaviours more accurate, it depends on whether the situation is right, such as both competition firms participate to advertise their products in the same time case, it is not right to apply above economic principle to predict consumer behaviours. They will get wrong prediction when they apply this principle to predict consumer behaviours.

However, demand and supply principle can predict below any one of these cases. I shall indicate as below:

The problem of need-based scholarships: Most systems for providing college scholarships are based on some definition of financial needs, with scholarships generally being given only to those students who must need financial help in order to attend school.

Is need, rather than academic ability, the best basic on which to choose those students who are to be encouraged to attend college? Which way of choosing who gets aids is the more just? Which is the more efficient ? Is the overall educational level of society increased more by giving financial aid to bright students or to needy students? Presumably the aid offers more leverage to needy students, since they all need the money in order to attend college, whereas, many of the bright students would attend college in any case. But is a smaller number of bright students the more important addition?

So, the school can apply demand and supply principle to predict whether how many parents feel need financial assistance and evaluate how much financial amount is the right to borrow. It aims to calculate how many parents feel real financial need and how much to lend to them in order to let these students to get the most fair financial assistance.

Assuming the school wish to use need as a basis, how does the school determines " financial need"?

Is need a function or parents' income? What, then , does the school about children of wealthy parents who are living independently of them and get no aid from parents? Should they be punished for their parents' wealth? But if they are given aid, won't all students, in order to get aid, claim to be independent of their parents?

Is need solely a matter of family income, or should not the school takes a family's financial obligations into account? Does not it make more sense to give aid to someone whose parents must put night more children through school than to someone from a family of five or one only with the same income? But in a possible parallel situations, should a family that carries mortgages on one or two large homes get preference simply because they do not have much money left to spend on college? Does doing this reward ? Is there a difference between the case of night children and the case of the

large mortgage? How should parents who are not married , but are living together and supporting their children jointly be counted? Most parents are supporter to their children , although they are married in possible.
So, the school needs to gather all these data to evaluate how many parents are not married or married or living with their children together, how much salary they earn as well as every family has how much children as well as whether they have mortgage for their houses. So, these number will be the financial education assistance demanders, but it does not represent their real financial needs. It is possible that someone does not feel any financial need, although their children apply financial assistance to your school. Then , your school needs to evaluate whether how much financial assistance can lend to every real financial need student family. It can not exceed your final financial expenditure budget (supply) , when your financial expenditure is not enough. SO, demand and supply principle can be applied to research this school real family financial demand to lend to the real financial need families and evaluate whether the reasonable financial amount to lend to every child family to study in your school.

Something Behavioral (e.g., Prospect Theory) applies to immigration to decide wage reasonal decision

● Supply and demand principle applies to immigration to decide wage case
A fascinating and important example of supply and demand, full of complexities, is the role of immigration in determining wages. If you ask people , they are likely to tell you that immigration into California or Florida US, surely lowers the wages of people in those regions. It is just supply and demand analysis of immigration. According to this analysis, of these to these two regions in US. Immigration in to a region shifts the supply curve for labor to the right and pushes down wages. Why has it relationship between immigration to US these two regions immigrant number and wage?
Careful economic studies cast doubt on this simple proposition, however, a recent survey of the evidence concludes:
The effect of immigration on the labor market outcomes of natives is small in US. There is no evidence of economically significant reductions in native employment. Most analysis, finds that a 10 percent increase in the fraction of immigrants in the population reduced native wages by a most 1%.
How can we explain the small impact of immigration on wages? The main mistake is to forget how mobile the American population is and that the

impact of immigration on wages, we must examine the effect of new immigrants when the strength of the local economy and the number of native-born residents in a city are unchanged, that is , when these other things are held constant. Unless you exclude the effects other changing variables, you can not accurately predict the impact of immigration. The same principle holds in doing a supply0and demand analysis of any market. As much as possible, when you are examining the impact of a supply or demand shift, you must try to keep all other things constant.

● Rationing by prices

By determining the equilibrium prices and quantities of all inputs and outputs, the market allocated or rations out the scare goods of the society among the possible uses. Who does the rationing? A planning board? Congress or the president? BO, the marketplace, through the interaction of supply and demand, doe the rationing. This is rationing by the purse.

What foods are produces? This is answered by the signals of the market price. High oil prices stimulates oil production, whereas low food prices drive resources out of agriculture. Those who have the most dollars votes have the greatest influences on what goods are produced. All of these considers how demand and supply to the market.

For whom are goods produces? The power of the pursue indicates the distribution of income and consumption. Those with higher incomes end up with larger houses, more clothing, and linger vacations. When the most urgently felt needs get fulfilled through the demand curve.

Even, the how question is decided by supply and demand. When corn prices are low, it is not profitable for farmers to use expensive tractors and irrigation systems, and only the best land is cultivated. When oil prices are high, oil companies drill in deep offshore waters and employ novel seismic techniques to find oil.

IN sum , any thing needs through demands, interact with costs of goods, as reflected in supplies in our economic world. Hence, demand and supply theory ought be the most accurate method to help any businesses or governments to predict their shareholders behaviours when they will change as well as how and how their behaviours change.

Consumer choice theory solves consumer problems

What is 'consumer choice theory'?

'Consumer choice theory' is a hypothesis about why people buy things. Put simply, it says that you choose to buy the things that give you the greatest satisfaction, while keeping within your budget. At the heart of this theory are three assumptions about human nature.[1]

The first assumption is that when you shop, you choose to buy things based on calculated decisions about what will make you happiest. In economics language, this is known as utility maximisation (Economists really like to put quite simple concepts into long complicated terms.)

Secondly, the theory assumes that no matter how much you shop, you will never be completely satisfied. In other words, you will always be happier consuming a little bit more. This is known as the principle of non-satiation.

Thirdly, even though you always get more happiness from more consumption, the amount of pleasure you get from each good decreases with the more you consume. So if you eat two ice creams rather than one, you get more overall pleasure, but the second ice-cream won't be as satisfying as the first. This is known as decreasing marginal utility.

Consumer choice theory has influenced everything from government policy to corporate advertising to academia. But the theory has been criticized for not being the most accurate description of how people actually make choices. A whole new branch of economics, called 'behavioral economics', has emerged essentially to use findings from psychology to disprove the assumptions behind consumer choice theory. This has also led others to argue that consumer choice theory is less about describing how we do actually behave, and is more about describing how people should behave.[3] In other words, by portraying people as self interested shopaholics, economists are saying that is it okay and natural for us to be avid consumers.

Lemons Problem Influences Consumer Choice During Economic Growth Period

Adverse Selection and the Lemons Problem

What Is the Lemons Problem?

The lemons problem refers to issues that arise regarding the value of an investment or product due to asymmetric information possessed by the buyer and the seller.

Lemons Problem Explained

The lemons problem was put forward in a research paper, "The Market for 'Lemons': Quality Uncertainty and the Market Mechanism," written in the late 1960s by George A. Akerlof, an economist and professor at the University of California, Berkeley. The tag phrase identifying the problem came from the example of used cars Akerlof used to illustrate the concept of asymmetric information, as defective used cars are commonly referred to as lemons.

The lemons problem exists in the marketplace for both consumer and business products, and also in the arena of investing, related to the disparity in the perceived value of an investment between buyers and sellers. The lemons problem is also prevalent in financial sector areas, including insurance and credit markets. For example, in the realm of corporate finance, a lender has asymmetrical and less-than-ideal information regarding the actual creditworthiness of a borrower.

Causes and Consequences of the Lemons Problem

The problem of asymmetrical information arises because buyers and sellers don't have equal amounts of information required to make an informed decision regarding a transaction. The seller or holder of a product or service usually knows its true value, or at least knows whether it is above or below average in quality. Potential buyers, however, typically do not have this knowledge, since they are not privy to all the information the seller has.

● Consumer choice theory can be applied to solve consumer problems during the country can have economic growth , the reasons may include as below:

The scenario leading to inflation starts with poor growth. Forget about everything that comes next and focus on that most important factor. Because it happens that the scenario leading to a budget crisis also starts with poor growth, and the scenario leading to a long-term unemployment crisis starts with poor growth, and a scenario leading to a better-the-neighbor trade crisis starts with poor growth, and so on. So a very important question is: what can be done to improve the prospects for economic growth? In particular, what is the right countercyclical approach to take to best situate the economy for future growth? I shall indicate during US, America's economy growth occurs, then economists can attempt to apply customer choice theory to solve US itself country's consumer problems more easier.

In no small part, the question comes down to interpretations of charts like the one at right. On the one hand, long and deep downturns seem to have almost no effect on the long-term rate of growth. On the other hand, in the long run we're all dead, and those who live during an extended period of economic weakness suffer for it. Meanwhile, it's also difficult to see where high debt levels influence the long-run rate of growth, at least where this chart is concerned.

During to the medium-term growth stage, is the bigger threat to American growth rates a market revolt against American debt levels? Or is it structural unemployment stemming from the slow, jobless recovery? Or is the cyclical shortfall in public investment? Or something else entirely? Of course, there's no real reason one has to choose a problem to address at the expense of others. More aggressive monetary expansion could make the finding of a solution to all these problems easier, but the Fed is unwilling to oblige me on this score. It may well be concerned that lack of fiscal discipline will lead to increasing inflation expectations, making its job harder (but then fiscal problems are trace able to growth). If that is the worry, however, one has to ask why the Congress has been unable to strike a deal for $20 billion in stimulus this year for $80 billion in fiscal tightening in a year or two (fill in whatever amounts you wish). But the outlook for the American economy vis-a-vis any number of potential crises will hinge on growth, and growth will hinge on the ability of private business to exploit promising opportunities as they arise. And the question is: what's likely to hurt that ability most? High interest rates? Lack of consumer demand? A shortage of adequately prepared workers? Right now firms appear to be most worried about demand shortfalls. So how much can you boost demand without making the primary fear high interest rates? A lot, if the expansion is on the monetary side.

● How to supply consumer choice theory to predict Consumer Behavior Marketing at Apple Computer

During US economy growth, Apply computer applies consumer choice theory to solve its computer buyers' choice problems among different kinds of brand computer competitors. Have you ever wondered why Apple is so successful? They were not the first company to invent the personal computer, portable music device, the tablet, the smartphone, software to download music, or the set-top box to name a few. Apple has amassed a brand loyal following like no other brand backed by significant sales, market share, and profitability. So, how does Apple do it? What's the secret behind their success?

Marketing using consumer behavior insight is how Apple succeeds. Even though Steve Jobs and Apple, did not use consumer research in the initial development of most products, consumer behavior plays a huge role in their marketing and ultimately the success of the company. Once a consumer purchases a product or downloads iTunes Apple has access to data the company leverages. Apple uses this information to gain significant insight into the consumer and what drives purchase behavior.

Consumer behavior marketing is an essential ingredient in the current business climate. The companies that apply this type of marketing well have a distinct competitive advantage that distances them from their rivals. Consumer behavior research is the primary driver at the core of any good strategy. Research provides actionable insight and ensures business success. If you answer no to the following questions, this post is for you?

•Are you applying consumer behavior marketing currently?

•Have you conducted consumer behavior research within the last two years?

•Do you have consumer behavior marketing in your marketing plan with well-defined marketing strategies and tactics?

•Are you achieving the maximum results for your organization?

Every business has a target audience and consumer behavior marketing provides the fundamental methods for understanding your target. Consumer behavior research provides the underlying element that drives quality strategies and ensures business results.

"Marketing is understanding your buyers really, really well. Then creating valuable products, services, and information especially for them to help solve their problems."

The organizations that have an intimate understanding of their target audience possess a competitive advantage over those that do not. Establishing a one-to-one relationship and thorough knowledge of your target audience is a core responsibility for business in the 21st century and beyond. Regardless if you are B2B, B2C, B2G or a hybrid organization you have a target audience. The information in this post can be applied to any business type. This post focuses on Apple (B2C) employing consumer behavior marketing as a critical ingredient for their success.

Hence, Apply computer shops have several computer teachers to teach any visitors how to use its laptops, hen they enquire its any computer salespeople. Due to its salespeople had been trained to learn how to use the different kinds of laptops. So, anyone enquires them, they can answer their enquires concern any computer questions immediately. Then, they will feel Apple laptops are the first choice to compare other kinds of laptops brands. It is one salespeople answering strategies to persuade any Apple computer visitors to feel its any laptops are the first or preference choice to compare its competitors in this computer market, so customer choice economic theory is the most suitable strategy to solve Apple computer's customer individual purchase decision problem.

Microeconomics Models and Theories solve customer problems

Microeconomics is concerned with the economic decisions and actions of individuals and firms. Within the broad church of microeconomics, there are different theories that certain assumptions and expectations of economic behaviour. The most important theory is neo-classical theory, which places emphasis on free-markets and the assumption individuals are rational and seek to maximise utility. However, there are many critiques of the neo-classical model, arguing economics is more complex with issues of market failure and irrational behaviour.

Pre-classical microeconomic theory

Before, Adam Smith, economics was more disparate with no commanding overall theory. Philosophers like Aristotle and Plato made references to issues in economics such as division of labour. The dominant ideas, pre-classical economics, were based on theories of mercantilism – the idea a nation should try to accumulate gold.

Classical microeconomic theory

Classical microeconomic theory was developed by Adam Smith (Wealth of Nations, 1776) and later economists, such as David Ricardo The essential aspect of classical microeconomic theory include:

Adam Smith mentioned the 'invisible hand of the market.' He noted how when people act out of self-interest, markets tend to provide goods and services which are demanded by the population. It needed no central price setting, but market forces responded to changes in demand and supply, e.g. a shortage pushes up the price and causes demand to fall.

Smith also investigated topics such as the division of labour, specialisation and economies of scale. The early classical economists emphasised the importance of costs to firms and consumers.

Utility maximisation

An important development of classical economics towards the end of the nineteenth century is the concept of utility maximisation. The concept of utility was developed by philosophers/economists – Jeremy Bentham and John Stuart Mill. In microeconomic theory, it was believed a consumer will buy goods depending on the marginal utility (satisfaction) they get from the good. This theory assumes consumers are rational and seeking to maximise the satisfaction they get.

Neo-classical theory

Neo-classical theory is a modern re-interpretation of classical economics of the nineteenth century. Neo-classical theory places importance on markets, but developed new ideas, especially regarding utility and rational choice theory. Elements of neo-classical theory.
1. Market distribution of goods and services.
2.R ational choice theory. This is the idea individuals hold rational preferences and make rational choices; seeking to maximise their outcomes – be it profit, wages, consumption or investment.
3. People act independently and make use of available information.
4. Marginalism. In neo-classical economics, more emphasis was placed on concepts of marginal utility and marginal cost. We make choices depending on satisfaction we get from one extra unit of a good.

Economists such as Carl Menger, William Stanley Jevons and Marie-Esprit-Léon Walras. and Alfred Marshall developed ideas such as diminishing marginal utility. Many of these neo-classical economic theories were brought together in Alfred Marshall's very influential textbook, Principles of Economics. (1890)

•Note there is some blurring between classical economics and neo-classical economics.

•Neo-classical economics has also come to mean 'orthodox economic theory. To a large extent, it has incorporated new developments in microeconomics, such as theories of market failure, market structure and econometrics.

Theories of Market failure

Neo-classical economics has become associated with a belief in the efficiency of markets. However, microeconomic theory has also incorporated the criticisms and limitations of free-markets.

•Monopoly. Adam Smith was well aware of the problem of monopolies and how firms could use their market power to set excessive prices.

•Imperfect competition. In the 1930s, Joan Robinson developed a model of imperfect competition, an awareness many markets were somewhere between monopoly and perfect competition often assumed in neo-classical economics.

•Externalities. Developed by Arthur C.Pigou in The Economics of Welfare (1920) this is the awareness production and consumption decisions can have harmful (or positive) effects on third parties. Therefore, a free market can lead to overconsumption of demerit goods and negative externalities.

•Game theory. An awareness, decisions are not linear or simple, but the interdependence of agents influences what we decide to do.

Behavioural economics

The most important trend in recent decades in economics is the greater emphasis placed on aspects of behavioural economics, which uses many insights from related fields such as psychology.

•Disputes rational choice theory. The essential element of behavioural economics is that it argues individual agents are often not rational and often do not seek to maximise utility.

•Behavioural economics examines how agents can be influenced by biases, and make decisions not predicted by neo-classical economic theory. Behavioural economics can explain the irrational exuberance of booms and busts.

Econometrics

In the post-war period, economics became increasingly mathematical with economists attempting to use mathematics to explain models and theories. Econometrics looks at economic data and seeks to extract simple relationships. The basic tool is the linear regression models and can be used to try and predict consumer spending and demand for labour.

Heterodox models of microeconomics

Heterodox models differ substantially from microeconomic foundations of neo-classical economics. Schools of thought include

Marxist economic theory

Karl Marx developed an alternative perspective on economics. He focused on the surplus value created under the capitalist economic system. To Marx, the invisible hand of the market would be better described as the invisible hand of capitalist exploitation of workers. Marx claimed workers did receive their full labour value but were compensated for their necessary labour only – enabling capitalists to profit from the surplus.

Institutional economics. The role of society and institutions in shaping economic behaviour. For example, Thomas Veblen looked at theories of 'conspicuous consumption' and noted how the desire for social status could drive much economic theory. Institutional economics could be seen as a forerunner for later behavioural economics.

Environmental economics Argues traditional economics wrongly places value on increasing output. The most important thing is creating a sustainable environment which maximises living standards. So, manufacturers need to consider how to manufacture their products , but pollution can not be raised as the same time, because human will face to raise cost of living and living experiences to be poor , even food shortage, water pollution , air pollution , death rate raises when technological productivities brings pollution to our natural environment. Hence, environmental economoic theory is the most suitable to solve manufacturers' pollution problem.

Buddhist economics/non-profit goals. Like environmental economics, this questions the assumption higher incomes and higher output are desirable. The theory of hedonistic relativism suggests higher incomes do nothing to increase happiness levels, and traditional economics can encourage society to pursue materialistic goals which actually create more problems of stress, conflict and environmental degradation.

Some of the basic models you might find in A-Level economics :

•Price Discrimination
•Perfect competition
•Price Mechanism
•Monopoly
•Oligopoly and kinked demand curve
•Game Theory Pricing strategies
•Market failure
•Behavioural economics

ON conclusion, any macro economy theories can be applied to find the most reasonable methods to solve any customer problems in societies by economists as above. So, I believe that any economic and customer and social problems can be solved by economic theories in our society.

Demand and supply theory solves social problems

Over the past 20 years, many researchers believe to apply behavioral economic macroeconomic models which can predict market behavioral change. The reasons are based on assumptions of optimizing behavior in many cases have difficulty accounting for key real-world observations. Hence, researchers have used behavioral economics assumptions with the aim of making their model predicting better fit the data. The reason for behavioral economics results into macroeconomics will be more accurate to predict market behavioral change in macro-economy view point, such as economic fluctuation prediction, the consumption, formation of expectations and determination of wages and employment how to aggregation supply and the possibility of consumer individual demand product or service number prediction more accurately.

- How to apply behavioral economy (demand and supply) theory to predict marketing behavioral changes more accurate?

Anyway, economists aim to develop models of human behavior and interactions in market in order to build useful models. Economists make simplifying assumptions to analyze why the market will be changed by consumer individual consumption behavior changing.

Why do I assume consumers are as economic man ? In behavioral economy view point, how the perception of the economic man's behavior (including consumer choices) of economic models with the development of economics as a science. Economists explain the concept of economics as a science. It is the concept of consumer as an economic man, the essence and complexity of consumer behavior.

The consumer and consumer purchasing behavior are an important area of interest of many scientific disciplines. The process of economic decision making as well as consumption choices are connected with wider human activities. The terms of both consumer individual attitudes and group social behavior will influence group social behavior will influence consumer individual final consumption decision in every consumption choice process. Thus, behavioral economy method can predict consumer behavioral changing, it can apply these sciences to research, includes sociology, psychology, anthropology, operational research, decision theory etc. different literature research aspects. I assume that businessmen can apply behavioral economy method to predict market changing behaviors successfully if they own behavioral economy knowledge.

In this part, I shall concentrate on explain how the perception of the economic man's behavior (including consumer choice) is applied to predict market behaviors. After explaining the concept of consumer as an economic man, the nature and complexity of consumer behavior are discussed to below different industries' marketing behavioral changing every case studies in US or UK countries.

Why is consumer as an economic man? IN behavioral economy view point, the concept of answer is one of the fundamental concepts in economics because the consumer is the case market participant along with the producer. In general, lecturers define the consumer in various ways, but in behavioral economy view point, consumers mean economy man. Because who will compare cost and benefit to any product or service to decide to choose to buy the product or consume the service. Consumers are as "economic man", who will make own subjective preferences (tastes), habits and traditions and existing objective constraints (i.e. disposal income) market prices of products and services in order to satisfy whose needs to a maximum degree and in the most rational way.

Thus, economic man means consumers need to make psychological mind to decide whether who either prefer to buy this product or another product or prefer to consume this service or another service more suitable. Thus, any markets or industries need have themselves benefits and consumers must need to evaluate whether the product or service has more benefits to compare other products or services in the consumption market to satisfy whose needs. It means that if the product or service has more benefits to compare other similar products or services. Then the product or service will persuade many consumers to choose to but the product or consume the service.

Consequently, in first part, I shall indicate how to apply behavioral economy theory : economic man psychological method, benefits and costs benefits method, how to predict these US and UK enterprises marketing behavioral changing more accurate.

In the second part, I shall apply micro employee behavioral economy concept to explain how to solve these US and UK inter-organizational management challenge.

I believe that behavioral economy method can be applied to research organizational employee behaviors change, e.g. how any why the employee chooses to do this action in whose organization. Moreover, behavioral economy method can be applied to consumption market to predict how any why the consumer choose to buy the product or consume the service. So, any consumers and employees personal psychology and external environment economic factor will influence how to choose to do decision in any organizations or consumption environment.

Bibliography

Bandiera, O., I. Barankay, and I. Rasul (2005). Social preferences and the response to incentives: Evidence from personal data. The quarterly journal of economics 120 (3), 917-969.

Exadaktylos, F., A.M. Espin and P. Branas-Garza (2013). Experimental subjects are not different. Scientific reports 3, 1213.

Lazear, E.P. (1979). Why is there mandatory retirement? Journal of political economy 87(6), 1261-1284.

● Behavioral economic method (demand and supply theory) predicts stable basic income consumer individual spending behavior

Can apply behavioral economic method to predict that the consequences of a stable basic income consumer's consumption behavior? It may be significantly different than the ones are predicted by the standard economic model if more realistic assumptions of human consumption behavioral prediction success.

Behavioral economic method assumes that consumer will compare whether whose benefits are more than costs after they buy the product or consume the service. I assume the consumer is only the who have stable basic income source consumer target. This stable basic income target consumers who will evaluate or feel they will earn more benefits than costs to every product in their consumption process, after they will make final decision to choose to buy the product to use or consume the service. Otherwise, if they feel they won't earn more benefits after they buy the product or consume the service in the consumption process. Then, they won't choose to buy the product to use or consume the service. In behavioral economic view point, it indicates their consumption behaviors are depend on comparing the product or the service whether it can satisfy their desire benefits and their desire benefits to the product or service must be more than their consumption cost.

There are four points to apply behavioral economic method to predict each stable basic incomc individual income spending. They include: motivation, conspicuous consumption, social preferences and crowding theory.

Each stable basic income consumer individual spending amount will be different and it is represent that every high stable basic income consumer must decide to consume any high cost services or buy high cost products to use. Although some economic teachers assume general high income people will accept to spend more expenditures for enjoyment or buy high cost of products to satisfy basic high level necessary expenditures. But, applying behavioral economic analysis, it is not absolute true, some low income people also accept to spend more to buy high cost of products or increasing spending expenditures for enjoyment for their basic necessary expenditures.

The field of behavioral economic can be fined as a combination of economics and psychology that tries to capture human behavior in a more realistic. Understanding each consumer individual consumption behavior, we need to know how who does each decision to influence each consumption choice. Consequently, analysis reaches the conclusion. Every high or low level stable basic income consumer individual behavioral consumption that the microeconomic consequences of a stable basic income of individual consumer target consumption group could be efficiency enhancing, but at the same time incentives about positional concerns could lead to wasteful and inefficient spending to the stable low basic income consumer target group.

● How to apply demand and supply theory to contribute to the stable basic income target consumer group's consumption prediction?

What is basic income mean? A basic income is an income paid by a political community to all its members on an individual basis, without means test or work requirement. How to apply behavioral economic method to contribute to the basic income consumption prediction?

I assume high income tax is charged to one high income tax payee , it will influence the high income tax payee individual consumption desires to be fallen, also extrinsic incentives will effort and intrinsic motivation and how the labor market change these variables under and big changes predicting, how income security changes social consumption preferences, e.g. how a big change affects the overall level of status -seeking behavior and this effect with income inequality to influence consumer individual consumption attitude or habit.

How can behavioral economic methods predict consumer's consumption decision, in special the stable basic income consumer target group? In any consumption decisions are involving risk and uncertainty, the standard economic model usually assumes that decisions are based on final condition, regardless of the changes are caused by the results of a consumer's decision.

An alterative mode of how consumers make decision and judgement under risk and uncertainty. This situation is often occurred in consumption market.

In behavioral economic view point, it explains how consumer's consumption, however, which excludes the stable basic income earn factor can influence the stable basic income earn target consumer group decides to make final consumption decision to compare to the non-stable basic income earn target consumer group. The reasons include as below:

(1) Consumers evaluate decisions over gains and losses with respect to some natural reference point, when they feel need to consume, which is assumed to be judgement about a sequence of outcomes are based on changes in wealth, rather than whether how much absolute basic income

earn to influence whose consumption desires.

(2) Thus, behavioral economic theory assumes the consumer is the low level of income group in society, but when who feels that he is still gains more than losses when who decides to buy the expensive product or consumes the expensive service. Then, the low level of income consumer who will accept to buy the expensive product or consume the service easily. Due to whose gains feeling is more than losses feeling, when who buys the product or consumes the service.

(3) Behavioral economic theory also assumes the taxpayer will pay high income tax in this year. The, even the high income taxpayer can earn high basic income, but due to whom needs to pay high income tax in this year. Then, he/she will reduce much spending, even he/she reduces spending on cheap products or cheap service consumption for enjoyment. This is the taxpayer's economic decision to influence whose consumption behavior, due to the high income tax expenditure factor influences whose consumption behavior to change to be reduced spending expenditures in this year.

How to apply behavioral economic method to predict labor market changing behavior?

Instead of applying behavioral economic method to predict every consumer individual consumption effort. Behavioral economic method can be also be applied to predict every country's labor market changing behavior. Particularly, how salary clerical workers or low wage labor workers should move from one type of job to another based on these factors. They include as below:

Their intrinsic motivation and how their levels of effort would change after this movement, investigates the effects of income security on social preferences in labor market changing behavior, and how cooperation in social contribution is affected when income security is guaranteed, how to predict the role of positional externalities on conspicuous consumption and how would change the incentive to influence consumption. So, it seems that general labor market job changing behaviors will not influenced by external economic environment better or worse changing factor, or salary changing factor etc. different environmental condition changing factors influence to employees' job changing. Generally, employee's job changing behavior is more influenced to persuade who changes job by himself/herself intrinsic motivation negative emotion influence mainly.

How to apply motivation crowding theory to predict labor productivity? One of the main challenges of economic theory is to find what are the optimal incentives that increase productivity of labors. The standing point is usually extrinsic incentive be it is form of monetary compensations for high effort or fine for low effort.

It is a kind method of reward or punishment to increase or decrease number of productivity to every labor. But it can only raise short term number of productivity in possible and it can not guarantee high quality of productivity. So if one employer wants a labor to do more of an activity or with a higher quality, consider paying the labor for working hard on punishing whom if for providing a low level effort.

This idea is that people do not like to work, and therefore they used some sort of compensation for doing a specific activity, and that the more they are paid the harder, they will work. So, payment better compensation is only beneficial to encourage labors to do one specific task or activity in short term. This method can not be suitable to rise long term beneficial productivity and high level quality of production or excellent performance in long term and it can only keep in short term raising productivity and high level quality of production or excellent performance benefits.

Consider paying the labor for working hard on punishing whom if for providing a low level effort. This idea is that people do not like to work, and therefore they used some sort of compensation for doing a specific activity, and that the more they are paid the harder they will work. So, payment better compensation is only beneficial to encourage labors to do one specific task or activity in short term. This method can not be suitable to raise long them beneficial productivity and high quality of products.

However, economists would argue that, is a labor has high intrinsic motivative to perform a task, who will provide a high level of effort without compensation by himself/herself but an even higher level of effort of whom is compensated. If a labor does not have any intrinsic motivation to perform a task or an activity, who will provide no effort or a low effort of whom. There is no compensation, but who will increase this level of effort of an extrinsic incentive is implemented.

Hence, in behavioral economic view point, the labor individual high level effort is a main psychological factor to influence whose productivity to be raised or the qualities of products to be raised, when the products are manufactured by the high level effort labor. It means that high compensation is not the good method to encourage labor productivity or raise quality. Otherwise, how to influence the one low level of effort of labor to change to be one high level of effort labor. It is the best psychological method to influence the labor to raise productivity and quality and service performance to any products or services in manufacturing process or service process for any organizations in long term beneficial possible.

● How can apply demand and supply theory raises basic stable income consumer consumption desire

Economists aim to develop models of human behavior and interactions in consumption markets. But consumers behave in complex ways, such as how to predict consumers to make rational decisions in consumption processes. Moreover, self-consumption control and motivation can vary significantly across different individual consumer.

In order to build useful consumption prediction models, economists make simplifying assumptions, aims to predict how to raise stable basic income consumer target group consumption more success. However, behavioral economy method is one kind of accurate consumption prediction method. It can be applied to predict economic decision-making to every consumer consumption choice more accurate raising whose consumption desire?

I shall indicate how to apply different behavioral economy methods (demand and supply theory) to raise stable basic stable income target consumer group consumption desire in these different consumption situation (consumption environment) aspects as below:

1. Stable basic stable income consumer group consumption great or small amount desire

The consumption of products and services is a fundamental part of consumer's welfare. Basically, every one who has stable basic stable income, who will like to consume any products and services. Even, consumption great or small amount desire won't be depended on whether the person whose income is more or less. It means low income level of people will still like to consume great amount to buy expensive products or consume expensive services, because consumption is human's part of life and basic needs.

This stable basic income people will like to consume, because they have stable income source when they do not worry about unemployment occurrence to cause them have no enough money to support their life. Otherwise, non-stable basic stable income people won't like to consume because they feel they have no stable basic income source to support their life and they will worry about unemployment occurrence any time. Hence, stable basic income people will have more consumption desire to compare non-stable basic stable income people in any countries usually. Behavioral economic method indicates they feel their economic benefits will be loss if they planned to buy any products or consume any services easily. So, they prefer to save money in bank more than consumption.

1. Demand systems and micro-economic factor influence basic income people consumption attitude

Why stable basic income people will like to consume? Because who have more demand, a demand system shows the level of consumer demand for different products and services: e.g. one basic stable income person may refer to the demand for clothes, another the demand for food etc.

How the demand for that particular product varies with the prices and demographic factor will influence who to accept consumption. Such as stable basic income people who will not consider to decide to buy the cloth to wear or the food to eat if who feel the cloth or food price is even more expensive to compare other kind of cloth or food.

Otherwise, non-stable basic income people who will consider to decide to buy the cloth to wear or the food to eat if they feel that they still have enough cloths to wear or enough food to eat at homes , even these food or cloth price are less expensive to compare others. Because they feel they lack stable income effort to support them to consume. Hence, basic stable income factor can influence the consumer's consumption decision.

2. Life-cycle advertisement method can influence consumer individual consumption behaviors to be increased

Consumer behavior makes strong assumptions about the informational and computational bases of consumer behavior. Generally, consumer behavior is reasonably characterized as the maximization of expected lifetime utility subject to budget constraint and conditional on the available information.

Generally, consumers prefer to buy any discounted products or it is reasonable that consumers accept to buy many attractions to persuade them to buy any kinds of bargain discount products. Hence, low bargain discount product is one good behavioral economic principle to encourage or persuade or attract any consumers to increase consumption.

What is behavioral life-cycle model? This model explains consumer behavior can be persuaded to buy any discounted products by advertisement, e.g. television, radio, newspapers, magazine etc. promotion channels. Because frequent advertisement promotion method can let any consumers often remember the product's brand, discounted price, style, color and image from advertisement content.

So, advertisement can be one part of consumer behavioral life-cycle. For example, when the television audiences often watch TV. Hence, when the brand of product advertisement often makes fun image and discounted message to let TV audiences to remember this brand of product, when they are watching TV. Then, it has possible to persuade any potential consumers to choose to buy this brand of any products or consume this brand of any services, due to its advertisement of discounted sale message is very attractive to every one to let this advertisement audience's attention to remember this brand of products or services are selling or serving in market at this moment. So, it is advertisement image behavior influences audiences to buy the brand's any products attractively and persuasively.

3. Raising electricity consumption from electricity user individual habit

For electricity use market case example, how to analyze people's behavior in consuming electricity using a behavioral economic framework ? Electricity consumption is modeled by the means of consumer's individual useful habit, electricity price, consumer satisfaction level, willingness to invest in new technologies, social interactions, and marketing strategies by the power utility. Because electricity is necessary to every home or electric vehicle users needs or businessmen office etc. different needs every day.

Power companies supply electricity to a region's homes and industries. However, electricity needs modernization of power system companies expect to increase price. Due to competitive factor, such as other fuel resource choices, outdated kind of energy electricity supply, and renewable fuel energy source competition.

Hence, applying behavioral economic concept, I assume electricity consumers will compare to electricity and other kinds of energy choices to weigh up the costs and benefits of all alternatives, aiming to maximize their benefits, before making a decision to choose to use electricity for their house electricity demand or electric vehicle or shop or factory manufacturing etc. function of different aspects of electricity users.

For example, electricity business clients, they aim to reduce cost, such as energy expenditure, when they use any energy to manufacture their products in factories. If they feel electricity is expensive price to compare other kinds of energy power supply. When, they feel that they can not earn much beneficial advantages to use electricity to produce their products. Otherwise, if they feel other any kinds of energy supply can replace electricity to give more benefits to compare electricity energy. Then, many business electricity users will change to use other kinds of energies to consume to replace electricity power.

However, electricity can have competitive ability in electric vehicles market, if many drivers feel environment protection is more important to compare vehicles will be popular to be driven, due to many drivers don't want air pollution. They will like gas vehicles. Hence, the main attribute from the consumer side is one their habit electricity consumption behaviors, satisfaction level, energy efficient interaction with the power utility.

Consequently how to predict electricity consumer's demand. The important factor is how to let electricity users to feel power companies are changing a reasonable level to compare other similar energy supply products. When electricity users feel electricity which can bring more benefits to compare other kinds of energy products. Then, in energy supply market, if the demanding number of electricity consumers can increase more than other kinds of energy demanding number. Then, it is right time to raise electricity price to charge electricity consumers. Hence, how to persuade electricity consumers to feel that they can have more benefits to compare other kinds of energy products. It is the main successful factor to electricity power supply companies.

- Consumer confidence is as a predictor of consumption spending

Behavioral economists believe it has link between confidence and economic decisions to cause consumers to choose spending, if the consumer has confidence to believe the product is worth to use, then who will accept to buy the product to use.

Concentrated on the conceptualization of confidence and its role in mode in theories of consumption. It also concerns on whether the confidence indicators contain any information beyond economic fundamentals. The concern is whether confidence can be explained by current and past value of variables, such as income, unemployment, inflation or consumption or in other way.

Whether confidence measures have any statistical significance in predicting economic outcomes once information from the above variables is used. Economic variable factor will also influence consumer confidence to decide consumption spending, e.g. real consumption expenditures (income, wealth or interest rate).

Finally, it will identify under which circumstances confidence indicates can be a good predictor of household consumption. Hence, survey is one good measurement method to predict whether how much every household has confidence to spend to consume the brand of products to use. Why is survey a good confidence consumption measurement prediction to every household in every country?

The reasons include survey can gather every household consumption habit history data to evaluate whether every survey person has how much confidence to consume the brand of products. Which in most cases correspond to periods where there are large changes in household survey indicators, liking during financial crises or geopolitical tensions to measure or predict whether the country's future good or bad economic condition factor will influence every household consumption desire in the year.

This modelling approach assumes that there is a certain (unknown) in confidence index changes beyond which confidence starts impacting consumption behaviors. So, sample household surveys can show the contribution of confidence in explaining consumption expenditures increases when household survey indicators feature large changes. So that confidence indicators can have some increasing predictive power during the survey investigation period in the year.

Other view point, surveys have been concerned on whether the confidence indicators contain any information beyond economic fundaments. The concern is whether confidence can be explained by current and past values of variables, such as income, unemployment, inflation or consumption or the other way. Whether confidence measures have any statistical significance in predicting economic outcomes once information from different external variable factors to influence the survey household group.

What is confidence in consumption survey ?

Confidence in consumption. For example, to measure whether how much degree of strong inflation in the economy, such as recessions and recoveries will influence the country's household confident consumption in the year.

The surveys consumers' questions usually concern on major expenditures and changes in the respondent's financial situation, focus on job availability and current business conditions etc. questions. It is then possible that about consumer confidence depending on the relative performance of the variables that may be more relevant balances, with respect to the factors that determine unemployment and other labor market related issues. It aims to investigate whether those any one of variable factors will influence consumers general loss confident consumption desire in this year.

What is a confidence indicator ?

A confidence indicator is considered as an explanatory variable for consumption together with standard variables used on predicting consumption expenditure. However, the natural real personal consumption expenditure is unexpected and unpredicted easily.

In conclusion, consumption expenditure depends the consumer individual confidence. If the consumer has much confidence to feel this year economic change will be better and he/she is easily to find job, then he/she will accept consumption easily in this year. It seems financial wealth and unemployment etc. economic factors will influence every household consumption desire. So, survey is one kind of good psychological consumption prediction method to predict consumption spending for any country in the year. I recommend manufacturers may choose to apply survey method to attempt to enquire sample survey people to gather data to predict whether what degree of consumption desire to them and find solution methods to solve low degree of consumption desire challenge.

How to apply behavioral economy methods to influence employee individual psychology to achieve raise productivity of long term incentive intention?

Increasing salary is short term incentive productivity method. Behavioral economy assumes labors will choose to do beneficial behaviors to themselves when they feel their work behaviors can earn more benefits to themselves more than their employers in the organizations. Otherwise, if they feel their work behaviors can earn more benefits to their employers more than themselves. Then, they won't choose to do their work behaviors, e.g. raising productivities or work hard. Due to they feel work hard or raise productivities behaviors that only give more benefits to their employers more themselves.

Whether does cheap product price incentive consumption desire to influence effective consumption behavior? Whether is monetary increasing salary payment incentive labors might be willing to work on task? I feel raising labors productivities is similar to raise incentive consumption, which both have similar point, such as increasing salary payment or cheap product price is the main factor to influence incentive consumption or raising productivities. Hence, it seems monetary factor is not the main

effort to encourage labors to work hard.
In labor's behavioral economic view point, for example, if an employer pays an employee more doing a task, who might be less willing to work on it, who might be less productive given whose efforts and who may enjoy the task less. If you want your employees to save more for retirement. You may want to give them fewer investment options. If you want them to engage more in a task, you might want offer them an additional alternative, instead of increasing salary to that task. Thus, increasing salary is not only method to encourage productivities of incentives.

How to improve the design of incentive structures to encourage productivities in any organizations?
Any monetary incentive can only encourage productivities in short term. It can not only encourage productivities in long term in any organizations. It is similar to cheap or discount product price can only attractive consumers to buy the product in short term, it can not attract consumers to choose to buy the product in long term, it prefers to have more options to encourage labors to incentive productivities, e.g. investing good beneficial retirement plans. Suggesting that employees do not have free disposal of their investment options. These standard incentives seem irrelevant raising salary monetary factor, they can be quite effective in inducing labors to take particular actions to incentive productivities in long term. Due to when they can hard work, then they have more beneficial retirement plans or investing plans for their retirement. It means when they can achieve the most effective or efficient productivities to the employer for long term. It will give better retirement benefits and investment benefits to the better or even the best performance of employees. Otherwise, the worst performance employees won't earn good retirement benefits and investment benefits, when their employers feel their perform very poor in the organizations in long term.
Hence, increasing salary level method is not one successful long term incentive method to persuade every employee to raise productivities or encourage excellent performance optional method. Increasing salary level is only similar to reduce product price and it is only short term encouragement to consumption or productivities method.
In conclusion, extrinsic monetary factor can not incentive labor's raising productivities more than every employee themselves intrinsic motivation to raise productivities as excellent performance in any organizations. Thus, organizations need to let employees to feel that they can give long term

economic benefits to encourage their intrinsic motivation effort to be raised their productivities or performance more effective or efficient in order to achieve long term both win-win economic benefits to employees and employers both.

Building employees and managers kindly co-operational relationship method

If you are an economist, your employer has no without any financial incentive to encourage your economic research tasks in your organization. It is equally difficult to certify that such activity will contribute to your growth of human capital and increased productivity in research or teaching. The standard model, which explains employee's effort only through the way (determined by productivity), is therefore incomplete. In particular, it doesn't consider that incentives to work do not have to be monetary in other words, that there are other things besides the disutility of labor (Kamenica, 2012) and section 1.3 have.

Why will short term wage increasing method only influence short term labor supply to raise productivities? The effect of reference raising wage can be most easily identified on short term labor supply to raise productivities. For US, New York city taxi drivers case, they have to decide every day for low long they are going to offer their services, given the day-to-day variable ability of demand they face (peaking during bad weather and/or when big conferences and public events are taking place in the city).

In the standard model, houses worked should grow with any growth in demand for New York taxi drivers‘ services. (one day's earning will have only a negligible income effect in the longer run). And yet actual cabbies work less on a demand heavy day. One of possible explanations suggests that New York city taxi drivers expect a certain income, they have set themselves a specific target income, who expect to achieve every day. During low demand for their taxi services, then they work longer hours to reach the target, when during peak demand, their referential income is achieved quickly and they only work short hours. Elasticity of hours worked with respect to their earnings is therefore negative (Lamerer, Babcock, Loewenstein, & Thaler, 1997).

However, taxi driver is either one self employment business or one taxi company employment driving service occupation. It is similar to other kinds of service jobs in societies. Servicing employees, such as waiters, salespeople, securities, customer services, bus drivers etc. different kinds of service occupations. They are not similar to manufacturing occupation to be applied how many amount of piece of products production to evaluate their productivities efforts. Thus these any one of service job nature is depended on their service performance to clients to feel their service performances are excellent to compare general service performance effort of service employees.

Considerably, respectively, I assume that if these service employees' managers can build kindly working environment, e.g. manager individual attitude and behavior can let their employees to feel happy to work together in their teams. Then, the managers' kindly as enthusiastic behaviors or attitudes will let every employee more positive encouragement of service attitude to serve their clients in their teams. Then, the client complaining number will be possible reduced, even none of any complains. Hence, building kindly relationship between managers and employees will raise excellent service performance to any organization service nature employees.

Can bonus method encourage service performance to be raised ?

In service job nature of bonus method can also raise employees' overall productivities or service performance. For example, when employees got a provisional bonus before the start of the workweek, but were warned that they would lose it on payday, unless they achieve the productivities or excellent service performance norm, they worked more productivities or let many clients to satisfy their service performance. Hence, managers can achieve bonus plan to compensate any excellent productivity or excellent services to them. Then, they can let clients to feel their service performance more satisfactory than employees of a control group who were merely given the standard promise to receive a bonus upon achieving the norm.

The effort was relatively small, however, productivity grew 1%. Interestingly, the effect of a loss was stronger when how teams were rewarded this way, social pressure came to bear on the less productivity team members. When the team members won't earn any bonus. So, long-term productivity gains were achieved through bonuses paid by excellent performance compensation method to compare to low service performance employees receiving no bonuses at all.

Economic views of human motivation nature

There are only two main types of economic actors and by making simplifying assumptions about how these types of actors behave and interact. The two basic sets of actors in this model are firms, which are assumed in this model are firms, which are assumed to maximize their profits from producing and selling products and services, households, which are assumed to maximize their utility (or satisfaction) from consuming products and services.

It seems any employees will choose to do behaviors to achieve to earn much benefits from their organizations. The models of economic behaviors that consider considerate employees' choice of goals, the actions they take to achieve these goals and the limitations and influences that affect their choices and actions.

For university students choose which universities to study case, suppose that any college enrollment students are deciding which courses to study. Thus, it implies that if the university can provide many different kinds of suitable or right courses to any college enrollment students to choose to study. It means that if the university can provide many different kinds of courses to enrollment students to choose to study. Then, it will have much chance to attract enrollment students to choose this university to study. It's competition can be raised by many courses choice factor. but, in fact, it is not absolute right, although the university can provide many courses to provide to enrollment students to choose to study. But, it is not guarantee to represent it must attract many students to enroll this university to study.

For example, suppose that college enrollment students are deciding which courses to choose to study. Although, it has right course to prepare to these enrollment students to choose to study. But, they see a summary of evaluations from hundreds of other students indicating that a certain course is very good in this university. Then, suppose that they match a video interview of just one student to give a negative review of this university of the course. Even when students were told in advance that such a negative review was worse to this university of the course. They tended to be more influenced by the negative review than the summary of hundreds of evaluations, even although such behavior seems irrational. Hence, although many right courses choice has much chance to attract students to enroll this university to study. But, if its bad educational quality from this course from negative review factor, which will influence the enrollment students number to be reduced.

It implies that students will compare this university's the course educational quality whether is better or worse to compare other universities' similar course educational quality, even this university's this course fee whether is reasonable in educational market. This is cost and beneficial comparison behavioral economy principle to all enrollment

students before they decide to choose which universities.
Hence, this case implies that universities how to train teachers' teaching skills to let students to feel that they can learn new knowledge from their teaching staffs absolutely. It means how to raise education training skills to raise teachers' teaching performance. It is very important factor to influence the university's teaching development success. So, many courses choice is not important factor to attract many students to enroll the university. Otherwise, although the university can not provide many courses to let students to enroll, but it's teachers can provide excellent teaching service to teach whose students. This is important factor to attract many students to choose to enroll this university to study.

- Under-level productive efficiency and low-consumption desire behavioral economic influences

In behavioral economic influence view point, I feel that under-level productive efficiency is the represent low production number to the manufacturer as well as low-consumption desire is not represent less consumers demands or customers lose confidence to the product.
On the one hand, I shall apply behavioral economic method to analyze why under productive efficiency is not represent low production number influence. Otherwise, I feel under-productive efficiency will have possible to increase production number after the manufacturer can review what factor(s) to influence under-productive efficiency.
I shall give reasons to explain as below:
As Jim, P. & Brendan. M. (2013) indicated who had ever been experiencing failure to do their businesses. Although, they had lost a million dollars, but they felt that they can be taught to learn undiscovered knowledge to know how to do their businesses successful by their wrong judgement and decision learning experience. They explained that " in ll risk taking, speculation, business ventures, entrepreneurial activities, it is the loss side on which you must focus first. This is even true for gambling, the gambler determines how much he's willing to bet, and loss, before the game is played. He doesn't wait for the game to end and then let the croupier or dealer assign his wager for him. How do you determine the downside, and how do you control or minimize it? With objective decision making and a plan that has as its starting point the stop-loss parameters"
Hence, it explains any business will have under-level productive efficiencies and low consumption desire business risk. However, to any one entrepreneur, who needs to know it is one game between the himself/

herself and whose clients. They also need to know with objective decision making and a plan that has as its starting point.

Hence, I assume that if the entrepreneur has wrong decision to cause under-level productive efficiency, it is possible that, due to there is no enough employee number to manufacture the product or many employees are not skillful to manufacture all product in normal time or many employees are lazy etc. different factors to cause under-level productivities. However, when they discover their productivities are very low to compare similar competitors their employees‘ productivities and efficiencies. Then, they can attempt to find what factor(s) to cause low productivities and low efficiencies. it is possible that any one among of these factors case. They include many employees’ lazy to influence low productivities or there is no enough employee number or many employees are not skillful to manufacture their products in production process.

Hence, wrong decision or plan is not represent failure. Otherwise, it can give chance to let the entrepreneur to learn whether what the factor(s) is (are) to cause low productivities and low efficiencies in whose product manufacturing process. As I feel that under-level productive efficiency is not represent low production number. Because I assume that if one worker lacks enough skills and manufacturing experiences to manufacture the product, but who can spend less time to manufacture the product and whose spending manufacturing time is same to the another owning enough skillful worker’s time to do the product. Hence, I believe that the product quality from the low-skillful worker’s manufacturing skill, it’s quality will be worse to compare to the product quality from the high skillful worker’s manufacturing skill. Hence, if the low skillful worker needs to spend much time to produce the product, but the product quality can be same to the high skillful worker’s product quality. It means that it is sure because the low skillful worker has no excellent skill to compare to the high skillful worker to produce the product. Hence, his manufacturing spending time must be longer than the high skillful worker’s time. It implies that the low skillful worker spends less time to raises high production number, but his product must be poor quality to sell. Then, his fast and efficient manufacturing speed that is not achieve economic beneficial to the organization’s manufacturing process, e.g. less electricity spends to manufacture the product. Otherwise, the low skillful worker’s fast and efficient manufacturing speed of behavior will raise the organization’s cost in manufacturing process because consumers would not like to choose to buy

any low quality product when they can choose which similar products to compare which one has the best quality and cheap price to buy.
Hence, efficient production is not the main factor to influence the business's success. Otherwise, good quality of the product factor is more important to compare it to influence the business's success.
On the other hand, I shall apply behavioral economic theory to analyze why low-consumption desire is not represent consumer demand lose to the business. As Jim. P. & Brendan. M. (2013) also identified " rather than looking for success to follow, who explained the formula for failure to avoid. As an Wang, founder of Wang laboratories said " it is my belief that there are no secret to success." The formula for failure is not lack of knowledge, brains, skills or hard work and it's not lack of luck, it's personalizing losses, especially of preceded by a string of wins or profits. It's refusing to acknowledge and accept the reality of a loss when it starts to occur because to so so would reflect negatively on you."
Thus, as whose feeling to explain why low-consumption desire is not represent less consumers demands or customers lose confidence to the product. The reasons include the causes of low-consumption desire are possible due to worse economic environment factor influences consumption desire to be reduced. It is not due to whether the product price is too high or quality is worse to compare others. Hence, as Jim & Brendan indicated the formula for business failure is not lack of knowledge, brains, skills or hard work and it's not lack of luck. It's not lack of luck. It's personalizing losses, means its reflecting to knowledge and accept the reality of a loss when it starts to occur. As it is applied to explain why low-consumption desire is not represent less consumers demands or customers lose confidence to the product. It's possible that external economic environment changing worse factor to cause the business personalizing losses, it is not reflect who lacks knowledge, skill, hard work factors to cause failure. Hence, ho to predict when and how and why economic environment changes worse will be important factor to predict when and how and why consumption behavioral changes to cause business's success.

- Demand and supply theory solves business sale problem

Any organizations can let salespeople feel happy to sell their products. Then their sale performance will also raise. The question concerns that how to make them to feel happy to help the organization to sell their products? I shall explain some methods as below:

How to manage sales for predictable revenue? In order to hold salespeople sale psychology whether they feel happy or unhappy, executives need to understand the essential activities, sales managers must focus on to be analysts for change, foster continuous improvement and create a sales culture that drives results. Sale executives need to know how to achieve top objectives of sales management is to drive sales, capture new revenue and exceed monthly sales and margin objectives, e.g. performing sale straregy development with each salesperson on Monday morning at a minimum, and in a formal one-on-one meeting during the week;using strategy tools and questioning techniques to ensure the prospects are qualified and the strategy is valid; knowing the ratio between future values and future monthly quotos to raise sale opportunities; six month on-going sale plan aims to make sure there are coordinated to achieve sale to various market segments; developing on ongoing series of networking events to build market awareness in order to ensure all salespeople attend specific events involved in networking by salespeople to, understanding the market how to influence salespeople sale method to sale number, understanding trends and seeking some channels to raise additional sales opportunities; how to create trained or warm sale environment to let sales teams feel happy to sell.

How to design and utilize efficient control sale procedures? The sale cycle procedure may include these market activities, such as advertising, sales promotion, market research, physical distribution, pricing , sale place, sale staffs seeking. SO, any organizations need have good sale planning, direction and control of the personnel, selling activities of a business with including recruiting, selecting, training, rating, supervising, paying or reward system, motivating strategy , as all these tasks apply to the personnel sales-force.

The factors may influence salespeople psychology, they may include fair income reward system, or appreciation methods and sale career development plan to every salesperson. It aims to encourage them to achieve the highest sale effort. Anymore, methods to train sale managers have the right direction to guide, lead and motivate their salespeople, e.g. knowledge of salespeople psychology needs how to satisfy them, understanding why they choose to do or act themselves sale behaviors in order to improve their weakness to motivate salespeople to achieve company's sale target goal every month easily, e.g. raising profitability, sales volume, market share, growth and corporate image building raise clients' confidence to choose to buy this company's any products more easily.

The sales organization is required for the following purposes, they may include: enabling top-management, to devote to more time in policy making for the growth and expansion of business to divide and fix authority among the subordinates , so that they may shirk work, to avoid repetition of duties and functions, so that there may not be any confusion among them to locate responsibility of each and every employee , so that they can complete the whole work in stipulated time, if not then the particular person must be responsible, to establish the sales effort to enforce proper supervision of sales force.

What does the concept of salespeople replacement value mean? What is a sales force turnover management tool? Sales force turnover is defined as the rate at which salespeople leave an organizations, resignations, retirements or dismissals. So, if the organization can raise the sales force turnover ratio, because many salespeople can be promoted or the retirement, or the sales force turnover ratio raising reasons as well as they are not resignation or dismissal reasons. I believe that the organization ought have good sale environment and reasonable reward and welfare strategy to let its salespeople feel happy to help this company to sell its products every day.

However, sales management's actions have direct or indirect effects to impact on turnover. Direct effects may include the firm's firing or dismiss policy. The indirect effects on sale turnover may include new salesperon recruiting and selecting policies affect the quality and performance of the sale force as well as the speed at which salespeople are replaced. The same policies have an impact on the sales force turnover rate through the characteristics of the newly recurited salespersons and the promotion , training, retraining policies, support, supervision, compensation. ALl of those factors have an impact on salesperson's personal satisfaction or dissatisfaction absolutely. So, any sale organizations need to concern how and why whether any one of above these factors may influence their salespeople how to perform or act sale behaviors in order to excite their sale number more effective in long term.

How to achieve sale force management effectively? Sale management is one strategy to many organizations, because organizations expect their salespeople can only raise product sale number. So , they will consider whetther how to implement the sale management strategy to be the most suitable to themselves sale organizations in order to excite their sale teams to sell their products to achieve sale growth aim effectively. So for organization's long term sale growth development, it seems that one excellent sale management strategy can help the organization has stable sale number growth in long term possible.

However, the term " selling" includes a variety of sales situations and activities. For example, those sales positions where the sales representative is required primarily to deliver the product to the customer on a regular or periodic basis. The emphasis is this type of sales activity is very different to the sales position where the sales representative is dealing with sales of capital equipment to industrial purchasers. IN additions some sales representatives deal only in export markets whereas others sell direct to customers in their homes. So, sale organizations need to sell to local or overseas market as well as its target customer is businessmen or individual consumer or both in order to implement to choose their most suitable sale management strategy to train their salespeople more effective or achieving sale growth objective only. Because these its sale major target and where sale market place both factors will influence how it ought train its salespeople, so any organization's training method ought be influenced to change by whom is its major sale target and where is its major sale market location factors.

How to know the psychology of salesmanship? WHen the organization can predict or find reasons to explain why its salespeople feel unhappy to help
this organization to sell its products. Then, it can attempt to improve its weaknesses in order to let its salespeople to feel more sale service satisfactory feeling to continue to help this organization to sell its products. THen, it won't need not often to train or recruit new salespeople to replace its old salespeople in consequence. How to know what its salespeoples' real need in order to raise their sale service satisfactory feeling ?

Psychology means that " science of the mind" and psychology plays to important part in business and it is quite worth to bring to influence any organization salespeoples' posivitive or negative sale emotion in their every sale process between themselves and their every client in personal. For example, if the salesperson often have negative emotion or he feels unhappy in every sale process, then he will encounter or increase many times of sale failure possibilities. He will feel that he is one poor verbal advertiser or seller or promotor to help his organization to promote its products to sell again as well as he will lose confidence to sell any products next sale chance, because his failure sale experiences are accumulated to influence his sale emotion to be poor or difficult sale.

Hence, the poor performance salesperson needs have more successful sale experiences to compensate his / her prior many sale failure times feeling, if the organization hopes this poor performance salesperson can raise sale number easily. Overall, any organizations need to concern how to improve or raise the more failure times of sale experience salespeoples' sale techniques or methods or attitudes more than choose to fire or dismiss them as well as finding another new salesperson to replace him/her. Because it is possible that the salesperson 's poor sale performance that is not due to himself/herself poor sale effort and sale knowledge or lacking sale experience to the product, it may be due to the poor sale team cooperation relationship , feeling poor or not comfortable sale physcial shop environment, poor sale manager and other salespeople working relationship, the sale manager lacks leadership effort, poor family relationship etc. external factors more than himself/herself personal poor or negative emotion or poor health etc. personal factors. Hence, the organization ought enquire him/her why he/she feels unhappy to sell its products and it needs to attempt to find methods to solve his/her challenges immediately. If his/her challenges can be solved. It is possible that his/her sale efforts can be also raised for. So, if the organization can know how to utilize positive sale emotion psychological methods to predict or know why and how every salesperson perform his/her sale behavior in whose daily sale tasks, then it can concentrate on implementing effective and the most suitable sale training to raise their sale abilities more easily.

However, the sale training may include: How to build or improve long term good salesperson and his/her customer sale service relationship between every salesperson and every client in every buying and selling cycle process, how to using right communicating styleds for better understanding every client's real needs, powers and negotiating, e.g. every salesperson needs to review why there are many clients do not choose to buy any products from his sale presentation or promotion, finding every time sale failure reasons can let the salesperson makes himself/herself sale failure reasons evaluation or judgement in order to find what is the major reason influences his/her sale failure, e.g. lacking product knowledge, he/she often let many clients to feel that he lacks patience to listen the client's enquiry or feedback, his sale presentation is not attractive to let many clients like to stay longer time to listen his sale presentation in whole sale process, the salesperson himself/herself emotion is negative and he /she can let many clients feel he / she is not happy or does not enjoy to sell this product from himself/herself face impression or sale behavior impression easily, lacking enough sale techniques to persuade his/her clients why he/ she ought choose to buy this product in whole sale process etc. these factors may influence the salesperson's sale failure chance to be raised. Hence sales manager ought need to spend long time to meet the poor sale performance salesperson to discuess what his/her sale challenges are the most major to influence his/her every sale successful chance in order to improve his/ her sale performance more successfully.

IN conclusion, the reasons why salespeople often encounter sale failure possibilities. The factors may include these aspects, such as they lask the desire to help customers to make satisfactory purchase decisons, they only concern how to achieve sale final objective or aim only, it will cause clients feel they do not real concern their real needs. They only concern to sell the product in success. They do not know how to describe the product whether what characteristics or features it owns accurately in order to increase sale chance to persudade them to make final decision to by the product, they do not attempt to participate the whole sale process to help them to choose the most right product in order to satisfy their any purcahse needs, they ought avoid deceptive or manipulative influence tactics, avoid the use of high pressure sales techniques etc. Thus, if any organizations can spend time to investigate what factors cause why any one of salespeople choose perform his/her sale behavior often in order to know or understand their salespeople' sale psychology absolutely. Then, I believe that their sale number will only grown more easily.

CHAPTER TWO

Behavioral economy predicts house buyers purchase living desire

Something Behavioral (e.g., Prospect Theory) applies to property buyer choice

What Is the Prospect Theory?

Prospect theory assumes that losses and gains are valued differently, and thus individuals make decisions based on perceived gains instead of perceived losses. Also known as the "loss-aversion" theory, the general concept is that if two choices are put before an individual, both equal, with one presented in terms of potential gains and the other in terms of possible losses, the former option will be chosen.

How the Prospect Theory Works

Prospect theory belongs to the behavioral economic subgroup, describing how individuals make a choice between probabilistic alternatives where risk is involved and the probability of different outcomes is unknown. This theory was formulated in 1979 and further developed in 1992 by Amos Tversky and Daniel Kahneman, deeming it more psychologically accurate of how decisions are made when compared to the expected utility theory.

The underlying explanation for an individual's behavior, under prospect theory, is that because the choices are independent and singular, the probability of a gain or a loss is reasonably assumed as being 50/50 instead of the probability that is actually presented. Essentially, the probability of a gain is generally perceived as greater. Although there is no difference in the actual gains or losses of a certain product, the prospect theory says investors will choose the product that offers the most perceived gains.

Tversky and Kahneman proposed that losses cause a greater emotional impact on an individual than does an equivalent amount of gain, so given choices presented two ways—with both offering the same result—an individual will pick the option offering perceived gains. For example, assume that the end result is receiving $25. One option is being given the straight $25. The other option is gaining $50 and losing $25. The utility of the $25 is exactly the same in both options. However, individuals are most likely to choose to receive straight cash because a single gain is generally observed as more favorable than initially having more cash and then suffering a loss.

Types of Prospect Theory

According to Tversky and Kahneman, the certainty effect is exhibited when people prefer certain outcomes and underweight outcomes that are only probable. The certainty effect leads to individuals avoiding risk when there is a prospect of a sure gain. It also contributes to individuals seeking risk when one of their options is a sure loss.

The isolation effect occurs when people have presented two options with the same outcome, but different routes to the outcome. In this case, people are likely to cancel out similar information to lighten the cognitive load, and their conclusions will vary depending on how the options are framed.

•The prospect theory says that investors value gains and losses differently, placing more weight on perceived gains versus perceived losses.

•An investor presented with a choice, both equal, will choose the one presented in terms of potential gains.

•The prospect theory is part of behavioral economics, suggesting investors chose perceived gains because losses cause a greater emotional impact.

•The certainty effect says individuals prefer certain outcomes over probable ones, while the isolation effect says individuals cancel out similar information when making a decision.

Prospect Theory Example

Consider an investor is given a pitch for the same mutual fund by two separate financial advisors. One advisor presents the fund to the investor, highlighting that it has an average return of 12% over the past three years. The other advisor tells the investor that the fund has had above-average returns in the past 10 years, but in recent years it has been declining. Prospect theory assumes that though the investor was presented with the exact same mutual fund, he is likely to buy the fund from the first advisor, who expressed the fund's rate of return as an overall gain instead of the advisor presenting the fund as having high returns and losses.

How and why behavioral economic method can predict house buyers house purchase need or desire whether the country's house buyers their house purchase need or desire will increase or decrease in the year. I shall explain the reasons as below:

Supply-side economists say that increasing business growth, not consumer demand, will boost the economy. They agree the government has a role to play, but fiscal policy should target companies. They rely on tax cuts and deregulation. So, supply-side economists believe that raising house buyers' house purchase or long term renting or instalement payment desires. Government or business organizations will play a important role, e.g. decresing salary tax, banks can charge low interest to encourage many people to borrow much long term loan or money to spend long term expenditure, e.g. buying house. So, it seems that other parties will encourage house buyers' house purchase more more than themselves psychological feeling influence. Otherwise, demand-side economists say that any house buyer individual psychological living need desire is more influential to encourage they choose to buy house in preference. On one hand, in demand-side economists view, I shall apply behavioral economic concept to explain why and how causes house buyer individual house purchase choice in preference than rent choice . On the other hand, in supply-side economists view, I shall apply demand and supply economic concept to explain why and how casues house buyer individual house purchase choice in preference than rent choice in property market.

What does behavioral economy mean ?Think about supposing you plan to buy a house. You may have decided to simplify your decision making by opting for the house price, living environment, such as air and noise pollution, income level, school, public library, public park, public swimming pool, transportation facilities etc. different factors to influence you house purchase decision in the location. You may then have visited the house location to view its environments before you decide to choose the location to buy the house to live. But the decision making process did not stop there, as you now had to customize your model by visiting from different house location . You aim to compare whether anywhere location(s) can let you to feel the location is better to let you feel to live.) Instead the house location and environment factor, you were still considered the house appearance and design and comfortable feeling features you really needed. At this stage, most property developers will show a base model with options that can be changed according to whether the house buyers their preferences are environment, house design, house price, facilties before they decide to buy the house to live. The way in which these different location of house choices are presented to house buyers will influence the final house purchases made and illustrates a number of concepts from behavioral economic (BE) theories.

First, the base model shown in the customization engine represents a rational choice to any house buyers‘ purchase decision usually. Usually, house buyers, they will visit the house location to feel its living environment, entertainment facilities supply, transport facilities supply and house design and comfortable feeling to decide to buy the house to live, instead of income factor in house market. The more uncertain house customers are about their rational house feeling , such as comfortable living, environment and facility and house design decision, instead of income factor influences can change their earlier first house purchase decision if they feel the house price is more expensive to compare the other houses choices.

Second, the house developer can frame options differently by employing either an 'add' or 'delete' customization mode (or something in between). In an add mode, house buyers start with a base model and then add more or better options. In a delete frame, the opposite process occurs, whereby house buyers have to deselect options or downgrade from a fully-loaded model. Such as this house market case, past research suggests that house buyers end up choosing a greater number of features when they are in a delete rather than an add frame (Biswas, 2009). Finally, the option framing strategy will be associated with different house price anchors prior to customization, which may influence the perceived value of the house. If the final house ends up with one million house price bid, its cost is likely to be perceived as more attractive if the initial default configuration was two million house price (fully loaded) rather than one million house price. Why does the more expensive house price will still attract some house buyers to choose to buy in preference—an option framing strategy that maximizes sales, but set at a default house price that deters a minimum of potential house buyers from considering a purchase in the first place. When the house buyers group is high and stable income group, they won't consider the more expensive house price issue to influence them to change to buy the one million house price houses to live easily. Instead of after they view the house location to let them to feel that there have less transport facilities, e.g. bus, taxi, underground train, tram etc. public service transport tools are close to their living location, or tehy feel the natural environment is polluted to let they feel the can not breathe fresh air , or there are many factories are close to their houses to cause they feel dirty air, or traffic jam is serious to cause air pollution and noise pollution , or they feel that the two million house design is poor, they can not let them to feel comfortable to live in the appartments, it means that the house price is under value to be accepted to same to two million price. Then, the stable and high income house buyers will change their earlier house purchase first choice to accept the other house opitions to decide to buy in preference.

Rational Expectations And Rational Choice Theory

Rational Expectations in Theory to predict property market buyers property choice desires

What are Rational Expectations?

Rational expectations is an economic theory that states that individuals make decisions based on the best available information in the market and learn from past trends. Rational expectations suggest that people will be wrong sometimes, but that, on average, they will be correct.

Understanding the Concept of Rational Expectations

The idea of rational expectations was first developed by American economist John F. Muth in 1961. However, it was popularized by economists Robert Lucas and T. Sargent in the 1970s and was widely used in microeconomics as part of the new classical revolution.

The theory states the following assumptions:

•With rational expectations, people always learn from past mistakes.

•Forecasts are unbiased, and people use all the available information and economic theories to make decisions.

•People understand how the economy works and how government policies alter macroeconomic variables such as price level, level of unemployment, and aggregate output.

The rational expectations theory comes in weak and strong versions. The "strong" version assumes that actors are able to access all available information and make rational decisions based on the information.

The "weak" versions assume that people lack the time to access all relevant information but make decisions based on their limited knowledge. For example, if they buy cornflakes, it is "rational" to keep buying the same brand and not worry about getting perfect information about relative prices of other cornflakes brands.

Most macroeconomists today use rational expectations as an assumption in their analysis of policies. When thinking about the effects of economic policy, the assumption is that people will do their best to work out the implications.

The rational expectations approach is often used to test the accuracy of inflation forecasts. For example, Pet is an individual's forecast in year t-1 of the price level in year t. The actual price level is denoted by Pt. The difference between the actual price level and individual's forecast is the forecast error for year t.

Pt – Pet = rt is the individual's forecast error in year t. With rational expectations, the forecast errors are due to unpredictable numbers. However, if people systematically under-predict or over-predict numbers, the price level expectations are not rational.

Under rational expectations, what happens today depends on the expectations of what will happen in the future. But what happens in the future also depends on what happens today. Many macroeconomic principles today are created with the assumption of rational expectations.

The theory is also used by many new Keynesian economists because it fits well with their assumption that people want to pursue their own self-interest. If people's expectations were not rational, the economic decisions of individuals would not be as good as they are.

Adaptive Expectations

While individuals who use rational decision-making use the best available information in the market to make decisions, adaptive decision makers use past trends and events to predict future outcomes. This is also known as backward thinking decision-making.

Adaptive expectations can be used to predict inflation. If inflation increased in the previous year, people expect an increased rate of inflation in the following year. The formula for adaptive expectations is Pet = Pt -1. It shows that people expect the trend of inflation to be the same as last year.

People will change their expectations of any variable if there is a difference between what they were expecting and what actually occurred. However, if their expectations turned out to be right, their future expectations likely will not change.

Limitations of Adaptive Expectations

While adaptive expectations allow us to measure expected variables and actual variables, they are not as commonly used in macroeconomics as rational expectations because of their limitations. The adaptive model is simplistic because it assumes that people base their decisions based on past data. However, in the real world, past data is just one of the factors that influence future behavior. Rational expectations incorporate many factors into the decision-making process.

What is house buyer individual Rational Choice

In an ideal house market world, defaults, frames, and house price anchors would not have any bearing on consumer choices. House purchaser decisions would be the result of a careful weighing of costs and benefits and informed by existing preferences, such as whether the house future price will appreciate to raise value or reduce under value, the house living location will increase public transport facilities, public entertainment facilities, build more schools, offices to close to the house location. We would always make optimal decisions. In the 1976 book The Economic Approach to Human Behavior, the economist Gary S. Becker famously outlined a number of ideas known as the pillars of so-called 'rational choice' theory. The theory assumes that human actors have stable preferences and engage in maximizing behavior.

Mental Accounting

The economist Richard Thaler, a keen observer of human behavior and founder of behavioral economics, was inspired by Kahneman & Tversky's work (see Thaler, 2015, for a summary). Thaler coined the concept of mental accounting. According to Thaler, people think of value in relative rather than absolute terms. They derive pleasure not just from an object's value, but also the quality of the deal – its transaction utility (Thaler, 1985). In addition, humans often fail to fully consider opportunity costs (tradeoffs) and are susceptible to the sunk cost fallacy. Why are people willing to spend more when they pay with a credit card than cash (Prelec & Simester, 2001)? Why would more individuals spend $10 on a theater ticket if they had just lost a $10 bill than if they had to replace a lost ticket worth $10 (Kahneman & Tversky, 1984)? Why are people more likely to spend a small inheritance and invest a large one (Thaler, 1985)? Such as this property market case, if the house living needer , he/she does not choose to pay all money to buy the house, although he/she has enough money to buy the house. He/she chooses to pay instalement or rent the house to live. If he/she own visa card. Then, he/she will choose to use visa card to pay rent or pay month instalement to the property developer's house in order to earn accumulated money reward or any benefits after he/she use the visa to pay the house rent or instalement every month. So, the visa card can encourage the house buyer to achieve the house rent or instalement payment house purchase long term transaction easily.

According to the theory of mental accounting, people treat money differently, depending on factors such as the money's origin and intended use, rather than thinking of it in terms of the "bottom line" as in formal accounting (Thaler, 1999). An important term underlying the theory is fungibility, the fact that all money is interchangable and has no labels. In mental accounting, people treat assets as less fungible than they really are. Even seasoned investors are susceptible to this bias when they view recent gains as disposable "house money" (Thaler & Johnson, 1990) that can be used in high-risk investments. In doing so, they make decisions on each mental account separately, losing out the big picture of the portfolio.

Another concept related to mental accounting captures the fact that people don't like to spend money. We experience pain of paying (Zellermayer, 1996), because we are loss averse. The pain of paying plays an important role in consumer self-regulation to keep spending in check (Prelec & Loewenstein, 1998). This pain is thought to be reduced in credit card purchases, because plastic is less tangible than cash, the depletion of resources (money) is less visible and payment is deferred. Different types of people experience different levels of pain of paying, which can affect spending decisions. Tightwads, for instance, experience more of this pain than spendthrifts. As a result, tightwads are particularly sensitive to marketing contexts that make spending less painful (Rick, 2018). Hence, such as this property market purchase case, because some house buyers do not hope to spend much money to buy one house to live. They will feel to use visa card, it can replace money to let them to feel they won't lose much money to spend in the moment. So, in mental spending feeling view, they will feel visa card will help them to reduce to spend much money to rent or pay instalement to live the house in long time. So, in psychological view, visa card is one good spending money replace tool to influence these non- accepted spend money buyers to make final house rent or paying instalement decision to live the house decision more easily.

Choice Overload

Humans' bounded rationality is particularly well illustrated by the concept of choice overload. Also referred to as 'overchoice', this phenomenon occurs as a result of too many choices being available to consumers. Overchoice has been associated with unhappiness (Schwartz, 2004), decision fatigue, going with the default option, as well as choice deferral—avoiding making a decision altogether, such as not buying a product (Iyengar & Lepper, 2000). Many different factors may contribute to perceived choice overload, including the number of options and attributes, time constraints, decision accountability, alignability and complementarity of options, consumers' preference uncertainty, among other factors (Chernev et al., 2015). Choice overload can be counteracted by simplifying choice attributes or the number of available options (Johnson et al., 2012). Hence, such as this property market case, when the month has too many properties are supplied to let house buyers to choose in the country's property market. Then, it will bring properties choice overload effect to cause the increasing houses number of options to cause the country's house buyers feel need to spend long time to make the house purchase preference decision in order to avoid any loss after they bought the under value houses to live. So, Choice overload usually cause long time choice process to any consumers, such as this property market consumption case.

Limited Information: The Importance of Feedback

Bounded rationality's principle of limited knowledge or information is one of the topics discussed in the 2008 book Nudge. In the book, Thaler and Sunstein point to experience, good information, and prompt feedback as key factors that enable people to make good decisions. Consider climate change, for example, which has been cited as a particularly challenging problem in relation to experience and feedback. Climate change is invisible, diffuse, and a long-term process. Pro-environmental behavior by an individual, such as reducing carbon emissions, does not lead to a noticeable change. The same is true in the domain of health. Feedback in this area is often poor, and we are more likely to get feedback on previously chosen options than rejected ones.

Information Avoidance

Behavioral economics assumes that people are boundedly rational actors with a limited ability to process information. While a great deal of research has been devoted to exploring how available information affects the quality and outcomes of decisions, a newer strand of research has also explored situations where people avoid information altogether.

Information avoidance in behavioral economics (Golman et al., 2017) refers to situations in which people choose not to obtain knowledge that is freely available. Active information avoidance includes physical avoidance, inattention, the biased interpretation of information (see also confirmation bias) and even some forms of forgetting. In behavioral finance, for example, research has shown that investors are less likely to check their portfolio online when the stock market is down than when it is up, which has been termed the ostrich effect (Karlsson et al., 2009). More serious cases of avoidance happen when people fail to return to clinics to get medical test results, for instance (Sullivan et al., 2004).

While information avoidance is sometimes strategic, it can have immediate hedonic benefits for people if it prevents the negative (usually psychological) consequences of knowing the information. It usually carries negative utility in the long term, because it deprives people of potentially useful information for decision making and feedback for future behavior. Furthermore, information avoidance can contribute to a polarization of political opinions and media bias.

The impact of smoking, for example, is at best noticeable over the course of years, while its effect on cells and internal organs is usually not evident to the individual. Traditionally, generic feedback aimed at inducing behavioral change has been limited to information ranging from the economic costs of the unhealthy behavior to its potential health consequences (Diclemente et al., 2001). More recent behavior change programs, such as those employing smartphone apps to stop smoking, now usually provide positive and personalized behavioral feedback, which may include the number of cigarettes not smoked and money saved, along with information about health improvement and disease avoidance.

Predictably Irrational and Nudge alerted the public to a new breed of economists influenced by the study of behavioral decision making that was pioneered by Kahneman and Tversky's work (sometimes referred to as 'choice under uncertainty'). The psychology of homo economicus—a rational and selfish individual with relatively stable preferences—has been challenged, and the traditional view that behavior change should be achieved by informing, convincing, incentivizing or penalizing people has been questioned (Thaler & Sunstein, 2008). The field associated with this stream of research and theory is behavioral economics (BE), which suggests that human decisions are strongly influenced by context, including the way in which choices are presented to us. Behavior varies across time and space, and it is subject to cognitive biases, emotions, and social influences.

Decisions are the result of less deliberative, linear, and controlled processes than we would like to believe.

Hence, such as this property market case, if the property developer can not provide more property advertisement to the property buyers to receive to let them to feel whether what benefits or enjoyment benefits that they can enjoy after they lived the property developer's houses to live. Due to lacking clear property information message to let many property buyers to know the property developer's property sale advertisement from property magazines, newspapers, TV, wesbite etc. channel. Then, it will influence the property developer's houses , they won't be many property buyers' choices, before they make final property purchase decision at the moment. So, property market purchase need desire change will be influenced by the time and space external unpredictable factor , such as visa card promotion , unemployment ratio rises up or falls down, the property advertisement attractive effort etc. unpredictable factors to excite any property buyers' living need desire in any time indirectly.

Dual-System Theory

Daniel Kahneman uses a dual-system theoretical framework (which established a foothold in cognitive and social psychology of the 1990s) to explain why our judgments and decisions often do not conform to formal notions of rationality. System 1 consists of thinking processes that are intuitive, automatic, experience-based, and relatively unconscious. System 2 is more reflective, controlled, deliberative, and analytical. Judgments influenced by System 1 are rooted in impressions arising from mental content that is easily accessible. System 2, on the other hand, monitors or provides a check on mental operations and overt behavior—often unsuccessfully.

Example 1: Availability and Affect

System 1 is 'home' of the heuristics (cognitive shortcuts) we apply and responsible for the biases (systematic errors) we may be left with when we make decisions (Kahneman, 2011). System 1 processes influence us when prior exposure to a number affects subsequent judgments, as evident in the anchoring effects discussed previously (Tversky & Kahneman, 1974). One of the most universal heuristics is the availability heuristic. Availability serves as a mental shortcut if the possibility of an event occurring is perceived as higher simply because an example comes to mind easily (Tversky & Kahneman, 1974); for instance, a person may deem pension investments too risky as a result of remembering a family member who lost most of her retirement savings in the recent recession. Readily available information in memory is also used when we make similarity-based judgments, as evident in the representativeness heuristic.

Finally, another 'general purpose' heuristic is that of affect, namely good or bad feelings that surface automatically when we think about an object. Applying the affect heuristic can lead to black-and-white thinking, which is particularly evident when people think about an object under conditions that hamper System 2 reflection, such as time pressure. For example, consumers may consider food preservatives' benefits as low and costs as high, thus leading to a significant negative risk-benefit correlation (Finucane, Alhakami, Slovic, & Johnson, 2000).

The role of affect in risky or uncertain situations is also evident in the risk-as-feelings model (Loewenstein, Weber, Hsee, & Welch, 2001). 'Consequentialist' accounts of decision making tend to focus on expectations along with the likelihood and desirability of possible outcomes. The risk-as-feelings perspective explains behavior in situations where emotional reactions to risk differ from cognitive evaluations. In these situations, behavior tends to be influenced by anticipatory feelings, emotions experienced in the moment of decision making.

Example 2: Salience

Availability and affect are processes internal to the individual that may lead to bias. The external equivalent of these processes is salience, whereby information that stands out, is novel, or seems relevant is more likely to affect our thinking and actions (Dolan et al., 2010). For example, a technological device can be framed as being 99% reliable or having only a 1% failure rate, thereby emphasizing either positive or negative information. Salience also underlies heuristic judgments that rely on external cues. Some psychologists have derived effort-reducing heuristics that simplify consumer decision making. The brand name heuristic, for example, suggests that salient cues in the form of brand names can be used to infer quality (Maheswaran, Mackie, & Chaiken, 1992). In terms of degrees of visual salience, one study found a congruence effect between price and font size, where showing a lower sale price in a small print size relative to the regular price resulted in greater purchase likelihood than presenting the sale price in a relatively large font (Coulter & Coulter, 2005). Finally, the salience of options can also be manipulated by rearranging the physical environment; for instance, a change as simple as moving water bottles closer to the cashier in a cafeteria has been shown to increase the salience and convenience of this healthier drink choice and thereby significantly boost water sales (Thorndike, Sonnenberg, Riis, Barraclough, & Levy, 2012).

Hence, such as this property market case, if the propety buyer feels that the property developer's house price won't be influenced to decrease easily in long time , even there are many property buyers still choose to buy the property developer's houses to live as well as the property developer's houses number supply won't increase in the long time. So, in Dual-System Theory explains if the house buyer felt that the property developer's house number supply won't increase, even decrease after there are many property buyers still chooce to buy its properties to live in preference in the country's property market. Then, the property developer's house high price and limited house supply factors will not influence the house buyer's prefer house choice decision more easily.

2.1 Property market demand and supply view

How can demand and supply determine property market price ? Property price is arrived at by the interaction between house buyers demand and property developers' houses number supply. Property price is dependent upon the house design and environment and facilities characteristics of both these fundamental components of a property market. Any properties demand and supply represent the willingness of house consumers and property developers to engage in properties buyers buying needs or desires. An exchange of a house purchasetakes place when properties buyers and properties sellers can agree upon a agreed property price. This module will look at property price in a competitive market. When imperfect property market competition exists such as with a property developer monopoly or single peoperty selling firm, property price outcomes may not follow the same general rules.

Equilibrium Price in property market

When a property exchange occurs, the agreed upon price is called an "equilibrium" property price, or a "market clearing" price. This equilibrium property price occurs at the intersection of house demand and house supply as presented are in balance at the moment in property market short time, e.g. one month.

Property price determination depends equally on the moment house buyers‘ living demand and the moment house number supply. It is truly a balance of the two market components. To see why the balance must occur, examine what happens when there is no balance, for example when the moment property market price is below than the past property market price, the property quantity demanded is greater than the property quantity supplied. In such a situation, property consumers would be clamouring for a property that property developers would not be willing to supply; a property shortage would exist. In this event, property consumers would choose to pay a higher price in order to get the property they want, while property developers would be encouraged by a higher price to bring more of the properties onto the property market.

The end result is a rise in property price, when the moment has many proprety buyers feel living desire needs. where the property supply and demand are in balance. Similarly, if a property price is above were chosen arbitrarily the property market would be in shortage properties are supplied, too less properties supply are relative to high living desire demand. If that were to happen, properties developers would be willing to take a higher price in order to sell, and property consumers would be induced by higher prices to increase their property purchases desire , because they feel afraid that there will have less properties to be supplied to sell later and their prices will continue to raise in long time.

Hence, a property market price is not necessarily a fair price, it is merely an outcome. It does not guarantee total living satisfaction on the part of house buyer and property seller. Typically some assumptions about the behaviour of property buyers and property sellers are made, which add a sense of reason to a property market price. For example, property buyers are expected to be self-living comfortable interested and, although they may not have perfect property living and house price knowledge, at least they will try to look out for their own living interests. Meanwhile, property sellers are considered to be profit maximizers. This assumption limits their willingness to sell to within a price range , high to low, where they can stay in business.

Change in Equilibrium Price of property market

When either property demand or supply shifts, the property equilibrium price will change. Look at the modules on understanding property number supply for a discussion of why of that property market component may move. So, what factors can influence the property equilibrium price to be raise.

Example 1: Unusually environment and facility factor

When the property's location , it's environment and facilities are improved to let property buyers feel to compare before. With no immediate change in property consumers' willingness to buy the property developer's houses to live in the location at the moment because they feel that its environment and facilities can not let them to feel enough and comfortable to live in the location, there is a movement along the reducing demand curve to a new low equilibrium market price. Property consumers will buy more but only at a lower house price, becaue they feel poor environment and not enough facilities supply to influence they do not choose the property developer's houses location in preference. Otherwise, if the property demand curve in this example were more vertical (more inelastic, it means that the property developers raise their price won't influence less property buyers because their living desire is increasing), the property price-quantity adjustments needed to bring about a new equilibrium between property demand and the new property supply would be different. Then compare the size of property price-property quantity changes in this with the first situation. With the same shift in property supply, equilibrium change in property price is larger when property demand is inelastic than when property demand is more elastic. The opposite is true for property quantity. A larger change in property quantity supply will occur when property demand is elastic compared with the property quantity change required when property demand is inelastic.

How Does Property Developer Supply and House Buyer Demand Affect the Housing Market?

Real estate is a tangible asset made up of property and the land on which it sits. Like other assets, real estate is also subject to supply and demand. The prices of homes, like stocks and bonds, depend heavily on the law of supply and demand. But just what kind of relationship does the housing market have to this law? I suppose house supply number and house demad number , they must have close relationship to influence their house price changes in any time. Although, houses are expensive and fixed tangible asset, but they are still similar to general cheap product price changes to be influenced by demand and supply as below:

•The housing market relies very heavily on supply and demand.

•Housing demand and low supplies normally cause prices to rise.

•Prices drop when there is low demand and a larger supply of homes on the market.

•Low interest rates generally impact demand, while natural disasters, changing lifestyles, and the lack of available lots affect supplies.

The law of supply and demand is a basic economic principle that explains the relationship between supply and demand for a good or service, and how their interaction affects the price of that good or service. When there is high demand for a good or service, its price rises. If there is a large supply of a good or service but not enough demand for it, the price falls. The theory of supply and demand is one of the most basic principles in economics. Supply and demand work against each other until the point at which the equilibrium price is achieved—that is the price where supply is equal to demand in the market, such as property market case.

The law of demand dictates that people will have low or no demand for a good that has a higher price. That happens, of course, when all other factors remain equal. People tend to sacrifice something that comes at a higher cost, which curbs demand. Similarly, lower prices drive demand, meaning consumers value and purchase something more when it's cheaper. In fact, general property buyers' preference house purchase decision will be influenced by price factor in earlier. It is such as general cheap product demand and supply factor to influence its house price changes in any time. When it comes to the law of supply, prices drop when there is an increase in the supply of a good or service in the market. But when prices increase, the number of goods and services tend to drop. That's because it tends to cost more to produce and sell goods at a higher price.

Real Estate Supply and Demand

The housing market relies very heavily on supply and demand, which is why it is very prominent in the industry. Each housing transaction involves a buyer and a seller. The buyer places an offer on a property, leaving the seller to accept or reject the offer. The law of supply and demand dictates the equilibrium price of a property. Hence, supply and demand work against one another until the point at which a property's equilibrium price is reached.

A low property supply may drive prices up, which is what tends to happen with bidding wars. A specific property may be in demand by multiple parties who try to outbid each other by increasing their purchase price offer. The bidding war ends—depleting the supply—when the seller accepts one of the offers. When there is high demand for properties in a particular city or state, and a lack of supply of quality properties, the prices of houses tend to rise. When a weak economy and an oversupply of properties leads to low or no demand for housing, the prices of houses tend to fall.

Factors Affecting Housing Supply and Demand

Supply and demand is never an easy thing to measure in the real estate market. That's partly due because it takes a long time to construct new homes and fix up old ones to put back onto the market. Similarly, real estate is not like other industries in that it takes a lot of time to buy and sell homes and other properties. Some of the factors that influence housing demand include lower interest rates or borrowing costs in economic environment view. When interest rates are low, people are generally willing to take on more debt. They may be able to finance the purchase of a home because the amount of interest they have to pay isn't burdensome. If more buyers flood the market, demand for housing increases. And if there's a limited supply of housing inventory, that makes people in a low interest rate environment want to purchase even more.

Meanwhile, the supply of housing is in a constant state of change. Inventory may increase when people are moving—some may downsize, others may be try to make more room for an expanding family, while others may purchase their first home. Similarly, there may be an increase in development and new home construction, adding to the existing inventory. On the other hand, housing inventory decreases during times of natural disaster—such as floods and earthquakes—and when existing properties are demolished. Land is also a finite resource, so the amount of new developments is generally limited. It is unpredicted environmental factor to influence property price changes in the moment.

Economic environment factor influences property price changes

One of the major causes of the Great Recession that followed the financial crisis in the mid-2000s was the housing market crash. It was a direct result of the law of supply and demand. During the lead up to the financial crisis, consumers were enjoying relatively low borrowing rates. Banks began to offer low rates on mortgages, and were encouraged to relax their lending standards. People who weren't otherwise able to afford a home now found themselves able to realize their dreams. These consumers, called subprime borrowers, were able to snag a home with low down payments and low credit scores.

During this time, speculative buyers also began entering the market, driving up demand for housing and, at the same time, cutting in to the available supply. All of this, in turn, drove prices up to very lofty levels. The market couldn't keep up, and investors who were merely in the market to make some money—many were buying and flipping homes in a very short period of time—began pulling out of the market. Demand started to drop and, so did prices. The collapse of the real estate market in 2007 created an oversupply of houses and decreasing properties prices. Real estate prices depend on the law of supply and demand. When the demand for property is high but property is scarce, prices skyrocket and it becomes a seller's market. When the number of available properties increases to glut the market, prices typically drop. Supply and demand in real estate aren't easy to balance. Creating more saleable properties takes time, considerable work, and a lot of effort. It's not possible at all in some cases, and even when it is, it might not be possible for supply to increase in time to meet consumer demand. So, salespeoples' house sale experiences can also influence the property developer's house sale number.

Understanding this basic economic principle can help consumers decide the best time to buy or sell their properties.

Property market Over-Supply Or Under-Supply factor

You can usually expect a drop in prices when there is an over-supply of homes or land in a given area. You can't move the overage to another area to keep prices stable. Scarcity causes prices to rise when there isn't enough land or if there aren't enough homes in a given area. Even if land is available on which to build more homes, the time it takes to construct them cannot meet immediate property needs, so demand will remain constant or rise. Many forces that might have little or no impact on other regions influence local markets and vice versa. Pay attention to the factors that influence your local market. Watch local businesses and make note of upsizing and downsizing trends if you do business in a market that has jobs and many workers relocating there. You'll also want to keep an eye on these issues if you're a homeowner looking to sell in such an area or if you're looking for property to purchase.

Things like divorce rates, death rates, and demographics can factor in. Factors that can greatly impact property market supply and demand—and by extension your business—might include local weather trends, an aging population, and investment trends if you do business in a resort area that includes vacation homes. Trends that impact discretionary income have more of an influence on this type of market than others. Trends in interest rates, national home prices, new housing starts, and many other economic indicators can influence real estate markets as well. These national events might not typically move real estate supply and demand directly, but they can render it less or more important. The mood and sentiments of the buying public cannot be overlooked. Supply and demand don't exist in a vacuum. But few could afford to pay those prices in a worsening economy and even those who could were understandably reluctant to part with their money at that time. So properties sat on the market, unsold. Worried homeowners in financial distress put their homes up for sale rather than risk foreclosure. Remember, almost 9 million jobs were lost during the Great Recession. Now what happens? Supply begins surpassing demand by leaps and bounds. The housing market is glutted and those healthy prices evaporate—which has little to do with local factors except as they're an extension of national woes.

Land Parcels Are Finite factor to influence property market price

If the country has high population, but land supply is less to let property developers to find lands to build houses easily. Such as Hong Kong is one high population and small city. So, its property prices must be higher to compare other countries, and it causes that its rooms and houses size or area is small , but house sale price or rent is still high.

Such as Hong Kong house market case, Hong Kong people cannot fill a real estate supply shortage by manufacturing more units of land. It's a finite supply, not a manufactured commodity. Hong Kong people might be able to create more units within a given space, such as condos or townhouses, but the land itself is unique and cannot be duplicated to accommodate a short supply. When a shortage of land for homes exists in a given area, Hong Kong people can't simply move in more land to alleviate the shortage. Real estate is where it sits. It will always be a local commodity influenced by local conditions. In short, keep up with the big picture but narrow your primary focus to your region. Supply and demand in real estate will always be foremost a local issue.

As with many other types of business market, the property market is driven by supply and demand. Property prices fluctuate depending upon the factors that influence both supply and demand. Knowledge of these factors equips you with the capability of knowing when to rent/buy and, perhaps just as importantly, when to sell. At the most basic level, when property supply is greater than demand, prices fall. That's the nature of almost every product. Similarly, when the demand for properties is greater than the available supply, prices rise. Even though property markets have these principles in common with many other types of products or business services, there are some differences worth mentioning. For example, the real estate market also takes into consideration factors such as location, seasonality, and durability. There are also different types of real estate – residential, industrial, commercial and land – each of which has their own factors that influence market supply and demand. "Real estate" is defined as more than just property. It also includes natural resources and land, too. So, Hong Kong property market's price is influenced by land supply factor more than other factors, such as facilities , environment , transport etc. factors influence.

Local factors that influence property rates include:

1 – Restrictions on property production – for instance, in the case of Manhatten, there is not much space for added supply. As a result, demand remains high and prices even higher.

2 – Credit access – this often depends on where individuals live. Rural communities may have less access to bank credit, for example – reducing demand.

3 – Job market – the more jobs, the greater the demand for properties.

4 – Transport – better transport translates into greater desirability for people to move – increasing demand.

5 – Retired persons – retired people often decide to downsize and opt for a smaller property in a different locality, thereby increasing supply.

6 – Families – as families begin to grow, they need greater sized properties. This increases the demand for larger homes, whilst decreasing demand for smaller homes.

7 – Meteorology – destinations with more favorable weather profiles and ones that avert the extremes of weather are preferable. Demand in places such as San Diego is significantly higher than the tornado alleys of Alabama.

8 – Income – if income levels in a locality are generally high, there is more money in the market to purchase homes, decreasing supply and increasing prices.

9 – Construction market – the greater the degree of construction of new properties, the greater the supply in the market.

Understanding the factors that drive market supply and demand, and hence property prices are important. The more informed about these nine factors, the better purchasing/selling decisions you can make. For example – designs and styles and fads come and go into "fashion", and what design/style/fad factors elevate a property price one-year can diminish the price of a property the following year. If you are managing a property, you can factor these decisions when determining optimum rent or a selling value.

When borrowing rates are lower, properties become more affordable. This, too, influences demand. Tax credits, for example – for first-time buyers – can encourage more buyers to seek interest in the property market. As well as this, there are various social factors involved, too – such as the social status afforded to people who own their own homes. Age can come into play here, too, depending on the city and what social expectations young professionals have.

What drives property market supply and demand, then, is an interweaving network of factors, many of which playoff on one another. It's important to appreciate the impact that each of these individual factors has and how they influence property prices throughout the country.

How to Analyze Supply and Demand For Apartment Buildings

One of the most important ways to use all of the data gathered in a real estate market analysis is to examine the supply and demand factors for a particular type of real estate. For example, an investor considering the construction or purchase of a new multifamily residential property uses the market analysis to determine what cash flows they can expect to receive given the expected demand for units. The demand must be high enough to generate cash flows that provide a rate of return high enough to make the investment feasible.

In order to estimate the demand for multifamily housing units, it is necessary to understand recent population growth trends for the city. Then, it's important to consider the major industries in the market area and the forecasted growth for those industries over the next few years. You can then put this information together to forecast multifamily housing demand and compare that demand to the existing and proposed supply of multifamily units. This case study takes data about population and industrial activity in the Orlando, Florida region and analyzes supply and demand of multifamily residential units in the region.

Population Trends and Apartment Building Demand

Recent data from the U.S. Census Bureau and the Orlando Economic Development Commission lists the total population of the Orlando metro area at 2,387,138 (2016). Between 2015 and 2016, the population of the Orlando metro area grew by 2.6%. That made Orlando the fastest growing region in the United States. The Orlando Economic Development Commission estimates that population growth in the region since 2000 equates to a gain of 138 people per day. Population growth is mostly fueled by domestic migration. Americans moving to Orlando for retirement in warmer weather or for new career opportunities account for about 40% of the population increase. International migration (mainly from Central and South America) accounts for 34% of the increase in population. People have been moving to the Orlando area due to the region's comparative advantages (climate, entertainment and lifestyle, and economic growth). Without these advantages, Orlando would not be one of the fastest growing regions of the country.

With an average household size around 2.5, that means there are an estimated 954,855 households in the Orlando metropolitan area. Data from the American Consumer Survey indicates that about 43% of the population is renters. So, 43% of households would give an estimated demand of 410,588 multifamily units. In reality, not all renters live in multifamily units since many rent single-family homes. Therefore, it is necessary to estimate how many of those renters occupy multifamily units. A 2016 report from Fannie Mae estimated that there were 156,000 multifamily units in the Orlando metro area with a 5.75% vacancy rate. So, in 2016 there were around 147,030 occupied multifamily units (156,000 x (1-.0575) = 147,030). This means an estimated 35.8% of the households that are renters occupy multifamily units while the remaining 64.2% of renters occupy single-family homes.

Economic Trends and Multifamily Housing Demand

Employment data from the Bureau of Labor Statistics confirms that economic growth is driving the population growth in the Orlando metro area. In fact, job growth from 2015-2016 in Orlando was over twice the national average. A strong economy and growth in the number of jobs indicates that the population should continue to grow over the next few years unless there is a major shift to the national economy or a natural disaster. Furthermore, the job growth rate of 4.22% exceeded the population growth rate of 2.6%. If the major industries in Orlando continue to grow at this pace, more new workers will need to move into the region to fill these new jobs. So, forecasted population growth may be higher than the average of 2% seen over the past 10 years. It might be more appropriate to estimate population growth of at least 3% annually.

As with commodities traded on the market, housing prices continually fluctuate, sometimes with drastic changes over a short period of time. Availability is a huge factor affecting prices within a set region, such as in a specific suburb of a metropolitan area. Likewise, demand for homes in that market also plays into that price, which is why two nearly identical homes in different cities may sell for vastly different prices. When buying a home in a seller's market, limit your contingencies and make your offer as favorable to the seller as possible.

For houses and virtually anything else available for purchase, supply and demand play into the ultimate selling price. When an item is in short supply and many people want it, prices tend to rise. When the market is flooded with an item or there's no demand for it, prices fall. Sporting event ticket prices tend to rise when a team reaches the championship level, yet tickets to the same team's events a few years later, when the team isn't doing well, cost far less. Prices on holiday decor are another great example: At the peak of any holiday's shopping season, some shoppers are willing to pay a premium for the decor. Three days after the holiday, the leftover stock of these items is marked down to clearance prices due to little demand.

Housing supply and demand works in exactly the same way. Sometimes there are so many single-family homes available in the same region that there aren't enough buyers for all of them. In this housing oversupply, prices drop to draw more attention from potential buyers. A lowered price may influence an interested buyer to choose one home over a similar house in the same general area. Without a lowered price, a house may sit on the market for months due to the abundant number of similar homes for sale nearby at the same time.

On conclusion, property price change can be influenced by house buyers living need and land and house number supply factor, but any house buyer individual rational will influence his/her prerference property choice decision before he / she decides to choose what kinds properties or anywhere locations to live. So, house buyer individual psychological factor will influence his/her properties choices.

CHAPTER THREE

Economic theories analyze market behavioral problem

Classical Theory analyzes whether internet invention whether influences smart phone sale number increases and creates long time mobile phones inventors and manufacurers occupations to bring real GDP growth

What is Classical Theory ?

The fundamental principle of the classical theory is that the economy is self-regulating. Classical economists maintain that the economy is always capable of achieving the natural level of real GDP or output, which is the level of real GDP that is obtained when the economy's resources are fully employed. While circumstances arise from time to time that cause the economy to fall below or to exceed the natural level of real GDP, self-adjustment mechanisms exist within the market system that work to bring the economy back to the natural level of real GDP. The classical doctrine—that the economy is always at or near the natural level of real GDP—is based on two firmly held beliefs:

Say's Law and the belief that prices, wages, and interest rates are flexible. According to Say's Law, when an economy produces a certain level of real GDP, it also generates the income needed to purchase that level of real GDP. In other words, the economy is always capable of demanding all of the output that its workers and firms choose to produce. Hence, the economy is always capable of achieving the natural level of real GDP.

The achievement of the natural level of real GDP is not as simple as Say's Law would seem to suggest. While it is true that the income obtained from producing a certain level of real GDP must be sufficient to purchase that level of real GDP, there is no guarantee that all of this income will be spent. Some of this income will be saved. Income that is saved is not used to purchase consumption goods and services, implying that the demand for these goods and services will be less than the supply, in demand and supply view. So, Say's law indicates that the real GDP growth, it can not depend on reflecting the people's income level, because one person has high income, it can not represent that he will often like to consume or buy anything.

If aggregate demand falls below aggregate supply due to aggregate saving, suppliers will cut back on their production and reduce the number of resources that they employ. When employment of the economy's resources falls below the full employment level, the equilibrium level of real GDP also falls below its natural level. Consequently, the economy may not achieve the natural level of real GDP if there is aggregate saving. The classical theorists' response is that the funds from aggregate saving are eventually borrowed and turned into investment expenditures, which are a component of real GDP. Hence, aggregate saving need not lead to a reduction in real GDP. Consider, however, what happens when the funds from aggregate saving exceed the needs of all borrowers in the economy. In this situation, real GDP will fall below its natural level because investment expenditures will be less than the level of aggregate saving. Aggregate saving, represented by bank increasing interest rate; as the interest rate rises, then many people are encouraged to save money in bank more than spend, the economy tends to save more. Aggregate investment, is a downward-sloping function of the interest rate; as the interest rate rises, the cost of borrowing increases and investment expenditures decline. Initially, aggregate saving and investment are equivalent at the interest rate between investment and savings. Aggregate investment will be lower than aggregate saving, implying that equilibrium real GDP will be below its natural level. Flexible interest rates, wages, and prices.

Classical economists believe that under these circumstances, the interest rate will fall, causing investors to demand more of the available savings. In fact, the interest rate will fall far enough—to make the supply of funds from aggregate saving equal to the demand for funds by all investors. Hence, an increase in savings will lead to an increase in investment expenditures through a reduction of the interest rate, and the economy will always return to the natural level of real GDP. The flexibility of the interest rate as well as other prices is the self-adjusting mechanism of the classical theory that ensures that real GDP is always at its natural level. The flexibility of the interest rate keeps the money market, or the market for loanable funds, in equilibrium all the time and thus prevents real GDP from falling below its

natural level.
Similarly, flexibility of the wage rate keeps the labor market, or the market for workers, in equilibrium all the time. If the supply of workers exceeds firms' demand for workers, then wages paid to workers will fall so as to ensure that the work force is fully employed. Classical economists believe that any unemployment that occurs in the labor market or in other resource markets should be considered voluntary unemployment. Voluntarily unemployed workers are unemployed because they refuse to accept lower wages. If they would only accept lower wages, firms would be eager to employ them.

● Classical Theory analyzes whether internet invention whether influences smart phone sale number increases and creates long time mobile phones inventors and manufacurers occupations to bring real GDP growth

Why does internet can influence smart mobile phone consumers' purchase desire? Has internet have direct relationship to influence smart mobile phone buyers' purchase desires ? Can the smart mobile phone talking product still attract phone buyers' preference choice, if it lacks internet function? Can internet raise smart phone sale number and create many mobile phone inventors and manufacturer occupations to raise GDP real GDP when smart phone buyers number and smart phone related occupation needs increase. I shall apply behavioral economic theory to attempt to explain the reasons how and why internet has direct relationship to influence smart mobile buyers' preference talking product choice in this traditional home telephone talking product market as below:

Is the internet putting up a barrier between people, even in bed? Does internet influence mobile phone consumers have not choose to buy because they are influenced to use mobiles when they use mobile to link internet to see any movies, or phones or news and influence their sleeping time in habit and they won't have nervous to work or learn on day time. We compulsively carry our smartphones with us wherever we go. The classroom, the bathroom, the bedroom, the outdoors — our phone is always in hand as if it were some magic self-defense tool capable of protecting us from all that is evil in the world. It all happened so fast. We didn't have the time to set any boundaries for smartphone usage, and now we find ourselves unable to save our relationships and form meaningful interactions with those dear to us.Smartphones are very useful in many circumstances. However, although not ruining your relationships per se, they can harm it in devious ways.

A smartphone is a modern day distraction that is so common, it's hardly noticed any more. It accompanies us wherever we go, demanding our attention multiple times a day. A phone call, a Facebook notification. We become irrevocably immersed in our digital lives, prioritizing the virtual world over anything else. Is it really that important to Instagram your dinner, rather than actually savoring it and sharing your impressions – or maybe a forkful of the dish – with the person next to you?Smartphones get in the way of our relationships, making it impossible for us to wholeheartedly devote our attention to the present moment. As a result, we lose many moments of wonder that are unique and never to be lived again.

Addiction to smartphone usage is a common problem among adults worldwide. It manifests itself in the excessive usage of their phones, while engaged in other activities such as studying, driving, social gatherings and even sleeping. However, many people fail to realize that addiction to smartphone usage is a serious issue that can have a negative effect on the person's thoughts, behavior, tendencies, feelings, and sense of well-being. In particular, it can be a risk factor for depression, loneliness, anxiety and sleep disturbances. As per the Mental Health Foundation in the United Kingdom, people with depression experience an unhappy mood, loss of interest or pleasure, feelings of guilt or low self-worth, disturbed sleep or appetite, low energy, and poor concentration. Depressive and anxiety disorders are two main common disorders that are highly prevalent globally, as over 300 million people are estimated to suffer from depression, which is equivalent to 4.4% of the world's population. It is speculated that not only addiction to smartphone usage can affect one's mental and behavioral status, but also that those with mood disorders are more likely to become addicted to using their smartphones .

Numerous tools have been utilized in literature to assess the same phenomenon, but with different terms such as excessive smart phone usage, smartphone addiction, dependency on smart phones, internet addiction, problematic mobile phone usage, and so on. Remarkably, there was a tendency to use a non-pathological terminology, such as "Problematic Smartphone Use," rather than the term smartphone addiction. Addiction manifests itself in various forms such as preoccupation, tolerance, lack of control, withdrawal, mood modification, conflict, lies, excessive use and loss of interest. Several studies have found that women are more likely to develop an addiction to smartphone usage than men. This was viewed as a positive way for people to stay connected in social relationships. One study clarified that women like to show affection to their families using their smartphones while men use phones for efficiency and practicality . Though there are several studies on this topic, no study has proven this connection so far. Smartphone addiction has been found to be correlated with various physical and psychological issues, as indicated in a number of studies that tested this relationship among various age groups. For example, one study found that people with depression, social anxiety and loneliness had different uses for their smartphones compared to others. People with social anxiety made fewer outgoing calls, as well as, fewer text messages than those without social anxiety. It was reported that high levels of smartphone addiction were correlated with low self-esteem, loneliness, depression and shyness.

Although, internet can bring smart mobile phone users to spend sleeping time to use this kind of mobile product to watch movies, watch TV, listen music, social media communication, searching etc. non-talking communication behaviors. It seems that internet may influence smart phone users to change their phone purchase choice to buy the kind common mobile product more. But, in behavioral economic view, internet can bring smart mobile phone product has more attractive strengths to influence common mobile phone kind product users to chooce to use smart mobile phone products in preference. Internet can also bring these positive emotion to persuade the common mobile users to choose to use them.

Convenient applying: Any smart phone users can apply smart phone to link to internet to replace home computers to link to internet to watch movies, watch TV, listen music, social media communication, searching etc. non-talking communication behaviors in anywhere and any time conveniently. It is one kind of small size and light talking communication tool, but it can also help any mobile users to apply smart phone product to apply internet to do the same computer tasks in any time and any places. Hence, smart mobile can bring many computer users to feel that they can apply computer to do similar internet search behaviors at home. Convenient internet search function is one attract function to influence traditional computer users to choose to apply smart phone tools to replace computers tools to apply internet to search information, news, watch TV, movie, lisen music etc. social media communication behaviors at homes. When they bring smart phone to any where, then they can apply this tool to click to internet to do the same computer and internet link tasks in order to enjoy their entertainment needs. So, they do not need to apply computer tool to link to internet to enjoy their visal entertainment at homes. They can bring smart phone to go to anywhere to link to internet to enjoy their visal entertainment in any time conveniently. So, smart phone can be replaced to home computer tool to solve any visal entertainment enjoyers' needs.

● Internet brings smart phone users to feel more visal entertainment enjoyment

The Internet has revolutionized direct communication, lead to the digitization of books and film, as well as made convenience even more important. Companies have developed strategies that capitalize on the growing desire for easily accessible goods and services in only a few mouse clicks. As technology grows increasingly local and more connected to all aspects of the customer purchasing process, small business owners need to be more efficient in how they target their markets. Understanding why convenience plays such a large role in the purchasing process is vital in growing a successful business. Here are five trends that have popped up in recent years as businesses looked for ways to help their customers take advantage of well-timed opportunities. Internet can bring more attract to smart phone users, instead of visal enjoyment needs, the reasons may include as below:

1. Prior Consumer Knowledge

In today's digital world, consumers are looking for retail solutions which allow them to maximize their free-time and to stretch their disposable income. Due to this economic climate, small businesses which are able to provide their customer with a more convenient experience than a large retailer, are cashing in. H.M Cole, a custom clothier, offers its customers an entire planned wardrobe for the upcoming year after an hour's consultation. Other convenience services such as Trunk Club and Stitch Fix, personalized styling sites for men and women respectively, take that one step further in creating a complete look. These levels of convenience take a simple fitting and turn it into a way for consumers to spend less time deciding outfits, and more time doing other things they value.

2. Direct-to Store Delivery

Due to the "larger-than-life" nature of big box stores, they have begun to develop strategies which combat the convenience of a smaller retailer. The newest trend among these chains is to offer direct-to store delivery.

Shoppers are able to find what they are looking for online, and purchase directly on the site. Rather than having to wait the 3-5 days for delivery, chains are making their purchases available (sometimes at discounted rates) for pick up at their local store. Essentially, customers are taking part in shopping services where the store physically groups together the inventory, saving the individual time in their purchases.

3. Personalized Billing, Shipping Info

Customer profiles across frequently visited webpages allow for consumers to not only keep their billing information in one place, but also have access to similar products or content. Businesses are able to not only track purchases, but to specifically target an individual with the information provided for convenience sake. A user does not usually choose to re-enter billing or shipping information on a site they frequent, and so by saving this information, a company is removing an obstacle that might otherwise influence the purchase.

4. Time is Money

Fast food and drive-thru options have changed the world's nutritional demands, creating a society of cheap convenience foods. Although the nutritional value of these highly-processed foods is lacking, the demand for them has been on the rise across the globe. While these types of businesses are growing at a record rate, the pressure to remain affordable and convenient has driven them online.

Some innovative restaurant chains have transitioned to online ordering which provide an easy, personalized interface for their customers to select and buy all from the website portal. A restaurant receives the order digitally, packages the food, and then sends it out to delivery, often for an additional fee. Both Google and Amazon , as well as many startups, have launched services that deliver meals and groceries to your home. Time has shown that customers are willing to spend a little more for the convenience of having food arrive at their doorstep.

5. Subscription Services

Another recent convenience service trend is through subscription services. This can include streaming goods such as TV shows, movies, audio books, or music tracks. Companies charge their customers a fee to have access to a database of content whenever, wherever they want. Some providers have included commercials as a means to generate more income. Other subscription services include coffee of the month clubs, or deliver gift boxes. These companies charge a monthly (or yearly) subscription fee and compile a box of themed goodies for their customers.While some very big companies have struggled to make convenience a larger part of their customers' experiences, many small businesses that offer niche products and services have an advantage in this area. The Internet is helping them to level the playing field in a way. It provides a platform for small businesses to capitalize on the demand for goods by using convenience to win fans and new customers.

On conclusion, internet can bring smart phone users to do any activities when they need to apply computer tools at home in any time and anywhere. So, internet has direct relationship to persuade mobile phone or computer users to choose to buy mobiles for communication uses or internet uses in preference nowadays as well as internet can bring the different kinds of new or unique mobile phones design needs increase to achieve the creating mobile phone inventors and mobile phone manufacturers occupations need. So, it seems that internet can influence mobile phone product's occupations needs and mobile phone consumers number increase to raise real GDP growth to the smart phone maufacturing and sale country really.

Reference

Bigne, Enrique (2005). The impact of internet user shopping patterns and demographics on consumer mobile buying.

Falk, Louis, K. et. al (2005) " E-commerce and consumer's expectations: What makes a website work". Journal of website promotion, 1(1), 65-75.

Parasuraman, A., Zeithaml, V.A. and Berry L.L. (1988) SERVQUAL: A multiple-item scale for measuring consumer perceptions of service quality. Journal of retailing, 64, 12-40.

● (AI) -driven automation manufacturing skillful workers needs to China non-industrial country

● Solow Growth Model: Technology and Productivity

In the basic Solow model we hold technological progress and population growth constant. Capital stock and output was dependent on the investment rate in which a country accumulates capital and the depreciation rate of said capital. The Solow model equalizes an economy into a long run steady state, when inflows or savings rate directly offsets outflows or depreciation rate. At this equilibrium capital stock does not change and the economy is at the highest level of consumption that is attainable. Assuming population growth is held constant, the only way to effectively and positively change capital stock and output in the long run at new steady state equilibrium is to either increase technological advancements or the way we use technology.

After technological progress was incorporated into the growth model, we could essentially split labor up between efficiency of the workforce. Workers in less developed countries are not as productive as workers in developed countries. For the most part everyone has access to the technology, but some in developing countries do not know how to use the technology correctly. This is where a separation between more efficient and less efficient comes from. This helps us understand a component of the model. The impression Solow makes is that the further away from the steady state a country is in, developing countries, the faster its growth rate. When the country initially increased investment, in both human and physical capital, they would see massive growth because of the technology, but as they approached the steady state, since technology hasn't changed and because the laborers already learned how to use the technology growth would begin to flatten until they reach equilibrium. Technological progress, not the utilization of technology has to be exogenously shocked (e.g. Industrial Revolution, Digital Revolution, Information Age, etc.) to increase capital stock and output.

After an exogenous technology shock an economy would see a shift with both the savings curve and production function and the economy would be at a new steady state with both a higher capital stock and output. Holding the assumption that technology is information that both poor and wealthy nations recognize, a technology shock would theoretically increase the steady state for those currently at equilibrium and those who have yet to attain it. While rich nations have the knowledge to utilize new technology from a shock, mostly because their research and development was responsible for the shock, poor nations need an extra kick to help apply the technology to production.

Encouraging technological advancements: patents, tax cuts from research and development, government subsidized research to universities and specific industry based technology research incentives are some ways rich countries are attempting to make technological progress and increase the steady state output and capital levels. Rich countries' labor forces have the capacity to take what technology they currently have and develop it to become more productive. Poor countries are not as capable. While poor countries have the technology available to one day be more productive, they must first invest in human and physical capital before they can apply the technology and then further develop it.

Artificial intelligent technological invention raise productivities to bring China less developed country efficient benefits in factories case.

After technological progress was incorporated into the growth model, we could essentially split labor up between efficiency of the workforce. Workers in the less developed country, China will may apply robotics to assist workers to raise any products manufacture number increases in short time.

- New Growth Theory (Romer & endogenous growth)

How is it possible for income inequality to increase within countries and across countries, but to decrease for the world as a whole?The answer is long-run economic growth".Specifically, income per capita in China and India has grown rapidly over the last half century. So even though inequality has increased within China and India, this growth has led the living standards for hundreds of millions of people to converge towards those in Europe, North America, and Australia.

This convergence is nothing to fear. Economic growth is not a zero-sum-game. But what drives this growth? The source of growth is probably not what you think it is. Variation in standards of living across countries is clearly associated with different amounts of physical capital such as public infrastructure. So should we simply invest more in more roads and bridges to increase our standard of living?

The problem is that physical capital only explains about one-third of the variation in income per capita across countries. The other two-thirds are "explained" by a more nebulous concept that economists refer to as total factor productivity, or TFP for short. I have to put quotes around "explained" because we can only measure TFP as the residual component of income per capita not explained by capital.

The point is that massive investment in infrastructure would only ever get even the poorest country one-third of the way to catching up with rich countries. Worse yet, capital accumulation is subject to diminishing returns for all countries. In fact, income per capita would increase with the amount of machinery and equipment per worker, but nowhere near proportionately. Rather than an easy path to prosperity, capital accumulation quickly becomes a lot like squeezing blood from a stone.

Did the single-child policy help China grow?

China's single-child policy may easily have been the largest social policy experiment in history, with many negative social consequences. But did the policy in part explain China's rapid economic growth? The Solow-Swan neoclassical growth theory, which predicts a lower rate of population growth will boost income per capita, would say it is possible. Yet interestingly, empirical estimates of the effects of lower population growth on China's economic growth are relatively small in magnitude, even when assuming neoclassical growth theory is correct about the existence of such effects. In some sense, small effects of the single-child policy should not come as much of a surprise, because according to neoclassical growth theory, a decrease in population growth only generates a transitory increase in economic growth.

Specifically, the generally-accepted theory says, long-run growth depends only on "exogenous" technological change — that is, it is assumed to be unaffected by population growth or capital accumulation.

What explains technological change?

Economist Paul Romer has developed a theory of economic growth with "endogenous" technological change — that is, it can depend on population growth and capital accumulation. His endogenous growth theory ties the development of new ideas to the number of people working in the knowledge sector (think of this as effort devoted to R&D). These new ideas make everyone else producing regular goods and services more productive – that is, ideas increase TFP. There are many variants of endogenous growth theory, but a robust prediction is that an increase in population or an increase in the share of people working in the knowledge sector will increase economic growth. This theory is quite radical for two reasons.

First, the prediction of higher economic growth for a larger population suggests that neoclassical growth theory, not to mention even more pessimistic economic theories of population going back to Thomas Malthus, got things completely wrong. Evidently, China's single-child policy was a mistake, not just for social reasons, but also for economic reasons. According to endogenous growth theory, China and the rest of the world could have had more growth because China would have produced more new ideas with an even larger population.

Second, because ideas are what economists label as "non-rival" (meaning that my use of an idea, like a recipe or a mathematical formula, doesn't prevent your use of it), there will only be an economic incentive for more people to work in the knowledge sector if there are intellectual property rights such as patents and copyright. Thus, it is necessary to restrict competition in the knowledge sector in order to stimulate growth, even though this leads to other distortions and disparities in the economy.

The reasons that I beleive China's single-child policy can not help its long term economic growth. Otherwise, robotic technologic manufacturing method can help its long term economic growth, I shall indicate why and how robotic manufacturing technology can help its economic growth more than single child policy, though this policy can help it to reduce high population , then it can reduce social need increases, but it can not bring long term consumption increases in China's society.

What is dependency theory ?

Dependency theory, sometimes called foreign dependency, is used to explain the failure of non-industrialized countries to develop economically despite investments made into them from industrialized nations. The central argument of this theory is that the world economic system is highly unequal in its distribution of power and resources due to factors like colonialism and neocolonialism. This places many nations in a dependent position.

The dependency theory states that it's not a given that developing countries will eventually become industrialized if outside forces and natures suppress them, effectively enforcing dependency on them for even the most basic fundamentals of life.

What is Colonialism and Neocolonialism theory ?

Colonialism describes the ability and power of industrialized and advanced nations to effectively rob their own colonies of valuable resources like labor or natural elements and minerals. Neocolonialism refers to the overall domination of more advanced countries over those that are less developed, including their own colonies, through economic pressure, and through oppressive political regimes. Colonialism effectively ceased to exist after World War II, but this didn't abolish dependency. Rather, neocolonialism took over, suppressing developing nations through capitalism and finance. Many developing nations became so indebted to developed nations they had no reasonable chance of escaping that debt and moving forward.

An Example of Dependency Theory

Africa received many billions of dollars in the form of loans from wealthy nations between the early 1970s and 2002. Those loans compounded interest. Although Africa has effectively paid off the initial investments into its land, it still owes billions of dollars in interest. Africa, therefore, has little or no resources to invest in itself, in its own economy or human development. It's unlikely that Africa will ever prosper unless that interest is forgiven by the more powerful nations that lent the initial money, erasing the debt.

The concept of dependency theory applying to solve international trading problem to Africa, India and Thailand non-industrial countries

The concept of the dependency theory rose in popularity and acceptance in the mid to late 20th century as global marketing surged. Then, despite Africa's troubles, other countries thrived despite the influence of foreign dependency. India and Thailand are two examples of nations that should have remained depressed under the concept of the dependency theory, but, in fact, they gained strength. Yet other countries have been depressed for centuries. Many Latin American nations have been dominated by developed nations since the 16th century with no real indication that that is about to change.

The Solution of international trading problem between industrial and non-industrial developed countries

A remedy for dependency theory or foreign dependency would likely require global coordination and agreement. Assuming such a prohibition could be achieved, poor, undeveloped nations would have to be banned from engaging in any sort of incoming economic exchanges with more powerful nations. In other words, they could sell their resources to developed nations because this would, in theory, bolster their economies. However, they would not be able to purchase goods from wealthier countries. As the global economy grows, the issue becomes more pressing.

(AI) -driven automation industry will create wealth and expand economy growth to any countries, but it will be accompanied by changed in the skills that workers need to learn. One of main ways that technology increases productivity is by decreasing the number of labor hours needed to create a unit of output. It implies (AI) technology will influence low educated and low skillful labor number to be decreased (reduction employment number).

Whether how to demand robotic products in manufacturing and service markets as well as how it will bring supply to be suitable distribution to different kinds of manufacturing and serivce industries needs, e.g. non -manual driven vehicle, non-manual driven air plane, ship, warehouse robotics, shopping center artificial intelligent service robotics? Whether do robotic needs to service industry more or manufacturing industry more?

In contrast, technological change tended to work in a different direction throughout the nowadays. The advance of computer and the internet raised the relative productivity of higher skilled workers. So, routine-intensive occupations that focused on predictable tasks disappearance, such as switch board, operators, filming checkers, travel agents and assembling line workers etc. were particularly replaced by new technologies.

However, today, it may be challenging to predict exactly which jobs , such as service industry, shopping center robotic, or manufacturing industry, warehouse robotic manufacturing workers etc. which will be most immediately affected by (AI) driven-automation in demand and supply view. The reason is because (AI) is not a single technology, but rather a collection of technologies that are felt unevenly through the economy to influence job changing both negatively and positively. In positively view point, (AI) driven-automation will make many workers more productive and increase demand for certain skills. Consequently, new jobs are likely to be directly create in areas , such as the development and supervision of (AI) as well as indirectly created in a range of areas throughout the economy as higher incomes lead to expanded demand. Otherwise, in negatively view point, many traditional human needed (demand) skillful jobs will be threatened by automation are highly concentrated among lower-paid, lower-skilled and less -educated workers. It means automation will cause pressure on demand for this group, pressure and employment, if (AI) can replace the low skilled and less educated workers' jobs. Thus, (AI) will have negative influence to impact on the labor market.

(AI) capabilities will enable automation of some tasks that have long required human labor in service industry more or manufacturing industry more. Can (AI) replace some simple human jobs to service tasks or manufacturing tasks more? For example, advances in robotics are expanding machines' abilities to interact with and sharp the physical world. Combined , (AI) and robotics will give rise to smarter machines that can perform more sophisticated functions than ever before and brings more advantages that humans have exercised. This will permit automation of many tasks now performed by human workers and could change the shape of the labor market and human activity. So, we need to analyze whether (AI) roboic can help human to do whether tasks on service industry more or manufacturing tasks more. Then, we can evaluate whether our service industry will need robotics more or manufacturing industry more.

● How (AI) influences labor market change on service and manufacturing industries aspect

Today, it may be challenging to predict exactly which jobs will be most immediately affected by (AI)-driven automation. Because (AI) is not a single technology, but rather a collection of technologies that are applied to specific tasks. So, deciding whether future service or manufacturing tasks needs on robotics replacing manual tasks aspect more. They need to depend on whether either future many service simple tasks can be replaced by robotic to do more or future many manufacturing tasks can be replaced by robotic to do more. So, we ought need to consider whether many manual tasks can be replaced to do by robotics or whhether many manual tasks can be replaced by robotics to do more in demand and supply view. Then, robotic manufacturers can decide whether they ought invent more robotics on service industry aspect or they ought invent more robotics on manufacturing industry aspect in this robotic manufacturing supply and demand market.

Some specific future robotic service industry or manufacturing demand and supply need predictions are possible based on the current (AI) technology invention effort whether the robotics scientists can have enough technology to manufacture any kinds of robotic products on service tasks or manufacturing tasks aspects. For example, driving jobs and house cleaning jobs, bank counter service jobs, telephone enquiry service operators. Restaurant cooking jobs, simple accounting record service jobs etc. that require relatively less education to perform. Advancements in computer vision and related technologies have made the feasibility of fully appear more likely, potentially displacing some workers in driving-dominant professions. Seemingly similar robot, for which the operational tasks is less specific of navigating to a specific destination when following a set of given rules and preserving safety. But, I believe that robotic scientists ought not follow their robotic manufacturing technology to decide whether they ought manufacture robotic service machines more or robotic manufacturing machines more in future robotic supply market. Because their technology can not represent that future human will need more robotic supply on either service industry more or manufacturing industry more. Future whether what human tasks are more popular to be replaced by robotics. They are depended on whether what kinds of service tasks can be simple to replaced by robotics more or whether what kinds of manufacturing tasks can be simple to replaced by robotic more factor , it means that how many simple manual service tasks or simple manual manufacturing tasks can be replaced by robotic.

In the future, the effects of (AI) on the labor market in the decade ahead will continue the trend toward skill-biased change that computerization and communication innovations have driven in recent decades. Thus, some human driving occupation will be disappeared or replaced by (AI) automation driven. For example, bus drivers, light truck or delivery services drivers, heavy and tractor-trailer truck drivers, school drivers, tax drivers, travel bus drivers. These will be future robotics needs on public transport service industry.

However, (AI) technology could enable some workers to focus time on other job responsibilities, boosting their productivity, and actually raised wage growth among those still holding the reshaped jobs. For example, salespeople, who currently spend a considerable amount of time driving could find themselves able to do other work when a car drives them from place to place, or inspectors and appraisers could fill out paperwork, when their car drives itself. This (AI) -driven technology should make these workers more productive, with (AI) -driven technology serving as a complement, not a substitute. New jobs will also likely be created, both in existing occupations cheaper transportation costs with lower prices and increase demand for products and all the related occupations, such as service and fulfillment, and in new occupations not currently foreseeable. These are other kinds of transport part service tasks needs on robotics.

What kind of jobs will be created by (AI) technology in whole job process on service or manufacturing industry? Predicting future job growth is extremely difficult, due to it depends on technologies or substitute for existing today as well as they may complement or substitute for existing human skills and jobs. However, (AI) will also lead to substantial indirect job creation to the degree it raises productivity and wages, it may also lead to higher consumption that would support additional jobs from high-end draft production to restaurant and retail. The future(AI) " augmented intelligence", the technology's role is as assisting and expanding the productivity of individuals rather than replacing human work. Thus, based on the biased-technical change framework, demand for labor will likely increase the most in the areas where humans complement (AI) automation technologies. For example, (AI) technology , such as IBM's Watson may improve early detection of some cancers or other illnesses, but a human healthcare professional is needed to work with patients to understand and translate patients' symptoms, inform patients of treatment options, and guide patients through treatment plans. Shipping companies may also partner workers who pick up and deliver products over the last feet with (AI) enabled autonomous vehicles that move workers efficiently from site to site. In such cases, (AI) augments what a human is able to do and allows individuals to either be move effective in their specially task or to operate on a larger scale. Thus, it seems (AI) technology will also create new jobs, raise productivities and workers' efficiencies on future factory warehouse delivery tasks.

● Redefining management in the workforce of artificial intelligent clerical tasks need office industry

In the future, due to artificial intelligence influences to some kind of human jobs nature in office administrative productive tasks environment in order to help any offices to raise administrative efficiencies by robotics. So, the kind of human jobs of management methods will also need to change to adapt the artificial intelligence technology input to their organizations. It will cause challenges for every executive and manager if who won't have effort to manage their teams how to apply artificial intelligence technology to work efficiently and easily. For example, division of labor will change among humans and machines will increase. Thus, companies will have to adapt their training performance and talent strategies how to emphasize on work that how to make human judgment and skills and experimentation. Thus, (IA)'s greatest impact will be on administrative coordination and control tasks, such as scheduling , resource allocation.

In fact, mangers will encounter this challenges: How to apply human experience and expertise to judge critical business decisions and practices when the information available is insufficient to suggest a successful course of action? Due to this kind of work will require new skills and mindsets. I shall indicate these change management methods to adapt (AI) technology. Such as: administration and routine tasks, scheduling , allocation of resources and reporting will fall within the intelligence machines, responsibilities that have long been reserved for humans. For example, a typical store manager or a lead nurse at a nursing home most constantly arrange shift schedules, accounting for staff members' absences owing to illness, vacation time or sudden departures.

Thus, the managers need to learn how to arrange new division of labor within the organizations after (AI) technology had been implemented to the organization. Artificial intelligence is currently influencing into once considered exclusive to humans: assessing and acting on human emotions and personality traits. The influences to managers need to change their strategies to adapt (AI) technology implements include such as below:

Firstly, managers need to spend the bulk of their time on coordination and control tasks from intelligent system implements. Their time spending on these major three aspects from impact of intelligent system: coordinate and control, solve problems and collaborate and people and community , strategy and innovation three aspects. Thus (AI) will influence managers need to change their judgment method to teach whose teams how to adapt the (AI) system operations in any organizations.

Secondly, (AI) will influence top, middle and low level management needs to change to adapt the (AI) technology operations to any owned (AI) technology organizations in the future. Intelligent machines must be trained in context. Just like humans , on-the-job training is a requirement for such machines because they typically arrive with only very general capabilities. To get the most from (AI), managers at all levels must participate in the instructional experience and in the learning process and provides managers' familiarity with such systems on these aspects, e.g. How the system works and generate advice, how the system has a proven track record , how the system provides convincing explanations , how the system can make simple rule- based decisions.

Thirdly, managers need to learn how to make judgment more accurate (AI) systems assistance. Although (AI) will invariably take on more routine work and even augment human decision-making, it won't judgment work, the application of human experience and expertise to critical business decisions when the information available is insufficient to suggest a successful course of action or reliable enough to suggest an obvious course of action. For a sense of the nature of judgment work, consider big data marketing and sales analytics. Such analytics often provide insights that can inform promotional campaigns, including predicting which promotions will generate desired sales brand further into the future, marketing executives need use judgment, combining analytics with their own and others' insight and experience.

The application of experience and expertise to critical business decisions and practice represents the real value of human judgment. But, when artificial intelligent machines are implemented to any organizations to assist the low, middle and top level management to make any business judgment. These forms of judgment work that managers can gather data interpretation, idea development more absolute from (AI) machine assistance. Thus, why these level management executives need to learn how to apply (AI) machines to help them to make any business judgment more accurate. Future offices will need robotics to help their some staffs to do simple administrative tasks.

- (AI) influences organizational change to help senior management to do strategic decision tasks in office environment

Consequently creative and social intelligence will be in even greater demand as (AI) makes in management and the workforce. This development will represent a long term trend in labor markets , one characterized by intensifying demand and reward for social skills with a growing desire for creative capabilities, managers will seek to fashion of ideas and hypotheses from inside and outside of the enterprise to shape solutions to their most pressing business problems. Thus, (AI) will influence overall organizational team members who have chance to participate any decision to make more accurate business judgment.

Many managers mistakenly view judgment work as only an individual discipline, failing to appreciate that it can also involve decide interpersonal and organizational practices. In more complex settings, judgment is typically a collective outcome of individuals' and teams' diverse perspectives, insights and experiences. And often , the resulting choices are better informed than decisions that an individual would have arrived at on his or her own.

Thus, when any organizations apply (AI) technology to assist managers to gather data and ideas to make any judgment. In these cases, organizations can create the conditions for effective collective judgment by establishing structures , such as " shadow advisory boards" that prompt managers and employees to source and synthesize multiple perspectives. Thus, a traditional organization (firm) might freshen its thinking is t put together a shadow advisory board, comprised of young, digital people who can apply (AI) machine assistance to make judgment work more accurate whether related to people development, problem-solving or strategizing and innovating for considerable degrees of creative and social intelligence.

Thus, on the one hand, (AI) technology machine augmentation and automation can give these advantages to human (organization managers) , e.g. developing people and community, solving problems and collaborating, coordinating and controlling work, shaping strategy and leading innovation. Besides, on the other hand, the next generation managers need have these individual attitude to treat intelligent machines to be as colleagues.
When, judgment is a human skill, intelligent machines can accelerate human learning that supports it, assisting in data -driven simulations, scenarios and search and discovery activities. Focuses on judgment work, some decisions require insight beyond what data can tell them. This is the sweet sport for human judgment, the application of experience and expertise to critical business decisions and practices. Thus, managers will also need to find ways to learn how to use digital (AI) technologies to tap into the knowledge and judgment of partners, customer external stakeholders and role models in other industries after the (AI) machine had been implemented to the organization. Future robotics will have more needs on senior management strategic decision aspect in office environment.

● Future works change: Automation, employment
and productivity on sevice and manufacturing industries by service robotics and manufacturing robotics both

● How (AI) influences future service and manufacturing industries job change

Human future " micro to macro" industry trends will be affected business strategy and public policy by (AI) technology. In the future (AI) technology will influence those six themes: productivity and growth, natural resources, labor markets, the evolution of global financial markets, the economic impact of technology and innovation and urbanization. However, (AI) technology will bring economic benefits of tackling gender inequality, a new global competition, Chinese innovation and digital globalization.
Nowadays, advances in robotics artificial intelligence, and machine learning are in a new age of automation, as machines match or outperform human performance in a development to any countries. For example, automation of activities can enable businesses to improve performance by reducing errors and improving quality and speed, and in some cases achieving outcomes

that go beyond human capabilities. For example, some research indicated automation could raise productivity growth globally by 0.8 to 1.4 % annually; more than 2,000 work activities across 800 occupations. When less than 5% of all occupations can be automated using demonstrated technologies about 60% of all occupations have at least 30% of constituent activities that could be automated. Many occupations will change that will be automated away: Activities most susceptible to automation involve physical activities, in highly structured and predictable environments, as well as the collection and processing of data. They are most prevalent in manufacturing , accommodation and food service and retail trade and include some middle-skill jobs. For example, such as natural language processing is a key factor. Beyond technical feasibility, the cost of technology competition with labor including skills and supply and demand dynamics, performance benefits including and beyond labor cost savings, and social and regulatory acceptance will be affected by (AI) automation technology. Thus, (AI) automation will impact to influence global employment in those aspects as below:

Firstly, assuming that people are displaced by automation will find other employment. The anticipated shift in the activities in the labor force is of a similar order as the long-term shift away from agriculture and decreases in manufacturing share of employment. Both of manufacturing and agriculture industries which would be accompanied by the creation of new types of work not foreseen at the time.

Secondly, for business, the performance benefits of automation are relatively clear. Thus, the businessmen have opportunities for their micro economies to benefits from the productivity growth potential and macro economies to benefit to encourage continued progress and innovation , investment and market incentives. At the same time, employers must innovate policies to help workers and institutions adapt to the impact on employment.

This will likely include rethinking education and training, income support and safety nets , as well as support for those dislocated, when employees need to leave themselves homes to move to other cities to learn new (AI) automation works. Thus, individuals in the workplace will need to engage move comprehensively with machines as part of their everyday activities, and acquire new skills that will be in demand in the new automation age. Consequently , the scale of shifts in the labor force over many decades that automation technologies can be a similar order to the long -term technology

-enables shifts in the developed countries' workforces away from agriculture in the 21 th century. Those shifts did not result in long-term mass unemployment because they were accompanied by the creation of new types of work not foreseen at the time. However, human will still be needed in the workforce when the total productivity gains are caused by (AI) technology.

- What occupations will be influenced by (AI) technology on future service and manufacturing tasks aspects

In the future, scientists predict that these occupations will be influenced by (AI) technology mostly. They include : retail salespeople, food and beverage service workers, language or translation teachers, health practitioners. Since these work activities have a more relevant occupations are made up of a range of activities with different potential for (AI) automation . For example, a retail salesperson will spend more time interacting with customers, stocking shelves , or ringing up sales. Each of these activities is distinct and requires different capabilities to perform successfully.

Thus, these job activities have similar simple control characteristics. Simple activities include greet customers, answer questions about products and services, clean and maintain work areas, demonstrate product feature process sales and transactions. All these activities can have similar simple activities in order to (AI) machines can be learn how to do these activities from (AI) technology . For example, the capability perception includes sensory perception, cognitive capabilities, such as retrieving automation, recognizing known patterns(supervised learning), logical reasoning problem solving.

Thus, (AI) machine is such human, which has feeling and emotion, such as social and emotional sensing, judgement reasoning methods, natural language understanding and physical capabilities, such as mobility , navigation, gross motor skill, fine motor skills. It seems that the future, (AI) human invents machines which will have these human characteristics to do human similar behavioral job duties more easily and efficiently. It implies these above human occupations will be replaced by (AI) human invention machines in the future. Due to (AI) creation, it is possible to cause unemployment number of these above workers will increase because (AI) machines can do their similar job behavioral activities.

Consequently, employers won't need to employ many of these skillful labor.

Otherwise, they can buy less number (AI) machines to attempt to do whose job activities more easily and efficiently. So, it seems (AI) machines will have more high work performance to replace these occupation workers' work performance. Finally, these occupation worker unemployment number will only increase when the (AI) machines had been invented to achieve to do their work behavioral activities absolutely success in the future.

● Whether (A) technology machine labor will replace human worker more or assist human worker more

There is no single agreed definition of a robot how outcome of a task that is completed without human intervention. When some definitions require the task to be completed by a physical machine moves and respond to its environment, other definitions use the term robot in connection with tasks completed by software , without physical embodiment.
However, to answer the question : Whether (AI) technology machine labor will replace human worker more or assist human worker more. I shall indicate some examples to let readers to judge whether (AI) technology can create new jobs or reduce old jobs.
Firstly, I shall explain what (AI) function is. (AI) is a service robot that performs useful tasks for humans or equipment excluding industrial automation application . Thus, the classification of a robot into industrial robot or service robot is done according to its intended application. It is also a personal service robot or a service robot for personal used for a non commercial task, usually by lay persons . Examples are domestic servant robot, and pet exercising robot. It is also a professional service robot or a service robot for professional used for a commercial task, usually operated by a properly trained operator. Examples, are cleaning robot for public places, delivery robot in offices or hospitals, fire-fighting robot, rehabilitation robot and surgery robot in hospitals. Thus, these functions will be future (AI) application to our daily life necessaries or business necessaries.
However, some authors agree (AI) will bring negative outcomes of automation, due to raise competiveness, reduce human job nature. Otherwise, other authors argue (AI) will bring positive outcomes of automation, due to raise productivities, job creation, assist humans work.
On the positive outcome hand, robots can increase productivity . This

is particularly important for small-to medium sized businesses both are in developed and developing countries economies. It also enables large companies to increase their competitiveness through faster product development and delivery. Increased use of robot is also enabling companies in high cost countries to re shore, or bring back to their domestic base parts of the supply chain that will have previously outsourced to sources of cheaper labor. Currently , the greater threat to employment is not a automation, but an inability to remain competitive. Automation has led overall to an increase in labor demand and positive impact on wages. The reason is that the middle-income/middle-skilled jobs have reduced as a proportion of overall contribution to employment and earnings leading to fears of increasing income inequality, the skills range within the middle income bracket is large. Thus, robots are driving an increase in demand for workers at the higher -skilled and with a positive impact on wages. This issue is how to enable middle-income earners in the lower-income range to unskilled or retain. Finally, the (AI) positive impact supporter who argue the future will be robots and humans can work together.

However, on the negative outcome hand, robots can substitute labor activities, but don't replace jobs. They believe that less than 10% of jobs are fully automatable. Increasingly , robots are used to complement and augment labor activities, the net impact on jobs and the quality of work is positive. Automation can provide the opportunity for humans to focus on higher-skilled, higher-quality and higher-paid tasks. Robots can improve productivity when they are applied to tasks that which perform more efficiently and to a higher and more consistent level of quality than humans. For example, increased productivity is enabling some firms, such as Whirlpool, Caterpillar and Ford Motors company in the US restructure their supply chains, bringing back parts of the manufacturing process to the country of origin. Thus, productivity gains due to robotics and automation are important not just at the company level, but also for build industry and nation competitiveness.

I suppose that productivity can be raised. What are the impacts of robots on employment? Firstly, the main focus of development has been on personal entertainment, which does not drive worker productivity (manufacturing production). When the internet (information and communication technology (ICT)) innovation. This is borne and by findings that manufacturing productivity, which has been driven by innovations in automation rather than consumer technologies, has government strongly than productivity in the services sectors of the economy in most nature economies. It seems (AI) automation will create many jobs in internet communication entertainment game industry. For example, many young people like to use internet to play any electronic games from computer or mobile at home or outside home conveniently. Thus, (AI) automation will increase demand to be invented to any new entertainment game from internet channel. It will need to employ many (AI) entertainment game inventors to create many automation entertainment games. Thus, (AI) automation in internet entertainment game industry will need human (AI) entertainment game inventors to invent the knowledge-based capital of (AI) automation entertainment games. The (AI) entertainment game inventors will need own research and development skills, form specific skills, organizational know-how skills, databased knowledge, design and various forms of intellectual property to do these (AI) automation entertainment game invention occupations in the future.

International Federation Of Robotics(2016) indicated that China will be as a major robotics manufacturer and user of robots, benefiting from jobs created by robot manufacturing and productivity gains from robot use. Chins had sold of robots to any one single market every year since 2017 year. The Chinese government has included a focus on robotics in its 10 year strategy. In order to achieve its target of a robot density of 150 units per 10, 000 workers by 2020 year. Thus, Chinese companies will have to install around 650,000 new industrial robots between 2016 to 2020 year, 2.5 times more than installed globally in 2015 year.

Hence, China (AI) manufacturing industry will need to employ many workers . It implies (AI) manufacturing industry will create many new occupations in China. Also, ministry of economy, trade and industry (2015) also showed that Japan currently has the largest stock of industrial robots in operations, primarily in the automation industry. Driven by a rapidly aging population and low productivity rates, the Japanese government has sights on a 20-fold increase in the use of robots in the non-manufacturing sector and a three-fold growth rate of labor productivity in the service sector both by 2020 year. Thus, it also implies Japan will need many robots to be provide to service industry. Due to robots will provide to serve any businessmen's clients. Thus, it is possible that the service workers won't be dismissed as well as it is depended on the serving job nature to decide whether Japan's service workers can still serve to their employer when the service (AI) robots are applied to whose employers.

Consequently, it seems that (AI) can create employment, Ministry of economy, trade and industry (2015) showed that such as China will develop the major (AI) automation manufacturing industry. The (AI) employers will need to employ many workers to manufacture any these different kinds of (AI) robots to satisfy China or overseas individual or business buyers needs. But, (AI) can also cause unemployment to the low skillful service workers. Such as if Japan some service businesses choose to buy any (AI) service robots to replace their service staffs to serve their clients. It is possible that the service staffs will be dismissed, due to (AI) robots can do such as their same service job duties to achieve better service performance. Thus, today, it is increasingly common for people to use robots in various situations at home and in retail stores, hotels and hospitals these service industries. Robots are classified into server types based on their functionality (service and utility robots or those designed to communicate with humans) and appearance (humanoid robots or mechanical robots). The type of robot, to which each country allocated particular importance in the advance of robotics, reflects the sense of values and preferences of its population. Thus, if the country has high population needs to use robots, then they will influence either more new jobs creation or more old job loss in the country's (AI) manufacturing or (AI) service industries both. For example, Japan respondents often associate the term " robot " with humanoid robots that can communicate with human and they have a high level of familiarity with robot. The US has the highest level of robot utilization at home and in retail stores with its people being the most enthusiastic about the future use of robots. Germany shows a strong tendency to consider robots for industrial purposes and its people feel strong effort to the presence of robots in their households.

In conclusion, to judge whether how (AI) will influence the country's employment to be better or worse. It will depend on the country home buyers (users) or business buyers (users) how to use (AI) for their daily needs. If the country , such as US retail stores need to use (AI) , it will have possible to reduce some or many retail service workers. Even, if the country , such as Japan has many home users need to use (AI) , it will not influence the employment market. Otherwise, it will raise (AI) salespeople numbers. Even, if the country, such as Germany and China will have many (AI) manufacturers, then it will create many (AI) manufacturing occupations for these (AI) manufactory workers.

Consequently, (AI) robots manufacturing and service needs will have positive or negative impact to any country's employment. It will depend on the (AI) service provision and service workers' job nature as well as the manufacturing workers of (AI) knowledge level to decide their employment chance in their country's employment.

● Whether robotic will bring more attribution to our future social service industry more or manufacturing industry more?

Some scientists explain that artificial intelligence means which is an expert system, computer software that embodies a portion of the specialized knowledge of a human portion in a specific, narrow domain, owns decision making ability of human expert. The (AI)technology is based on the premise that what makes a person an expert is years of experience that enables who recognizes certain patterns in a problem as being similar to pattern. For example, in the future artificial intelligence system can be applied to control air traffic, design to computer configuration, medical diagnosis, instruction/training, speech/interpretation, monitoring to (nuclear plant), planning to mission, factory scheduling, prediction weather, repairing telephone, automatic driving etc. different industries.

Artificial intelligence characteristics include: creative, adaptive , common sense, fact processing, quick replication, broad focus permanent and consistent skill. Otherwise, traditional computer expert system disadvantage includes perishable, unpredictable, slow reproduction, expensive, slow reproduction, slow processing lacks inspiration, needs instruction, narrow focus only machine knowledge. So, artificial intelligence is a branch of computer science devoted to creating computer to influence software and hardware to attempt to create human intelligence or human intelligent behavior. It is learning from experience, responds flexibility in situation that are, new or not anticipated.

Thus, (AI) can be learnt programmed knowledge to solve problems, using reasoning in solving problem, understanding and inferring facts and rules, recognizing the relative importance of different elements in a situation. In summary, artificial intelligence is concerned with two basic ideas mainly: The first idea, it involves studying the thought processes of humans to understand what intelligence is; the second idea, it deals with representing thought processes using companies to create artificially intelligent entities for testing the theories of intelligence.

● Can (AI) impact human job nature change more on service industry or manufacturing industry?

Human need concern this question: Will artificial intelligence (AI) reduce some human jobs in order to instead of replacing machines to do? Due to artificial intelligence is the ability of machines to do thing, that people would require intelligence. For example, artificial intelligence machine man driving(self-driver), it (AI) machine man driving research is an attempt to discover and describe aspects of human intelligence that can be simulated by driving machine functions. Alternatively, (AI) mathematical research may be another viewed as an attempt to develop a mathematical theory function to describe the abilities and actions of things (natural or man-made) exhibiting intelligent behavior and server as a design of intelligent calculation machine function.

Why do humans need artificial intelligence machines to instead of traditional human service job? For example, can artificial intelligence machine man (self-driving) driver drive to replace human driver? I shall compare the differences between humans and computers : The characteristics of humans are good at recognizing various things, either seen before or not, recognizing the relationship patterns between things. Human thinking is common sense reasoning, combining all types of sensory input, acting appropriately in novel situations, learning new things and changing behavior patterns, making decisions , even when given incomplete information, working with noisy, incomplete information gathering behaviors . However, characteristics of computers are good at: The tasks humans do naturally are extremely difficult for a computer program as intelligent, which must be able to do the same kind of tack as humans do naturally.

Hence, (AI) is an combination of many different success and technologies: Linguistics - computational and socio, philosophy-logic, philosophy of mind and of language, electronical engineering -image and speech processing, pattern recognition, robotics, machine learning, neural networks, optimization scheduling, management information system and decision making. So, it is possible that (AI) can impact human job nature to instead of human working behavior in the future.

How can (AI) influence labor market?

- How can human social job nature

to be changed to accept to use whole tasks steps on artificial intelligent manufacturing industry or artificial intelligent service industry?

I believe that how to decide whether robotic needs are more on manufacturing industry or service indusry. It depends on whether they are how many whole tasks steps of any service or manufacturing occupations are accepted to be replaced by robotics ? From the first intelligent perspective reason view point, artificial intelligence is making machines " intelligent" acting as humans expect people to act. Artificial intelligence has ability to distinguish computer responses from human responses, it owns knowledge to solve expert problem. From another research perspective reason view point, artificial intelligence is the study of how to make computers do things which, at the moment, people do better (Rich & Knight, 1991, p.3).

(AI) researchers are native in a variety of domains, e.g. formal tasks (mathematics, games), tasks (perception, robotics, natural language, common sense reasoning), expert tasks (financial analysis, medical diagnostics, engineering, scientific analysis and other areas).

From the second business perspective reason view point, (AI) is a set of many powerful tools, and methodologies for using those tools to solve business problems. From a programming perspective reason view point, (AI) includes the study of symbolic programming problem solving and search .

From the third human technological perspective reason view point, today's computer can do many well-defined tasks, for example, arithmetic operations, are much faster and more accurate than human beings. However, the computers‘ interaction with their environment is not very sophisticated yet. How can human test whether a computer has reached the general intelligence level of a human being? Can a computer convince a human interrogator that it is a human? But before thinking of such advanced kinds of machines, human will start developing our own extremely simple " intelligent" machines. So, it is possible that human society job nature will to be changed to artificial intelligent society when (AI) technology is developed to the mature stage in the future.

- Why do some service or manufacturing providers need artificial intelligence machines to replace manual service workers or manufacturing workers in our future societies?

One of major division in (AI) is between humans who think (AI) is the only serious way of finding out how we (human) work and human who want companies to do very smart things, independently of how we (human) work. This is the important distinction between cognitive scientists vs engineers. One of another major division in (AI) is between symbolic (AI), which represents information through symbols and their relationships. Specific Algorithms are used to process these symbols to solve problems or deduce new knowledge and connectionist. So (AI) , which represents information in network. Biological processes underlying learning, task performance and problem solving are imitated from human mind behaviors. Thus, it is possible that artificial intelligence machines can do the better judgicious behavior to compare human.

- How does artificial intelligence influence future working changing in automative manufacturing or automative service tasks aspects?

In the automation changing influence aspect, as companies increasingly use robots on production lines or algorithms to optimize their logistics manage inventory, any carry out other core business functions. Technological advances are creating a new automation age in which ever-smarter and more flexible machines will be deployed on an ever larger scale in the marketplace. However, researching artificial intelligence with how influences human working nature. We need to answer these questions: How will automation transform the workplace? What will the implications for employment? And what is likely to be its impact both on productivity in the global economy and on employment?

Advances in robotics, artificial intelligence, and machine learning are growing in a new age of automation as machines match or outperform human performance in a range of work activities, including ones requiring cognitive capabilities. What factors are determined the changing in workplace adoption by artificial intelligence innovation? What advantages are automation? Automation of activities can be enabled businesses to improve performance by reducing errors and improving quality and speed, and achieving outcomes that go beyond human capabilities.

Some scientists indicated based on their scenario modeling. They estimated automation could raise producing growth globally by 0.8 to 1.4 percent annually. Almost, the activities people are paid almost $16 trillion in wages to do in global economy have the potential to be automated by adopting currently demonstrated technology. According to their analysis of more than 2,000 work activities across 800 occupations. When less than 5% of all occupations have of least 30% of activities that could be automated. They also indicated that technical economic and social factors will determine automation. Continued technical progress, for example, in areas such as natural language processing is a key factor beyond technical feasibility , the cost of technology, competition with labor including skills, and supply and demand dynamics, performance benefits including and beyond labor cost savings and social and regulatory acceptance will affect (alter) the scope of automation.

Other some scientists also indicate U.S. country for example, the anticipate shift in the activities in labor force of a similar order of magnitude as the long term sight away from agriculture and decreases in manufacturing. Share of employment in the United States both which were achieved. So, those factors can influence why artificial intelligence technology needs. So, it is possible that future agriculture and manufacturing both industries will apply (AI) technology manufacturer-kind of job nature to raise productivity instead of farmers, fruit picking workers, farming transportation labours as well as factory manufacturing workers and supervisors etc. human-kind of job nature.

● Is artificial intelligence possible to replace any service occupation or manufacturing labor to finish whole tasks steps of some service or manufacturing occupations in our societies ?

Not just intelligence, but also debating, if machines are capable of having a conscious minds. Artificial intelligence has those characteristics as below:

On functionalism aspect, artificial intelligence inputs mental states, sensory inputs, (beliefs, desires being in pain feeling) and behavioral outputs. Since mental states are identified by a functional role, which are thoughts to be manifested in various systems. Even, perhaps computers which are physical devices with electronic substrate that inform computations on inputs to give outputs similar to brains which are artificial intelligence composed of part any intrinsic relationship to each other. Thus, artificial intelligence activities is not the whole itself, but into parts or on external influence on the parts.

On dualism aspect, artificial intelligence is a set of views about the relationship between mind are matter. On materialism aspect, it builds the only thing that exists is matter, including consciousness.

On biological naturalism aspect, it is similar a human brain than feels pains makes mental situation. So, artificial intelligence is similar biologist which might to be excited to human labor work. Hence, it seems artificial intelligence can change (alter) or replace human labor work of nature in possible in the future.

On technological innovation reason view point, the history development of artificial intelligence studying the intelligence is one of most ancient scientific discipline. The history development of artificial intelligence what aims to achieve human use to sense, learn remember and think, logic probability, decision making and calculation develop from mathematics, instead of replacement human labor functions.

Artificial intelligence history development aim is the scientific analysis of skills in connection and practice with the appearance of computers from 1950 year beginning. The artificial intelligence (AI) can deal with the ultimate challenges. How can (either biological or electronic) mind sense, understand and manipulate a world that is much simple and more complex than itself? And what if would human like to construct something with such capabilities?

The general-purpose software of the early period of (AI) were only able to solve simple tasks effectively and failed when which should be used in a wider range or an more difficult tasks. One of the sources of difficulty was that early software had very few or mix knowledge about the problems which handled, and activities successes by simply syntactic manipulation. Moreover, the other difficulty was that many problems that were tried to solve by the (AI) were untreatable.

The early (AI) software whether trying step sequences based on the basic facts about the problem that should be solved, experimented with different combinations till which found a solution. From the end the 1960 year, developing the so-called expert systems were emphasized. These systems had (sue-based) knowledge base about the field which handled. Till to the beginning of the 1970 year, (Prolog) the logical programming language was born, which was built in the computation realization of a version of the resolution calculus. (Prolog) is a remarkably prevalent tool in developing expert systems (on medical, judiciary and other scopes), but natural language parsers were implemented in this language. Then, in 1981 s, the Japanese announced the fifth generation computer system project, a 10 years plan to build an intelligent computer system that use the (Prolog) language as a machine code. Nowadays, (AI) can be applied any industries, such as car manufacturing industry can use (AI) technological machine-men manufacture car, instead of replacing human labors in factory. Even, in the future, using (AI) machine-men drivers can drive any private cars or public transportation tools, instead of replacing human drivers, e.g. bus, train, tram, ferry etc. Also in the future, machine-men can replace housewives to serve families to do housekeeping clean job , e.g. cleaning toilets, bathrooms, kitchens, even cooking functions at home. So (AI) machine-man can reduce housewives works at home. Moreover, (AI) machine man can take care old people , when who are living at homes or elder care centers.

So, it seems artificial intelligence (AI) will be possible developed to manufacture a new generation machine-man to assist (serve) families to do any simply cleaning or cooking jobs at homes. Moreover, the overall demand of (AI) general social needs will also rise, such as security, driving transportation tools, restaurant cleaning, elder centers care service etc. So, it seems that individual or families or social needs of (AI) will be increase in the future. Thus, it will influence macro economy growth (GDP) if there are large house family consumer group and hotel or bus or taxis or ferry etc. different business consumer group demand any artificial intelligence machine numbers increasing. Then, the artificial intelligence products and material manufacturers must need to buy many artificaial intelligence materials to produce any kinds of artificial intelligence machines to prepare to satisfy consumer individual needs. Consequently, macro economy will grow to the owned artificial intelligence development countries, e.g. US, China, UK.

● Why can artificial intelligence satisfy human needs on some service or manufacturing tasks to some occupations in our future societies?

First, On machine-man satisfactory demand aspect view point, it makes computers that think, it is the automation of activities. We associate with human thinking: like decision making, learning. It is the act of creating machine that perform function that require intelligence when performed by people. It is the study of mental faculties through the use of computational models. It is the study of computations that make it possible to perceive, reason and act. It is a branch of computer science that is concerned with the automation of intelligent behavior. It is anything in computing service that human don't yet know how to do property.

Second, on thought aspect artificial intelligence means systems thank think like humans, systems that think rationally.

Third, on behavioral aspect, artificial intelligence systems that act like human and that systems act rationally. However, the basic objective of (AI) is to represent human's thought processes in computation . These machines are supposed to exhibit behavior that. It is performed by a human being, would be considered intelligent. However, some authors feel (AI) has disadvantages, such as it is not creative, it is excited in the use of sensory devices, it can't make use of a very wide context of experiences and it does not use common sense.

For speech recognition and understanding function needs example, (AI) can be applied in speech recognition and understanding function, which (AI) speech or voice recognition is a data input method. For example, the computer recognizes and understands one (or a few) word commands. Speech understanding on the other hand is the computer's ability to understanding a spoken language. That is , the computer understands the meaning of sentences, an paragraphs through (AI).

So, (AI) can be attempted to learn human language how to speak. It is similar to translate human language skill, instead of actual human speaking skill. Also, (AI) can assist handicap learning or language student how to listen different languages by machine-man sounds from computers more accurately. So, it seems that it (AI) can replace human language teachers speaking function and can change teaching language nature of job in language speaking and listening education industry.

- Is artificial intelligence one good choice for human future technological raising productivities or improving performance advantages ?

Nowadays, new technology development is popular. However, artificial intelligence is one kind of new technology choice among different technologies innovation. So it brings this question: Is artificial intelligence technology value to invest? To answer this question. I shall indicate some other new technology developments to compare (AI) technology development to judge which has urgent needs to achieve human expectation nowadays.

For example, why is green peace interested in new technologies? New technologies features prominently in our ongoing campaigns against genetic modified crops and number power. However, which are also an integral part of our solutions to environmental challenges, including renewable energy technologies, such as solar, wind and wave (water) power energy as well as waste treatment technologies, such as mechanical, biological treatment.

It seems humans need concern how to apply (AI) technology to solve environment pollution challenges in our future. So, environment protective, agriculture, natural energy technology will be popular demand to attempt to apply (AI) technology to solve their challenges or apply (AI) to assist to develop their industry.

- How can artificial intelligence technology bring robotic invention needs more?

Advances in artificial intelligence (AI) technology and related fields have opened up new markets and new opportunities progress in critical areas, such as health, education, energy, economic development, social welfare and the environment pollution.

(AI) automation will continue to create wealth and expand the global economy development in the future. However, when many will benefits that growth won't be costless and will be accompanied by changes in the skills, that workers need to increase productivity in the economy and structural changes in the economy. So, in the skills that workers need to succeed in the economy and structural changes.

I shall indicate why aggressive policy action will be needed to help Americans who are disadvantaged by these changes , due to (AI) technology is caused. For automation industry change example, artificial intelligence (AI) capabilities will enable automation of some tasks that have long required human labor. These artificial intelligence technology introduction can increase new opportunities for individuals. The economy and society, but (AI) has also the potential to disrupt be current livelihoods of many Americans. However, (AI) leads to unemployment and increase in inequality over the long run depends not only on the (AI) technology itself, but also on the institutions and policies that are changed. Thus, it is possible that (AI) technology will raise some countries unemployment number if the employer apply (AI) technology workers to work instead of human labor in their factories, but it can also raise productivities for these employers.

Technological progress is main driver of growth of GDP per capita, allowing output to increase faster than labor and capital . However, technology can increase productivity, but also decrease the number of labor hours needed to create a unit of output. So (AI) causes unequal to labor wage decreases, even reduces the number of labor to manufacture, e.g. artificial intelligence technology of automation car manufacturing industry; clothing manufacturing industry; plane manufacturing etc. high technology of artificial intelligence manufacturing method. But (AI) should be potential environment benefit, although it raises unemployment ratio. Moreover, it can rise production , due to many skilled craft were replaced by the combination of machines and lower-skilled labor. The result of (AI) technology introduction , it causes output per hour risen when inequality declined, driving up average living standards, but the labor of some high-skill workers was no longer as valuable in the market. Otherwise, if (AI) technology is continue developed to be success. Some routine intensive occupations will be loss, which focused on predictable, e.g. easily programmable tasks, such as switchboard operators, filing clerks, travel agents, and assembly line workers would be particularly replaced by new (AI) technology. However, at the same time, (AI) technology development will bring these benefits: improvement in education (training (AI) technology scientists) , due to (AI) manufacturing technology needs are raising to businesses and institutional changes, such as the reduction in unionization and raising in the minimum wage to the (AI) manufacturing technology skilled labor in factories.

Because (AI) technology is not a single technology, but rather a collection of technologies that are applied to specific tasks, the effects of (AI) will be felt unevenly though the economy. It will bring some tasks will be most easily automated than others , and some jobs will be affected more than others, both negatively and positively. Finally, new jobs are likely to be directly created in areas , such as the development and supervision of (AI) as well as indirectly created in a range areas though out the economy as higher incomes lead to expanded demand.

However, if (AI) technology could dominate global labor markets. If labor productivity increases, do not influence into wage increases, then the large economic gains brought about by (AI) technology could be increased wealth inequality, due to employers can reduce production cost, but workers (labors) wages will not be increased, even will be decreased. Hence, it seems the (AI) technology will bring disadvantages to labor market to cause unemployment or reduce wages in possible, although it can reduce employer individual salary (wage) expenditure and it can raise productivity.

Artificial intelligence (AI) technology is a branch of computer science that aims to create intelligent machines that work and react like humans. So, (AI) is a technology that appears to impact (influence) human preference by learning, understanding complex contents, enhancing humans in executing both routine and non-routine tasks. In the future, (AI) technology that can be virtual personal assistant, as well as it may exist, such as robots with human-like processing capabilities.

How can (AI) technology impact global service and manufacturing industries products needs over the next 10 years? During this time period, (AI) technology is predicted to have wide-ranging applications including: Machine learning that automates analytical model building by using algorithms that allow machines to operate without human assistance.

In global education aspect, potential applications include predicting cause-

and-effect relationships from biological data, identifying new drugs, self-driving cars, and protecting against fraud, improved natural language processing that allows computers to continue to better analysis, understand and generate language to interface with humans using natural human languages. For example, transcribing notes dictated by physicians, automatically drafting articles and translating text and speech. So (AI) technology can be applied to education aspect to improve humans' knowledge level.

In visual art aspect, (AI) machine vision that allows computers to identify objects, scenes and activities in images. Current applications of (AI) machine vision include providing objective descriptions for the blind seeing(visual) needs.

We except the economic effects of (AI) technology to include both direct GDP growth from sectors that develop or manufacture. (AI) technology and indirect GDP growth through increased productivity in existing sectors that employ some form of (AI). If (AI) technology is an increasingly critical component of more products, it will become an integral part of many people's lives. Thus, (AI)'s ability to influence economic activity, rather than the economic or development status of the region. (AI) has the potential to impact income classes and to bring significant gains to both developed and developing countries. For example, (AI) has the potential to optimize good production around the world by analyzing agricultural regions and identifying what is necessary to improve crop yields.

In estimating the future economic effects by (AI) technology innovation, it is important to note that it is challenging to accurately predict which applications of (AI) will ultimately be commercially successful. In micro level economic influence, we need to apply methodologies to estimate the economic effects of investment in firms developing (AI) technology since investment levels in a technology are a telling sign of the future potential of that (AI) technology.

How (AI)'s development may affect the global economy over the next ten years. In fact, (AI) technology has the potential to affect business across the global in a wide range of industries in ways only a number of technologies have done in the parts. For example, (AI) technology's expected to be a useful tool for enhancing human capabilities and in some instances replacing functions, such as driving a car, adoption of broadband internet, mobile telephone, industrial robotic automation have served to enhance human capabilities.

However, significant public debate has focused on projections of (AI) technology's effect on the labor force. However, large companies prefer to invest in (AI) technological industry. For example, face book's (AI) research lab., google machine intelligence lab. and micro soft machine learning and artificial intelligence research division are all making advances in (AI) technology and investing in the industry's top talent. Additionally, between 2010 year and 2015 year, nearly $5 billion in venture capital funding invested in firms across the global developing and employing (AI) technology (Facebook (AI) Research).

● How can artificial intelligence impact on workplace on future service or manufacturing industries ?

Modern information technologies and the labor economy growth of machines is powered by artificial intelligence have already strongly influenced the world of work in the 21 ST century. Computers, algorithms and software simplify every tasks and it is impossible to image how most of our life could be managed without them. How can be the information economy characterized by exponential growth replaces the most production industry based on economy of scales? What will the future world of work look like and how long will it take to get? Will the future world of work be a world where humans spend less time earning their livelihood? Alternatively, are mass unemployment, mass poverty and social distortions also possible scenario for the future, where robots, artificial intelligence systems play an increasingly central role? These questions concern how artificial intelligence further development . Can influence labor economy growth on workplace ? When the labor market has widespread impact on intelligence property, information technology, product liability, competition and labor and employment laws.

How (AI) technology impacts on labor workplace.

The future influence any organizations how labor economies use of (AI) can be analyzed, such as deep machine learning is based on a set of model high level data. Unlike human workers, the machines are connected the whole time in workplace. If one machine makes a mistake, all autonomous systems will keep this in mind and will avoid the same mistake the next time.

Over the long run intelligent machines will win against every human expert. Production robots have been replacing employees because of the (AI) technology. They work more precisely than humans and cost loss. Creative solutions like 3D printers and the self learning ability of these production robots will replace human workers, the automatic data recording and data processing, traditional back office activities are no longer in demand. Autonomous software will collect necessary information and will send it to the employee who needs it. Additionally, dematerialization leads to the phenomenon that traditional physical products are becoming software. For example, CD or DVDs are being replaced by streaming services. The replacement of traditional event ticket, e-travel ticket service products or hard cash will be the next step, due to the possibility of payment by smartphone. So, (AI) technology will impact human's daily life consumption behaviors in the future. For another example, transportation tools, such as boats and ferries and private vehicles will use sensors and navigating without human input. Taxi and truck drivers will become obsolete, the stock store applies to stock managers and postal carriers of the delivery is distributed by (AI) machine delivery method.

- Can (AI) technology impact on customer relationship management (CRM) on customer service tasks market ?

Nowadays , (AI) is a technology almost as old as the computer industry itself, it is similar with the advent of personal assistants function to businesses and personal promotion channel, such as (Amazon's Alexa, Apple's Siri, Google's Assistant) image recognition (face book), personalized recommendations (Netflix , Amazon). Those innovations have been driven by a increase in processing power, lower cost hardware, and the exploding creation and availability of data. It seems, (AI) technology can impact global customer service management method.

How to forecast economic impact modeling to (AI) will affect global economy? Can human forecast business revenue growth and job creation (or destruction) based on (AI) applied to customer relationship management (CRM) activities? In addition to the economic impact on (AI) or (CRM) which can include an estimate of the economic impact attributable to sales forces customer base. What can economic benefits be brought to (CRM) from (AI) technology?

Artificial intelligence(AI) comprises a set of technologies that use natural language processing, machine learning, knowledge graphs, and other tools to answer questions, discover insights and provide recommendations. Computer systems can use (AI) hypothesize and formulate possible answers based on available evidence can be trained through the ingestion of vast amounts of content, and automatically adapt and learn from (AI) self mistakes and failures.

So, any business organizations (customer service departments) can provide efficient and effective customer relationship management of excellent customer service quality if which applied (AI) technology system. The different type of (AI) systems include: (AI) system platforms, machine learning (AI) based data preparation and enrichment tools, machine vision/ image recognition, voice speech recognition, text analysis and natural language processing, bots , e.g. face book website and virtual digital assistance solutions, social media pattern analysis , sentiment analysis, advanced numerical analysis (e.g. IOT streaming , machine logs), supporting technologies, knowledge base dialog management, Q&A processing etc. different (AI) technology system customer relationship management (CRM) tools.

(AI) (CRM) of activity can include these categories, such as: corporate marketing, marketing operation, field marketing, customer support, digital commerce, customer analytics, customer influenced product or service design, product or service pricing, finance information, presentation, customer billing, inventory , logistics and fulfilment support, partner management etc. different CRM tools.

(AI) technology of CRM has been carrying on plan different stages to achieve CRM personal assistant tool for businesses. The stages are such as, in the beginning stage of (AI) projects in place, implement now, pilot phase next year in the final stage of (AI) customer relationship management tools are foreseeable future. So, this CRM technology has been improved to plan in different stages every year to prepare to achieve full capacity of CRM service quality for businesses to use in the future.

Hence, how to develop an estimate prediction of the economic impact (AI) technologies could have CRM activities, which depends on gathering macroeconomic information on business revenue and the basic marketing of business revenue and the basic markup of business expenses by major functions (customer support, marketing and sales , production etc.)

An economic impact model that can gather data together and forecast the results how (AI) artificial intelligence technology brings (CRM) customer relationship management benefits to businesses, e.g. surveys investigation includes IT spending by sample countries, GDP and population estimates and forecasts, revenue per employee and ratios of IT spend to GDP. Surveys (questionnaire questions) of forecast results are influenced by (AI) impact can include: results are projected from surveys and rely on estimates are made by respondents on the expected financial improvements in categories of (AI) –assisted customer relationship management activities. The forecast assumes that these estimates are correct; financial estimates are based on estimates of "first year" improvement from full (AI) implementation; forecasts are from planning to implement any artificial intelligence of customer relationship management (CRM) projects, the improvement forecast is of categories of activity , e.g. corporate marketing , digital commerce, and customer analytics. They are not estimates of ROI for the (AI) software. They rely on conservative estimates to which each of these entities might affect company revenue, expenses or productivity. They also rely on estimates of the penetration of software in customer relationship management activities . Net new jobs created are based on the ratio of new revenue to jobs required to support that revenue . They can assume that 50% of the net new revenue will support increases in labor and the rest will go for capital and other operating expenses that may replace jobs lost to automation.

In the future, some of the ways in micro economic benefits to any organizations. (AI) technology is expected to impact CRM activities include: Spending up sales cycles, improving lead generation and qualification solving customer support problems faster (raising service quality), helping companies improve brand campaigns and recognition, lowering costs of support calls when increasing resolution rates, lowering the cost of recruiting employees and partners, increasing revenue from optimized product marketing, optimizing price, distribution logistics and preventing loss through fraud detection. So, micro economic benefits view point, it seems that (AI) CRM technology can raise any companies economic benefits for care term.

Artificial intelligence enables machines or the in-build software to behave like human beings which allows these decisions and act. The advent of (AI) is leading , talking, making decisions and act. The advent of (AI) is leading to new technologies advances and transforming the economic and employment opportunities for humans in a positive way. (AI) related technologies can facilitate our live. For example, industrial robotics, robotic medical assistants, smart games, financial forecasting software, big data analysis, algorithms in health and bioinformatics, pilotless cargo places, drone ambulances and general purpose and workplace robots and others. (Disruptors technologies: Advances that will transform life, business and the global economy).

Artificial intelligence also known as computational intelligence is defined as " the human –like intelligence exhibited by machines or software. It is theorized that intelligence of humans can be described and intelligence machines or software can simulate it. These machines software can be reasonable , learn, perceive and process information, like human mind and thus facilitate human life. They can think and act for us. So, artificial intelligence is an interdisciplinary field of study including computer science, neuroscience, psychology, linguistics and philosophy.

However, (AI) research and developments have economically impacted many industries, such as robotics, telecommunications, computer applications , health, finance, heavy manufacturing, transportation, aviation, e-service and e-commerce, military , music and movie, toys and games entertainment etc. industries.

In fact, many ideas, systems and technologies have been developing in the world of (AI) technology. However, which are net called or considered (AI) products, rather which are mentioned with their specific names, such as smart graphics, machine learning, e-commerce etc. (i.e. this is called (AI) effect).

- How can (AI) technology influence digital industry ?

Nowadays, (AI) related industrial applications will replace most human power in fields, including call centers, customer services and air cargo transportation. (AI) technologies also help weather forecasting based on repeated rainfall pattern (data) recognition, through robotics (i.e. floor cleaning, moving lawns etc.) transporting people and products with unmanned vehicles, sending space unmanned smart shuttles, developing robotic arms, predicting market values in stock exchanges by internet, making homes safer, helping elderly and disabled using robotic servants etc.

Among the (AI) related technologies , there are a few that significance for the impact on society and especially on digital economy . (AI) is particularly influential in machine learning. Such as robotics, transportation, finance, health and bioinformatics, e-commerce , e-games, big online data gathering and internet-of-things. For example, machine e-learning is based in bioinformatics and robots that can learn new skills for better caregiving in healthcare. What is machine e-learning? Machines can e-learn from e-data gathering, coming up generalizations and making decisions to act in certain ways from internet.

There are important applications , such as e-machine perception, electronic online natural language learning processing, online search engines, online bioinformatics, online brain –computer interface, online game playing, online robot locomotion, online advertising, online computations finances, online health monitoring, online DNA classification and decision making, online in chemistry –cheminformatics . So, online machine learning can positively impact productivity and it can enhance information and analytical system from (AI) online channel.

What is robotics? Robotics is one of the most strongly influenced fields in (AI). For example, heavy manufacturing industries, robots and used and man power is replaced for effectiveness, precision, and accuracy, especially in respective or dangerous tasks, including welding, assembling , picking and placing .

So, robots can acquire new skills or adapt the changing dynamic environment. Also, artificial intelligence can be applied in developing transportation. For example, automated vehicles, driver assistance systems , safety systems, collision avoidance systems and public transportation. Moreover, (AI) technology has proven to produce some of the best tools to predict stock market fluctuations from internet data gathering method. It's predictions are based on ever-evolving predictions algorithms and systems learn new models and make connections between historical data and new data to measure stock market trading more accurate from internet data gathering channel.

In health field, especially in health data processing , analysis, decision making support and medical diagnosis. So, online data can show which patients will need what treatment and what alternative drugs could be used more accurate from (AI) online data gathering method. Bioinformatics is an interdisciplinary field combining statistics, (AI) online technology can help in discovering data patterns and modeling through the application of machine learning, artificial neural networks and genetic algorithms. For example, further (AI) technology development of human genome project of online data sequences.

Online shopping can be facilitated by virtual assistants developed through (AI) technology and these assistants can offer the best advice. (AI) online purchase coming after every product image recommendations and personalization bring important revenue to shopping online sites, like Amazon . Smart computer graphics and games, artificial intelligence is useful in smarter computer, graphics, scene modeling , scene rendering processes in order to create, for example, effective human –robot interactions , online machine learning, online strategic games techniques etc. online computer related (AI) software.

So, online big data analysis and big data does have a critical need in the world of online intelligence machines and software in our future. In other words, (AI) offers online technology to enable online big data analysis to provide industrial organizations with valuable information for effective decision making in short time. For example, what IBM's Watson achieved: this machine used 200 million of structured and unstructured content with a special technology of hypothesis generation, massive evidence gathering, analysis and scoring from internet channel.

Finally, (AI) online technology another related internet invention (internet of things) (IOT) is the network of machines or objects connected through internet. These connected objects can sense their internal and external environment, communicate with each other, can send critical data and finally can make decisions to act or correct their environment from (AI) online technology. For example, factories can monitor and automatically change production processes, hospitals can monitor and regulate the health conditions of their patients , schools can collect data from facilities and cars can send data to car makers from (AI) online technology.

Partner predicts that (IOT) market will create about trillion amount value by 2020 year. Although machines collect big data from their environment, whether which gain an insight or learn from these online data largely depends on the (AI) online machine learning principals and (AI) online technology. In 2013, Mckinsey estimated that disruptive technologies closely related with potential economic impact in 2025 year between $7.1 to $13.1 trillion amount (automation of knowledge work, advanced robotics, autonomous or near-autonomous vehicles).

- Could work activities in China be automated

making on service or manufacturing industries needs in the nation with the world's largest automation potential?

Can (AI) technology influence China economy? Could China workers be affected and jobs made up of routine work activities and predictable? Will programmable tasks be particularly impact to China employment market ? When impact on labor market is likely to be gradual at the aggregate level, it can be sudden and dramatic at the level of specific work activities, rending some job obsolete fairly. Overall (AI) technology will raise digital skills when reducing demand for medium incomer inequality for China workers. It seems (AI) technology's effect on productivity could be crucial to China's future economic growth as the population ages are increasing.

In China, some biggest technological companies driving significant investments in research and development. Moreover, China is one of the leading global (AI) technology development county. However, China will need to focus on building its innovation capacity. For example, United States and United Kingdom are currently producing more influential (AI) technological research. However, if China planed to achieve (AI) technology success, it's traditional industries will need to develop technical know-how –to and overcoming implementation costs prepare to develop (AI) . When (AI) technology is introduced into China society, China government needs to raise concerning ethical, legal, technological security etc. business questions. Also, surrounding issues include privacy, discrimination, legal liability and regulation. It aims to encourage overseas investors to choose to invest (AI) technological industry to raise GDP growth and manufacturing industries income growth for long term in China. If China encouraged overseas (AI) technology investment in its country. It is possible to influence China employment market to be changed. Because (AI) technology will impact to influence China people daily life. Due to (AI) technology is introduced to China society, many rich people will prefer to spend to buy any high (AI) technological products for entertainment or learning or machine man driving etc. daily necessity activities. Then it will raise GDP growth and will raise (AI) manufacturers or related-(AI) technological manufacturers profit. It is beneficial to China because it can become one high knowledgeable and (AI) technological economical society. But it will bring bad influences to raise unemployment chance for the low skillful labor. In labor economy aspect influence , how (AI) technology can influence China low skillful labor unemployment ratio raising. The raising low skill labor unemployment reason is because China low skillful human labors are argued or are replaced by (AI) technology creating new challenges to introduce to influence China society of simply human manufacturing job nature to be changed to be high (AI) technology manufacturing job nature in any China factories. Moreover, when (AI) technology introduction to China, it will cause other related social challenges in China. The varied (AI) related challenges, including the difficulty of creating safe and reliable hardware for sensing and affecting (transportation and education), the challenges of gaining public trust, a low resource comities and public safety and security, the challenges of overcoming fears or marginalizing humans in China employment and workplace and the risk of diminishing interpersonal trust because the low skillful labors won't believe any China employers will give chance to employ them , due to (AI) technology will replace their skills and man manufacturing of productivity is much less to compare to (AI) technology manufacturing method.

- How does (AI) technology influence

the future of employment change?

Are future nature of jobs changed to computerization from (AI) technology? Where are the probability of computing occupations from (AI) technology influence? What is expected impacts of future computing on labor market from (AI) technology influence? John Maynard Keynes's frequently cited prediction of widespread technological unemployment " du to our discovery of means of economic the use of labor outrunning the pace of which we can find new used of labor" (Keynes, 1933, p.3).

In the future, (AI) technology will impact some nature of occupations to change computing. This chance will also influence some countries' economic change. For example, some factory human labors hand routine manufacturing tasks will be changed to computerization of routine manufacturing tasks by (AI) technological machine men hand manufacturing method. it will cause a structured shift in the labor market, with workers reallocating their labor supply from middle-income manufacturing to low-income service occupations.

Arguably, this is because the manual tasks of service occupations are less computerization, as who require a higher degree of flexibility and physical adaptability. So, (AI) technology will influence the human hand labor skillful occupation nature of task cheaper , such as vehicle manufacturing , ship manufacturing, computer manufacturing, steel manufacturing, television, radio etc. home electronic products of heavy machine industry change. Due to (AI) technology machine man will be proper to be used to manufacturing these electronic products when the (AI) technology innovation can develop to the mature stage. Then, any countries manufacturers will choose to use (AI) technology machine man, instead of human hand production.

Supposing the future prices of computing are fallen, seriously, problem solving skills are becoming relatively productive, explaining the substantial employment growth in manufacturing occupations, involving cognitive tasks where skilled labor has a comparative advantage, as well as the increase education needs for (AI) technology computing of machine man subject study.

Prediction of education needs for (AI) technology student numbers will increase, due to manufacturing industry needs many (AI) technology students in future employment market. Another (AI) technology influence if the future (AI) technological innovation, e.g. machine man manufacturing or machine man service industries will both increase demand, then with more sophistic software technologies will be disrupted labor markets by marketing workers redundant.

For publishing industry, what is striking about the case in paper book publishing industry will be unpopular? Due to the electronic book publishing industry will be popular, e.g. Amazon publish . (AI) technology can influence paper book manufacturing method which is replaced by machine man electronic book manufacturing method as well as it will cause the computerization is no longer confined to routine manufacturing tasks. Due to (AI) machine man manufacturing technology will be proper to be used to manufacture any products in short time efficiently and effectively , e.g. electronic book products. In the future, if it is fact to occur this case, such as (AI) technological machine man manufacturing method will be adopted (applied) to manufacture electronic books or any products in possible. (AI) technology will cause many manufacturing workers are unemployed. It is beneficial to employers, who can reduce to spend much wages expenditure to employ manufacturing workers, but it will cause many manufacturing workers loss jobs and reduce income to support whose families lives. It will cause social challenges, e.g. increasing stealing crimes if the manufacturing workers had not other skills to find other jobs to do easily. So, manufacturers need to concern over technological unemployment which will be hardly future phenomenon if who decided to dismiss all manufacturing workers, due to (AI) technology machine men replace to them.

If (AI) technology can be innovated to produce any kinds of machine man to serve any service or manufacturing industries successfully. Then, it will bring these questions: Can future that workers be influenced to be automation employment and productivity by (AI) technology influence? Does it impact to influence the (AI) technology countries' productivity and growth and natural resources development and labor markets and evolution of global financial markets and economic impact of technology and innovation and urbanization etc. issues? How will automation transform the workplace? What will be the implication for employment? What is likely to be its impact both on productivity in the global economy and on employment?

In fact, automatic of activities can enable businesses to improve performance by reducing errors chance and improving quality and speed, and same cases achieving outcomes that go beyond human capabilities. Some economists indicate (AI) technology would give a needed boost to economic growth and prosperity have of the working age population in many countries. Based on the scenario modeling, they estimate automation could raise productivity growth globally by 0.8 to 1.4 % annually. They also indicated that almost half the activities people are almost $1.6 trillion in wages to do in the global economy have the potential to be automated adapting current demonstrates technology, according to their analysis of more than 2,000 work activities across 800 occupations. When less than 5% of all occupations can be automated entirely using demonstrated technology, about 60% of all occupations have at least 30% of worker made activities, that would be automated. More occupation will change to be automated. They also indicated for business performance benefits of automation are relatively clear, but the issues are more complicated by policy making to attract foreign investors. Beyond technical feasibility, the cost of technology, competition labor will include skills and supply and demand dynamics, performance benefits and beyond labor cost savings and social and regulatory acceptance will affect the automation. Their predictions suggest that half of today work activities could be automated by 2055 year, but this could happen 10 to 20 years earlier or latter depending on the various factors in addition to their wider economic condition.

Some scientists suggest (AI) technology is finally starting to deliver real-life business benefits. Computer power is growing significantly , algorithms are becoming more sophisticated and perhaps most important of all, the world is generating vast quantities of the fuel that powers (AI) technology data billions of gigabytes of it every day. Also, online firms are digital natives, such as Google online search service company is investing on (AI) technology. For new though most of the news if coming from the suppliers of (AI) technologies. And many new users are only in the experimental phase. Few products are on the market or are likely to arrive these soon to drive immediate and widespread adoption. As a result, analysts believe (AI) technology's potential will give true economic benefit in the future. (AI) industry will introduce to suppliers and users to raise economic potential of (AI) technology.

In the future, (AI) technology systems can solve business problems. Some

scientists categorized those into five technology systems that are key areas of (AI) technology development: robotics and autonomous vehicles, computer vision language virtual agents and machine learning , which is based on algorithms that learn from data without replying on rules-based programming in order to draw conclusions or direct an action.
Such as computer vision and language includes natural language processing, analytics, speech recognition technology, some are about learning from information, such as about machine learning and others are related to acting on information, such as robotics, autonomous vehicles and virtual agents, which are computer programs that can converse with humans. Machine learning and a subfield called deep learning are artificial intelligence applications.

Artificial intelligence (AI) is a term first defined in 1956 year. It is a branch of computer science that aims to create intelligent machines that work and react like humans. In contrast today, 60 years later, (AI) is characterized by a number of applications, including computers playing games against humans and understanding human languages, virtual personal assistants, and robotics which involve computers seeing , hearing and reacting to sensory stimuli. In the future, technologists predict for (AI) technology ranging from (AI) being used as a tool to aid relatively simple processes for robots with human like mental capabilities, who expect (AI) technology can emulate human performance by learning, coming to mind its own conclusions, understanding complex content, engaging in dialog with people, enhancing human cognitive performance or replacing humans in executing both routine and non-routine tasks. In existing industry, (AI) technology is used , such as targeted advertising and virtual used personal assistant as well as the (AI) technology that my exist in the future, such as robots with human vehicle processing capabilities.
The range of (AI) technology's progress in the future will determine the economic impact future of (AI) technology on the global economy with more limited advances and applications (i.e. weak (AI) only) corresponding to more limited economic impacts and more substantial progress, i.e. strong (AI) technology is corresponding to more significant economic impact.
(AI) technology learning that automates analytical model, including predicting cause-and-effect relationship from biological data, identifying new drugs, self-driving cars and protecting against fraud etc. functions. Also (AI) learning can improve natural language processing that allows

computers to continue to better analyze, understand and generate language to interface with human using the natural human language, virtual personal assistant, helps users by providing scheduling appointment, reminds organizing personal finance and finding providers of various services, machine vision allows (AI) machine man to identify object, scenes and activities in detect pedestrians and bicyclists.

We expect the economic effects of (AI) technology to include both direct GDP growth from sectors that develop or manufacture (AI) technology and indirect GDP growth through increased productivity in existing sectors that employ some from of (AI) technology. If (AI) producing sectors could grow, then it could lead to increase revenues and employment of (AI) technological professionals within these existing firms as well as the potential creation of entirely new economic activities to any countries' societies productivity improvement in existing sectors could be realized through faster and move efficient processes and decision making as well as increased (AI) technological knowledge and access to information available in societies easily.

In the future, if (AI) technology is an increasingly critical component of more products, it will become an integral part of necessary products of many people's lives. The extent of (AI)'s economy effort is also likely to vary from region to region, thought variation may be more dependent on the predominate economic activity of a region and the (AI) ability can influence economic activity, rather then the economic or developmental status of the regions. (AI) technology can move accessibility and can use source development to do international business between one country and another country.

So (AI) technology has the potential to give benefits to different income chooses and to bring significant gains to both developed and developing countries. For agricultural technology, (AI) has the potential to optimize food production around the world by analyzing agricultural regions and identifying what is necessary to improve crop yield. In total, (AI) technology gives greater economic impact to any countries agricultural regions if which implemented (AI) technology to grow crop , fruit etc. food production in the farms.

Investment in (AI) technology is such as capital investment to any countries' public or private enterprises. So, it will have large economic impact to the future . If the (AI) technology is reasonable invested to the different needs aspect by the public or private enterprises in the country.

Then, it will have good economic impact to the country in the future. However, when (AI) technology is likely to affect both the productivity and employment components of economic growth in many sectors. Significant public debate has focused on projections of (AI)'s effect on the labor force. However, for instance, some researchers have argued that the rise of (AI) technology and automation will led to significant unemployment as capital is substituted for the low skillful labor. So, they point to the concern that the increasing sophistication of (AI) technology may balance skilled and semi-skilled workers and the reduce the size of the middle class. However, this is not a new argument, due to (AI) technology negatively affecting the labor force and leading to mass unemployment. Because the (AI) technology is the substitution of machinery for human labor. Although, employment in certain industries, has been reduced in the past due to technological advancement. For long term, the labor market has adapted to the introduction of new technology, giving rise to new jobs in new areas. (AI) technology may also be accomplished without a reduction to total employment in the long-term to some Asia countries, such as Hong Kong and Japan. Because Hong Kong and Japan many low skilled labor, e.g. security, cleaner who complaint that employers need them to work long time hours. (abnormal working hours) e.g. one day 12 to 15 working hour per day. Hence, if (AI) machine means invention technology success. Security or cleaning job can be worked from (AI) machine man in some hours every day in order to reduce the long time working hours cleaners or security workers, e.g. one (AI) machine man works 4 hours for cleaning or security job, one day as well as another cleaner or security labor only needs to work 8 hours one day. So total security or cleaning employers can employ 12 hours machine cleaners or security workers and human cleaners or security workers in one day. For long term benefit, Hong Kong or Japan every security or cleaning worker does not need to work 12 hours minimum working hours one day. They won't feel tried and bore and without private with whose families, so who will accept to do these cleaning or security jobs, even they can raise work efficient and performance when who feel happy and health.

So, (AI) technology of machine man invention can raise low skillful labor efficiency and it can help them to avoid abnormal working hours demand in some busy work life countries, such as Hong Kong and Japan. Before, one Japan female labor feel unhappy to work, due to who often needs to work abnormal working hours for her employer and who has less sleeping and without any private time to enjoy her life with her families every day. So this abnormal working hours factor causes her to do commit suicide behavior, then she is die unlucky. So (AI) technology of machine man invention ought avoid abnormal working hours demand for employer in any countries in the future.

The most important occurrence to any employers, some researchers had attempted to do one experiment to find that private research and development , venture capital and public research and development investment all have strong net effect or economic growth with venture capital funding further having the strongest such effect from (AI) technology. The researchers hypothesize the venture capital investment contributes to economic growth through (AI) technology innovation and by the capacity of an economy to use existing (AI) technology knowledge to increase productivity. They predict the impacts of venture capital, business-research and development and public research and development can raise multi factor productivity from (AI) technology introduction.

Can (AI) technology influence the economic development to developing countries? The developing regions of the world contain most of natural resources. If one day, (AI) technology has invent one kind of machine man which can assist any gas or oil workers to seek any new oil/gas natural resource locations easily. I believe that (AI) technology can help these natural resource exploitation countries will gain economic benefit more easily. So, (AI) driven technology can be used to change to create any new opportunities to address poor management or resources and improve human well being, such as Africa Latin America and India can use (AI) technology machine man to seck any oil/gas natural resource countries exploitation activities to attempt to gain much economic benefits.

- Why will (AI) technology influence future service and manufacturing workers needs ?

Nowadays, increases in capital and labor are no longer driving the levels of economic growth, such as (AI) technology. The ability of increase in capital investment and in labor of traditional drivers of production, have no longer to be enjoyed in most developed economies ,e.g. developed country, US, UK . However, artificial intelligence has the potential to overcome the physical limitation of capital and labor to avoid missing out on this opportunity. So, policy makers and business leaders must prepare for and work toward a future with artificial intelligence. They must do with the idea that (AI) is another simply method to enhance productivity method .

Rather they must see (AI) as the tool that can transform thinking about how growth is created.

Economists have always thought of new technologies are as driving growth their ability to enhancing. It can replace labor and capital factor of production. So, it brings this question: What is the factor of production (AI) technology characteristics. They key factor is to see (AI) technology as a capital-labor .

(AI) can replicate labor activities at much greater scale and speed, and to even perform some tasks began the capabilities of human. For example, by using virtual assistants , 1000 legal documents can be reviewed in a matter of days instead of taking three people six moths to complete. Some (AI) technology may be one kind of factor of production in the future. For another example, people will work in workplace digitalization environment. So, in the future, working environment and information management are automated. Such as Konica camera sale company will use workplace digitalization. So , (AI) technology can provide workplace digitalization in order to raise productivity efficiency. (AI) technology will be one kind of production which is replaced by workplace digitalization and it will grow any organization productivity efficiently. Then, (AI) technology will assist overall social economy growth , due to productivity is raised and products can be produced in short time to prepare to sell in consumption market. So, time will be shortened to increase GDP growth fast for the development of (AI) technology countries.

What will be the development of (AI) technology and predictions concerning the future evolution? The computers and robots will develop conscious, intelligent and minds into humans, enhancing psychological and behavioral abilities and allowing for direct communication with (AI) minds. (AI) technology will be impacted human life by (AI) technology information communicative and environmental influence. A " world brain" and " world mind", this psychological system will be enhanced and enriched the capacities of both individual and collective cognition by (AI) technology of service industries.

(AI) technology with influence these human needs of service industries changes, such as , biological science, finance, entertainment, business, biological science, transportation, communication military etc. The personal computer evolution, the internet and the world wide web which exploded on the scene, linking business, homes, schools, social organizations which were a completely unpredicted phenomenon to influence human life. Kurzweil (1999) predicts that by 2029 year, most human communication will be with machines. According to Person, by 2100 year, there will be human machine convergence.

How can (AI) technology influence environmental protection to make benefits to farming economic growth? (AI) technology can be applied to predict how to solve environmental pollution challenge to avoid to damage any crop or vegetable or rice or fruit etc. food growth. Because environmental experts can gather global environmental pollution data from an environmental database to build a perform a systematic analysis from (AI) technology. The first step is this broad analysis can include understanding, statistical and data gathering techniques to obtain the relevant data, the correlation among the variables involved, and a list of possible models. The next step is to select a set of methods and models that cover all kinds of knowledge and functionalities needed for the decision making process. Once the models are selected, they must be fully implemented by means of machine learning , data mining, statistical or numerical technique. After that, those models must be integrated to build the whole EDSS. The EDSS must be tested to check its performance, accuracy, usefulness and reliability, both from the user's and (AI) technology/computer scientist's point of view. If these is any wrong feature in any development stage, such as model's integration, models' implementation, selection of models, database, problem analysis etc. the developers must come back in the update th required components. When the evaluation phase is all right, the EDSS is ready to be applied to the environment. The great contribution of artificial intelligence to EDSS the integration of several methods complementing the classical statistical models/simulation , statistical analysis, linear models, etc. and numerical models (control algorithms, optimization techniques etc.) .

This cooperation makes the resulting systems more reliable and powerful in coping with real world environment systems. Date interpretation has been a principal area of research in (AI) technology since the very beginning. The most demanding problem in the environmental assessment context. Knowledge representation permits the definition of the different types of data that the existing methods adapt to the process. There is also a lot of work to clean, repair and transform the huge available quantities of raw data. Apart from this, the availability of meta-information or background knowledge is required to guide the process. Data mining is multidisciplinary: It covers expert systems, data based technology, statistics, data visualization and unsupervised machine learning. These techniques operate at the level of data and background information, where numerous and often incompatible new commensurate pieces of information from disparate sources have to be brought together (K, Fedra, 1994).

So, it seems that in the future, (AI) technology with the increasing maturity in particular those related to knowledge and engineering, new dimensions can be assisted to users in environmental decision making are available. For example, many environmental systems are characterized both by incomplete models and by limited data. Hence, in the future, (AI) technology will be applied to predict climate change to reduce crop or fruit etc. food agriculture challenge by climate change bad influence.

- Will (AI) technology influence taxi transport service needs ?

To understand how the manufacturing business must adapt to prosper in the technology, we need to understand how (AI) technology will change us to shape our daily habits to satisfy our expectation of products to how we shop and even the immediate of the entire process. For example, taxi services are in the crosshairs as on demand transportation services like, available of the touch of a smart phone button expand. In fact, Yellow lab, US country , san Francisco city's largest taxi company is filing for bankruptcy as the industry starts to change faster than almost anyone expected. However, at this point, its more than an app that is changing, some our taxi passengers renting taxi transportation to catch consumption behavior.

(AI) technology will influence digital economy for taxi passenger's individual customer experience, offering a growing renting taxi to catch of service and feedback opportunities when any one taxi passenger who chooses to use mobile phone app online tool to prepaid to rent any taxi more easily.

Also in the long term, (AI) technology can influence vehicles drive themselves of behavior. Already, companies like Google and GM are working on projects to bring fleets of autonomous vehicles to cities at the path of a button.

Moreover, this on-demand service model is beginning to appear across a much broader range of markets. For example , Amazon company is investing in its own fleet of trucks, planes and even drone at the same time as it pushes for same-day delivery of products. As some point, vehicles will be autonomous too. So, it seems that (AI) technique will influence any transportations choose to use digital autonomous driving technology in the future . For Amazon company case, it is not stopping of logistics. It is also aiming to automatically manage the supply of consumer home products with its recently launched Amazon replenishment service, Dash. Dash is a digital service that enables that connected derive to automatically order physical products from Amazon when supplies are running low. So, it seems (AI) technology will be applied to logistic function by digital technology method introduction in the future.

Hence autonomous vehicles will optimize industry supply chains and logistics operations through increased efficiency and flexibility. In fact, fully automated and lean supply chains will keep reduce load sizes and inventory by leveraging smart distribution technologies and smaller autonomous vehicles by machine man assistance. If Amazon continues to grow market share for online sales by reducing effort required by the consumer to place an order, when also contributing the almost immediate delivery of products to the doorstep. So, it will further fuel the trend toward on-demand derive. As Amazon company fuels the on-demand economy, consumers will expect immediacy in more parts of the digital economy. On top of speed, consumers increasing expect more personalization options.

So, (AI) technology will influence digital manufacturing, such as Amazon publishing to monitor every aspect of every process in real -time and communicating to self-optimized deep learning robotics, new methods of high volume and high customization will become possible. Then, as products merge into product platforms and even services, manufacturers have the opportunity to provide components and platforms used by smaller players. So, (AI) technology will influence manufacturing industry to choose automated SMI lines, robots installed, automation engineers.

Another future (AI) technology development can be applied to space science aspect, such as Automation engineering space in manufacturing process to achieve digital manufacturing benefits to any businesses in the future. Such as reducing cost, shortening manufacturing time, raising efficiency, shortening delivery products to client individual time. How can artificial intelligence give the need and advanced fast and evaluation methods benefits for space exploration? When US NASA (space exploration organization) achieves any space exploration missions, it will answer this question:

When is it useful to have a machine use (AI) technology to achieve a decision? After all, after millions of years of space exploration and rough 10,000 years of civilization, humans are usually quite good at making decisions in complex uncertain environments. Through, Johns Hoplains University's Applied Physical Lab. Research in (AI) technology enabled systems, which has identified three general use cases for (AI) technology to explore space mission:

First, for some tasks (AI) technology is more cost effectiveness than human. Second, (AI) technology is better suited than humans at solving some, but not all problems. Third, (AI) technology allows NASA organization's space exploration mission to develop machines that ate capable of responding faster than when a human is in the decision loop (D. Scheidt, 2012, A. Castano et. al. 2008).

So, the use of (AI) technology to enable science by observing the pace of rapidly evolving phenomena was demonstrated. It is more effectively coordinating and (AI) technology utilizing to earn economic benefits to use for space exploration mission.

However, (AI) technology also have current risk for space exploration. Today (AI) technology is immature and requires further development to reach its potential. For instance, the (AI) technology algorithms that detected the dust derive could not have identified whether the Martain weather represented a threat to the cover. Also it can not yet use instrument input to determine what, where and how to autonomously make the next space science measurement. An equally important factor limiting (AI)'s deployment is that lacks the methodology and technology to effectively test (AI) technology. So, the challenge will testing (AI) enabled system is how (AI) performance can be measured. It would be NASA organization's difficulty to find (AI) technology to develop to carry on researching any space exploration missions in the future. However, (AI) technology will be a good economic benefit choice for space exploration mission in the future.

- What is artificial intelligence potential

benefits and ethical considerations to influence future global job market change?

The ability of (AI) technology systems to transform vast amounts of complex information into insight has the potential to help solve manufacturing or service challenges for human needs. However, to reap the societal benefits of (AI) systems, humans will need to trust then and make sure that which follow the same ethical principles, moral values, professional codes and social norms that we humans would follow in the

same scenario, research and educational efforts as well as carefully designed regulation in order to achieve the most effort of economic benefits goals. For example, international business machines corporation (IBM) is actively engaged both competitors , in global discussions about how to make (AI) ethical and as beneficial as possible for people as social economic benefits.
(AI) is usually defined as the " capability of a computer program to perform tasks or reasoning processes " that human usually associate to intelligence in a human being. Often, it has to do with the ability to make a good decision, even when there is uncertainty, too much information to handle. As an example, play chess or complex card games of entertainment activities is believed to need some form of intelligence in a human being, as well as choosing the best medical facilities in a difficult medical case, or creating something new, such as mathematical theorem or even some form of act, or even driving automatic machine man (self driving vehicle) replacing human driving in the middle of a crowded city.
(AI) needs depends on what we consider being intelligence in the behavior of a human being act a certain point in time. If human belief about human intelligence changes and we don't believe any longer that a certain task requires intelligence, then a computer program performing that task is no longer part of (AI), it becomes just another boring computer program. So, it means that (AI) technology will replace some old computer programs, if human can invent new generation of (AI) software for any functions or activities to satisfy human needs.
As IBM, it argues intelligence. This means that we aim to build systems that enhance and scale human expertise and skills rather than replacing them. We therefore focus on practical applications of (AI) capabilities that assist people in performing well-defined tasks of needs by exploiting and wide range of (AI)-based services. We also use the term " cognitive computing" it is mean a comprehensive net of capabilities based on technology. It comprises the fields of machine learning, reasoning and decision technologies, language, speech and vision recognition and processing technologies, high performance and high efficient functions for any industries or individual consumers needs. For example, robotics, which are usually very good at doing what which are supposed to in any environment, much have public shopping center, factory etc. places which need simply services from the robot (machine man), such as cleans the floor of our houses to the robot that can work together with humans in production chains, passing through the warehouse, robots can take care of the tasks of

an entire warehouse and the companion robots like Nao, Pepper, Aibo and Giraff, who can entertain use, talk to use and help elderly people to stay connected to their friends, relatives and doctors.

Google company is building automatic machine (self-driving cars) and has acquired more than 10 robotics companies. Facebook had opened whole new research facility only on (AI) research. Apply computer has developed Siri. Microsoft computer company has built a similar personalized assistant. Google has Deep mind, a UK company whose long term aim is to build general (AI) and has already great potential to win game to the world champion and IBM is investing a huge amount of resources in applying its Watson cognitive computing system to the medical domains to finance and to personalized education. In Europe, IBM is establishing new centers in Munich and Milan focused in the application of cognitive computer capabilities to the internet of things and healthcare respectively.

For example, automatic machine man (self-driving cars) are all about (AI), which used to be able to see what happens in the street (signals ,lanes, other cars, pedestrians, traffic lights, which need to able predict what other cars and pedestrians will do, and who need to be able to cope with unforeseen situations. Since, most car accidents are due to human fault, it is estimated that the adoption of self-driving cars will save about half of the lives that are usually last in car accidents.

IBM Watson company has to understand spoken language, make sense of massive amount to text , respond correctly to questions in many categories, as well as assess its own confidence in responding to such questions. In the future, (AI) technology can own question/answering capabilities that would be very useful, for example, in assisting a doctor when trying to some to the correct diagnosis for a patient and to propose the best therapy .

Intelligent machines can also rely on huge amounts of data to be used to learn how to make better decisions. This data comes from all of us over the years Facebook users have uploaded more than 250 billion pictures and every day who upload about 350 million more. Every second, we submit 40,000 google search queries. So, (AI) technology will be connected through the web from appliances to traffic lights from cars to watches. Other tasks that are very easy for humans are physical and manipulation tasks, such as walking , running, picking up an object to make its shape and location, restricted environment. But (AI) machine man technology still not able to have the general physical and manipulation capabilities even of a 6 year old.

So, it brings this question: Why do (AI) scientists need to concern ethics? Because (AI) technology is complex, information into insight has the potential to reveal long held secrets and help solve some of the world's most difficult problems. (AI) systems can potentially be used to help discover insights to treat disease, predict the whether, and manage the global economy. So, ethic issues is important to and (AI) scientists . If any one new (AI) technology research investigation could success, it will be a secret to and the (AI) scientists can not permit to their loyalty to any competitors to damage the fair (AI) technology products trading market. The country (countries) (AI) technology scientists need to concern ethic issues, who need to keep secrets for their countries economic or/and social benefits. This is moral issues to any countries/country loyalty is whose countries intangible assets. They can not sell (AI) loyalty to any their countries to assist whose economic benefits immorally.

- How can (AI) technology influence to global
health care service needs?

According to (AI) lecturer analysis, when combined key clinical health (AI) application can potentially create $150 billion in annual savings for the US healthcare economy by 2026 year. (AI) technology is re-winning modern conception of healthcare delivery. It enables machines to sense, comprehend, act and learn. So which can perform administrative and clinical healthcare functions (Accenture, 2017).

It will help health care service organizations to reduce health care cost, will improve and raise service quality and access. So, (AI) health market size will be predicted growth. (AI) applications in health care include robot-assisted surgery, virtual nursing assistant, administrative workflow assistant, fraud detection, error reduction connected machines, clinical trial participant identifier, preliminary diagnosis, automated image diagnosis and cybersecurity.

What kind of benefits (AI) technology can contribute to healthcare service? (AI) technology can deliver what many health care organizations need, such as financial and operational of labor costs, digital expectations from patient consumers how to use (AI) technology to solve interoperability challenges in any healthcare organizations. Also (AI) technology can be applied to wellness an d lifestyle management, diagnostics, delivers financially but also way of organizational and workflow improvement. So, (AI) technology will be continue to become most prevalent and adoption to healthcare organizations , which must need to enhance structure to be position to take full advantages of new (AI) technological capabilities. (AI) technology can change the nature of work and employment is rapidly changing to make the best use of both humans and (AI) talent in healthcare industry in the future. For example, (AI) technology offers a way to fill in gaps and the rising labor shortage in healthcare. According to Accenture analysis, the physicians shortage is increasing. However, (AI) technology will manufacture healthcare machine men to replace physicians in future one day(2017). Hence, (AI) technology will be invented to raise health care service staffs work efficiency and performance in any hospitals or clinics in the future.

In conclusion, (AI) technology will raise efficiency for any service or manufacturing industries in the future, although, it is possible that it will also rise low skillful workers unemployment numbers. But, the most important influence to human technological innovation will be risen and it will influence human life will be changed to be better, e.g. self drive cars, health care physician machine men, machine man cleaners etc. intelligent machine men will be manufactured to serve for our daily life. Furthermore, (AI) technological products will influence countries trading, some low technological development countries manufacturing businessmen can choose to buy any (AI) products to raise whose productivity and efficiency and reducing cost to achieve economic cost saving result. Also, GDP of trading growth income will increase to the (AI) products sale countries. Hence, it will be beneficial to economic development to both developed and developing countries both in the future as well as (AI) scientists time and money spending will be valued to continue to invest (AI) technology development for human life and economy benefits for long term.

In conclusion (AI) technology will raise macro economy growth and it can create many (AI) jobs , but it also raise the low level technological worker unemployment change. In the future, (AI) technology can be applied to digital technology to attempt to invent any new undiscovered (AI) and digital technology. So, it needs any scientists to continue to research how digital and (AI) technology can be mixed to satisfy human's future undiscovered needs. So,if America can choose robotic maufacturing industry is developed to China manufacturers to help them to manufacture any kinds of high technological robotics products., but Amercia robotic businessmen are still these robotic products sellers. Then, it may create many (AI) robotic manufacturing workers needs in China , so it can increase China, such as non-industrial developed country's real GDP growth when it has many robotic workers can earn wages from US robotic manufacturing employers in possible. Hence, it seems that China needs to train many robotics manufacturing workers in order to satisfy future manufacuting robotics skillful needs for US robotic manufacturing employers.

● Marxism theory

The fundamental philosophy of Marxism was developed by Karl Marx, who has been characterized as "one of the greatest economists of all time" and "one of the truly great thinkers". Marx was unhappy with the societal climate of his time, in which the working class (proletariat) were being exploited by the upper/middle class (bourgeois) by using the labor of the working class to fatten their own wallets. Marx envisioned a revolutionary society in which everyone's needs are met, and no class divisions exist. This system, also known as "socialism", was Marx's vision for the perfect society Marxism began with a "bottom up" approach; that is to say, the needs of a society should begin with economic need at the base, then build upwards to construct the economic climate that will provide for those needs. Marx held capitalism in complete disdain, claiming that it would be the ruination of all societies, leaving them no alternative but to claim socialism as the sole answer to survival. Marx contended that capitalism would inevitably lead to a revolution by the working class due to the strain that it placed upon the oppressed workers, thus separating them from their own humanity.

There are three basic doctrines of Marxism: Classical Marxism, Academic Marxism, and Political Marxism.

While Marxism itself has become diluted and divided, it is not a form of government in and of itself. Some have erroneously lumped Marxism with communism as being synonymous, but they are not. Marxism believes that capitalism is a misguided system that will result in a revolution between the classes, with communism as the only logical result.

Classical Marxism had nine main points of thought for consideration and resolution:

Alienation: The separation of a person from his humanity by the exploitations of capitalism.

Base and superstructure: Economic needs, according to Marx, are the basis of all societal action. The needs need to be determined, then the superstructure of the aspects which will provide for those needs will commence.

Class consciousness: The awareness of the classes of society and their importance to the overall picture.

Exploitation: Marx vehemently asserted that a society of classes will result in one class taking advantage of (or exploiting) another.

Historical materialism: Marx was the first to identify this phenomenon, which is the study of the way in which humans have been affected by, and struggled to attain, material wealth.

Means of production: The manner in which workers produce products.

Ideology: According to Marx, this is only a term that is used to express the manner in which people are persuaded to believe representations as if they were reality.

Mode of production: The means implemented to generate production. This includes machinery and human labor.

Political economy: Peruses the manner of production, and how it interfaces with the economy.

While the concept seemed altruistic, reality was not. As the communist societies lost their stations (classes), they also lost their humanity. Workers became slaves, working under inhuman conditions. This was especially true in countries such as China and the USSR.Other countries who embraced Marxism were easily identifiable by the phrase "The People's Republic of" before the name of the country. The names were deceptive however, because these governments became notorious for oppression and flat economic growth. China has modified its Marxist roots somewhat, and the results appear to be favorable. The USSR, however, failed in 1991 and began the uneasy transition into capitalism. They no longer follow the tenets of Marxism, socialism, or communism.

● New trade theory explains e-commerce influencess China " one belt, one road " strategy comparative advanages

● Globalization e-commerce

Development brings

China " one belt, one road

Strategy" advantages between industrial developed and non-industrial countries

Globalization can bring China " one belt, one road strategy" global social economic advantages, such as China's 21 St. century " one belt , one road strategy. It aims to bring the different Asia countries, even Western countries' business cooperation more easily after it had built high speed railway to go to different countries which had road transport to link to China on land. So, in long term benefits, China businessmen can cooperate to these participative "one belt, one road strategy businessmen to carry on buying and selling their unique products from road transport conveniently. Even, e-commerce can bring important economic advantages to influence this " one belt, one road strategy " in success. I shall explain the reasons that why e-commerce can bring business advantages to them as below:

China's "one belt, one road strategy " aims to achieve the global world share GNP 55% , as well as global consumer number of 77% and global energy saves 75%. Instead of existing trading investment, China also compromises to provide US one hundred billion dollar of basic facility fund, central Asia one belt, one road strategy fund of forty billion US dollar to invest this "one belt, one road strategy" of long term business development. I believe that it seems that China only hopes to build railway facility and encourage the participative countries to build factories to invest to do businesses between China and these countries as well as create jobs to solve China unemployment ratio, but in fact, I believe that China will apply e-commerce technology to assist its businessmen to do online trading more easily. I shall indicate the reasons to explain that why e-commerce and China 's one belt, one road strategy , they have close economic growth of case and effect relationship.

China will be only one globalization main essential " one belt, one road strategy" country to control all participative countries' businessmen activities and China can help the excess of developing countries' economic development in the same tie. In fact, internet can assist China's future economic development. The reason is that I believe that when China's " one belt, one road strategy " can develop to succeed. It can encourage many " one belt, one road strategy" participative countries businessmen to be persuaded to apply internet technology to do e-commerce in the same time after the railway transport facilities are built to let all of these participative countries businessmen can transport their products to their cities from road transport more easily and rapidly. So, it can being short time product transport advantages when the participative country's consumers buy the product from the online platform as well as the product can be delivered to his home from railway transport rapidly. So, e-commerce and railway transport has close relationship to cause this business activities in success. For example, one Asia "one belt, one road strategy country's participative businessman , he can apply e-commerce technology to sell its products to Western countries , e.g. US, UK online clients in short time rapidly.

The participative countries may include India, Greece, Serbia, Hungary etc.

66 countries. So, these one belt, one road strategy participative countries can cooperate to do e-commerce business to sell themselves unique products to the non-participative “one belt, one road strategy” countries from e-commerce channel. When these non-participative “ one belt, one road strategy “ countries consumers have none of the kinds products to buy from themselves countries, but they click to these participative “ one belt, one road strategy” countries participation businessmen themselves web stores to find the kinds of products which can buy from their web stores. Then, they can apply online to buy the products from these one belt, one road strategy countries’ businessmen web stores more easily and conveniently in short time. The important factor is railway transport, when these products can be delivered from railway from China to these participative countries. For example, when one participative country businessman , he has none of this kind of product to sell to the US or US client, but he apply internet channel to click to the China businessman’s web store to find the kind of product that he can sell. SO, he can apply internet channel to buy the Chins business’s product after he pays visa. The China e-retailer can deliver the kind of product to his store by railway transport rapidly. Railway transport can reduce the transport cost , when the e-retailer (buyer) does not need to pays air freight fee. It is more cheap transport cost. Then, the participative “ one belt, one road strategy “ e-retailer can deliver the kind of product to the US, or UK buyer by air transport rapidly when he find the kind of product which can be provided from the China e-retailer from online channel immediately. So, railway building and e-commerce channel will influence the “ one belt, one road strategy “ in success.

The 21 St century sea transport considers different countries consumers’ buying need when they feel that they can not buy the kinds of products from themselves countries easily. So, such as the participative “ one belt, one road strategy” countries , they can transport their products between China and themselves countries by railway transport, then the sea transport will not be popular to help them to deliver their products because sea transport delivery speed must be slower than railway transport. Any consumers won’t hope to receive their products in long transport time. So, railway transport must be one important transport factor to influence China ‘s “one belt, one road strategy” in success.

Moreover, e-commerce invention can help these participative “ one belt, one road strategy” countries e-retailers to apply web stores sale channel to cooperate to sell their unique products between them. When one country e-retailer can buy the another country retailer 's product from web store and it can be delivered to its country by railway transport , then it can still supply the kind of product to the e-consumer , even it has non any of this kind of product stock in its warehouse. Railway transport can help them to deliver their products from road in short time between China and these participative countries. So, they must have geographic advantage to deliver their products rapidly after railway transport facilities are built successfully between China and these countries. Moreover, web store can help them to advertise their products to let the non-participative "one belt, one road strategy" countries consumers to know whether which kinds of products these participative countries e-retailers , they can sell from themselves web stores when they click to their websites to see their product photos immediately. So, China's " one belt, one road strategy" can influence to achieve global online ecommerce advantage for China and the participative " one belt, one road strategy 66 countries e-retailers and e-commerce can help them to promote their any products to Western countries to let they to know in short time rapidly.

ON currency gain benefit aspect, in fact, e-commerce can help this " one belt, one road strategy" participative countries earn exchange rate transaction more easily because when the non-participative " one belt, one road strategy " countries consumers pay visa to buy their products from their web stores. Usually, they need to pay US dollar to buy their products by visa card for every online transaction. So, when these participative "one belt, one road strategy" online e-retailers receive their US payment by visa. They have more currency earn chance when US dollar needs to exchange high local exchange to their dollar. So, the currency exchange earn will have possible to occur from e-commerce. For example, when one e-US consumer buys one product from the China's online e-retailer , when the e-US consumer pays US currency to buy it by visa. Then, the China E-RETAILER can receive the US currency sale profit and change to Chinese dollar to earn the foreign exchange income when it find decides to change the US currency to Chinese currency in the right time.

So, e-commerce globalization can also raise foreign exchange earn chance between the countries' online consumers and the another e-retailers when they are carrying any e-commerce activities. Hence, e-commerce can assist the China's " one belt, one road strategy" development more success between Asia and Western countries.

However, the internet development can help China's 21 St century " one belt, one road strategy" to achieve these aspects of development, instead of e-commerce development. The five major achievements are such as , 1. Policy coordination, 2. Facilities connectivity, 3. Going out trade, 4. Financial integration, increased economic performance and productivity and 5. Encouraging people to people e-commerce transaction. Because internet development can help any countries consumers to search new products information as well as helping them to cooperate to analyze and achieving the best effective and efficient online shopping activities. So, it may reduce the incentives and opportunities for terrorist movement. Such as Beijing is becoming a top salesman city to promote the China made products and in big discount with some conditions when to achieve the global of made in China e-commerce in " one belt, one road strategy" 2025. ON conclusion, internet invention can help China and the 66 participative one belt, one road strategy" countries to gather any new products information as well as discusses how they can operate do this global e-commerce in success. Nowadays, the world is focus on the China movement on the one belt, one road strategy, how impact of the international financial crisis keeps rapidly, the world economy is recovering slowly, and global development is uneven. So, internet development can encourage the international trade and investment for the participative one belt and one road strategy countries and even these countries still facing big challenges to their e-commerce development. So, internet can assist the one belt, one road strategy cooperative countries' information exchange to achieve success. Internet can help them to bring an economic area through building infrastructure, increasing culture exchange and broadening global e-commerce development. This innovative conceptual strategy will bring China to take a bigger role in global affairs and it is an easy way to let China to export China's reserve products in area of " over production" , such as electrical appliances, steel aluminum , railway equipment and building's material manufacturing between China and the participative countries by railway transport. Internet can help it to apply e-commerce channel to promote its material products to let overseas buyers to know from their web stores in short time. So, internet can bring successful advertisement promotion development to China and the 66 participative one belt, one road countries on overseas online e-commerce sale chance absolutely. Finally, internet can also bring further deepening and expanding beneficial cooperation in such areas as trade, investment, finance, transport and communication aspects to these participative one belt, one road strategy countries. For China example, it is the world's largest producer of gold and also major importer and consumer. It can apply e-commerce trading method to promote its gold products to global gold buyers from the gold sellers' web stores in short time. When the country's one gold buyer research the China's one gold online retailer web store to find its quality and appearance is more attractive to compare his country gold shops. Then, he will pay visa to buy the China gold e-retailer's gold from its web store by visa immediately. So, e-commerce can help China's gold e-retailers to promote their gold products to let global gold buyers to know from their web stores in the short time. Hence, global e-commerce activity can help China to promote products and increase sale chance in short time after its one, belt, one road strategy can implement to achieve successfully.

GAME THOERY

Economics is just as much about consumer and producer behavior as it is about finance or the allocation of resources. With that in mind, game theory will explain one of the most fundamental tools economists use to frame competitive decision making.

Game theory solves the Prisoner's social criminal behaviors

Two small-time criminals are out breaking into cars, stealing what they can. They are working together in the same area of town. Fortunately, they get caught and booked down at the station. The detective goes in to question them separately and offers them both the same deal: they can either confess or stay silent. Their punishment will be determined by what action they take and what action the other perp takes. Here's what could happen:

a) If both perps confess, they each get 3 years.

b) If both perps stay silent, they each get 1 year.

c) If perp #1 stays silent and perp #2 confesses, perp #2 serves NO time and perp #1 serves 10 years.

d) If perp #2 stays silent and perp #1 confesses, perp #1 serves NO time and perp #2 serves 10 years.

So, if you were perp #1, what would you do? You could stay quiet and count on only getting one year, hoping that your friend stays quiet as well, and you'll both only serve 1 year. But, what if you admit to being involved and they admit being involved as well, then you'll both get 3 years. Or, what if you stay silent but your friend admits? Then you'll get 10 years; that wouldn't be good! Well, it is if your friend stays quiet.

The lesson to be learned from the prisoner's dilemma described above is how difficult it is to make an optimal decision when two competitors - and that's what these two perps are right now - can't collaborate. Typically, the economic man (or woman) is someone who makes decisions based on their own self-interest and chooses that which maximizes their own benefits. The entire idea behind game theory is that the result of your decision isn't known to you until you find out what your friend (or competitor) is going to do, so you have to make the best decision you can based on the information you have.

Game Theory in Real Life

We know how game theory works in a fictional situation that would never really happen, but what about how game theory applies to real life? Well, we can talk about that, too. Think about any strategic decision a business might make. The success or failure of that decision may very well depend on how the competition reacts. Perhaps a fast food restaurant wants to build a new location on the corner of a popular intersection. They complete their analysis of traffic flow, demand, other options in the area, etc., and ultimately decide it's a good idea. Then, once construction begins, another restaurant opens up a new location across the street, with a new building plan that includes drive-through ordering. What does our first restaurant do now?

Technology marketing cooperative strategy

Future when the thinking capabilities of computers approach our own is quickly coming into view. Raid process in coming decades will bring about machines with human –level intelligence capable of speech and reasoning, with a myriad of contributions to economics, politics and warcraft. The birth of true artificial intelligence will profoundly affect humankind's future. In our future technological development market, what it will bring much influences to economy. I shall indicate these several aspects, they may include as below:

On artificial intelligent invention brings high unemployment to low skill employees aspect, from the time the last artificial intelligence break through was reached in the last 1940s, scientists around the world have looked for ways of this " artificial intelligence" to improve technology, raising efficiency and productivity beyond what even the most sophisticated of today's artificial intelligence programs can achieve. Even now, research is ongoing to better understand what the new AI programs will be able to do, when remaining within the intelligence such as human brain. Most AI programs currently programmed have been limited primarily to making simple decisions or performing simple operations on relatively small amounts of data.

AI technological invention will bring much contribution to influence our future economic development. It had unique characteristics to compare common machines and it can help many industries to raise efficiency, productivity and improve performance as well as consumer individual self use. Such as the network is not taught to understand prose in any human sense. Instead, during its training phase, it adjusts the internal connections in its simulated neural networks to best anticipate the next word. It can be applied to read any article and understand any meaning to write any article as same to authors' mind and writing ability. For example, in the future, any one entered the first few sentences of any article, you are reading, the algorithm spewed out two paragraphs that sounded liked a freshman's effort to recall the gist of an introductory lecture on machine learning during which she was daydreaming. The output contains all the right words and phrases , not bad. So, (AI) technology can be applied to become just one more example of programs that do things thought to be uniquely human playing the real-time strategy game, translating text, making personal recommendations for books and movies, recognizing people in images and videos. But with the invention, of deep neural networks and the massive computational of the tech industry, computers improved until their outputs to longer appeared . In the future, algorithms can best humans, (AI) can help human to do any things in possible. Then, our society will encounter one automobile machine working environment. Does (AI) innovation will low skill employees lose their jobs because robotic can replace to any human to do simple jobs in any industries.

Whether machines can become sentient matters for ethical reasons. If computers experience life through their own senses, they cease to be purely a means to an end determined by their usefulness to us humans. Then our society will have many jobs which are needed to be worked by human, due to (AI) or robotic invention, it can replace human to do many simple jobs, e.g. factory manufacturing jobs, warehouse deliver jobs, public transportation , e.g. tram, train, ferry, underground train, bus etc. driving tasks, they are replaced by robotic auto driving, even pilot flying job will be also replaced to drive air planes by (AI) driving on sky impossible. Although, (AI) can help businesses to raise efficiency, increase productivity and improve performance, but it also bring these jobs to be replaced by

(AI) and it will cause many people lose jobs when (AI) is invented to be applied in popular in our future societies. On business benefits aspect, (AI) can bring working efficiency and productivity improvement, but it can also bring unemployment ratio raises as the same time when employers accept to apply (AI) to replace human to any simple or difficult tasks.

So, we need to limit or prohibit (AI) invention to exceed human's extent in possible. I mean that we do not need to limit to invent any (AI) skill, but we need to concern human need to work in the same time. If (AI) was real replaced to do any simple jobs in any industries, then there are many low skill workers , such as factory workers, clean workers, drivers ,even high skill workers, such as lawyer, teacher, pilot. They will lose their jobs in possible. So, how to invent (AI) technology will influence our future global employment chance to provide us to continue to work in any organizations. So, (AI) will may bring high unemployment ratio, if it is applied to any low skill , even high skill jobs aspects to different industries in global.

On conclusion , in economist view, technology market development must need, such as (AI) invention because it can help any industries to raise efficiency, productivity and improve performance, but we need to know how it can be applied to avoid human to lose jobs, due to (AI) is replaced to do their tasks for any industries in possible. Whether (AI) invention can create jobs or bring job lose? (AI) scientists must need to consider how to invent their skill to be applied to which tasks aspect if they hope human won't lose many jobs to do in future one day.

- How to apply robotic to raise efficiency and productivity and improving performance for manufacture as well as bringing long term productive economic benefit to manufacturers?

It is one good question. Can scientists only concentrate on researching artificial intelligent for raising productivity, efficiency and improving performance to businesses aspect, so neglecting on research other scientific researching aspects? Technological marketing economy is as a play between independent individual subjects. However, it has also become clear that the notion of play has to be interpreted within a different framework than that of classical functionalism. In mainstream classical economics, interaction or exchange is understood as the effect of the ends-means rationally of individuals. Smith's sympathy –based view of man and society avoids this functionalistic reduction of interaction and exchange. For example, the utilitarian or functional aspect of , the social process of producing and distributing wealth through free exchange, is in Smith's view on part of the value and belief system which people in ordered and prosperous societies employ to give sense and meaning to their experiences.

Hence, in our business society, technology can bring marketing economic change to be better. One free technology marketing economic society must have these advantages to bring to influence our living, such as below:

It interprets and explains improving social processes of producing and distributing to business, such as (AI) skill invention , it can help businesses to improve performance and efficiency and productivities for their manufacturing aim only, but (AI) ought not be applied to replace to do all low skill workers' jobs in any positions in any factories or warehouses. So, any employers ought not dismiss all workers and they are replaced by all robotics. They will need to consider overall economic benefit. I mean that avoiding low skill workers unemployment ratio raises. For example, one factory can still keep 50% workers and 50% robotics to cooperate to work together. Because some human workers can be such as assistants to do any simple tasks in factory every teams. Human workers can discover any errors to let manager to know in order to improve in their cooperation process with robotics. So, human workers and robotics cooperation , it is more efficient manufacturing method to compare any manufacturing process is needed to finish from robotics only in any future factory or warehouse working environment. So, robotics and human workers cooperation can bring the most efficient production and distribution benefits to future manufacturers in any factories or warehouses because human can help robotics to find any error in order to improve. Otherwise, if the factory or warehouse has only all robotics to work. Although, they may bring raising productivities or improving performance and efficiencies. But they can not know whether how to improve their errors or revises their every time productive performance to be better every day. SO, the most efficient manufacturing method is that human workers and robotics cooperate to work together in any factories or warehouses.

On innovation and information economic influence aspect, one of the most important topics in economics is the economics of information. Information includes things as varied as e-mail, and even the text book you are reading. Information is a very different kind of commodity from things like pizza and shoes because information is expensive to produce , but cheap to reproduce. Because of the unusual nature of information, it is subject to market failure, so we need to develop different kinds of public politics to regulate it, the law of " intellectual property".

We are encountering the essence of economic development is innovation and that monopolists are in fact of innovation in a capitalist economy. What does the economics of information mean ? Who do we need to develop information economy? Modern economics emphasizes the special problems involved in the economics of information. Information is a fundamentally different commodity from normal goods. Because information is costly to produce , but cheap to reproduce, markets in information are subject to serve market failures.

For the production of software program industry example, the windows software, developing this program took several years and cost Microsoft many money of dollars. You can purchase a legal copy for $5. The same phenomenon is at work in pharmaceutical, entertainment and other areas where much of the value of a good comes from the information it contains. In each of these areas, the research and development to software on the product may be an expensive process that takes years. But once, the information is recorded on paper, in a computer or on a compact disc, it can be reproduced and used by a second person essentially for free.

The inability of firms to capture the full monetary value of their invention is called inappropriability. Inventions are not fully appropriable because other firms may imitate an invention, in which case the other firms may derive some of the benefits of the inventive investments. Sometimes, imitators may drive down the price of the new product, in which case consumers would get some of the rewards. Information consumers can earn these benefits when the value of an invention to all consumers and producers is many times the appropriable private return to the inventor (the monetary value of the invention to the inventor).

However, information is expensive to produce but cheap to reproduce. To the extent the rewards to invention are inappropriable, we would expect private research and development to be underfunded, with the most significant underinvestment in basic research because that is the least appropriable kind of information. The inappropriability and high social return on research can lead most governments to subsidize basic research in the fields of health and science and to provide special incentives for other creative activities. Thus, special laws governing patents, copyrights, business and trade secrets and electronic media create intellectual property rights. The purpose is to give the owner special protection against the material's being copied and used by others without compensation to the owner or original creator.

On the Internet information economic market influence hand, inventions that improve communications are hardly limited to the modern age. But the rapid growth of electronic storage, access and transmission of information

highlights of providing incentives for creating new information. Many new information technologies have large sunk costs but virtually zero marginal costs. With the low cost of electronic information systems like the internet, it is technologically possible to make the large amounts of information available to everyone, everywhere, at close to zero marginal cost. Perfect competition is nowadays different e-commerce internet information business competitive feature, and any e-commerce merchants can not survive here because a price equal to a zero marginal cost will yield zero revenues and therefore no viable firms.

Hence, the economics of the information economy highlights the conflict between efficiency and incentives. On the one hand, all information ,might be provided free of charge, e.g. free e-book download, e-song download e-movie download from internet. Free provisions of information looks economically efficient because the price would thereby be equal to the marginal cost, which is zero. But a zero price on intellectual property would destroy the profits and therefore reduce the incentives to produce new books from authors, movies and songs from creators would earn little rewards from their creative activity. But with the costs reproduction and transmission so much lower for electronic information than for traditional information, so the future any electronic publishing industry 's products, e.g. e-books, e-songs , e-music, e-movies prices will be lower than traditional paper books, pack of songs and movies price, either consumers go to shops to buy them or consumers pay visa card to enter websites to buy any e-books , songs, e-music , e-movies from internet channel. Then, it will cause these traditional publishing and entertainment industries' competition to be raised because these e-publishers or e-entertainment can reduce their price to sell from their websites when their costs are nearly to zero. Hence, information technology can raise competition to the traditional publishing and entertainment industries. The traditional paper book, music, movie business merchants need to any authors or creators to help them to create any unique movies, songs, paper books to sell from their shops and they need to ensure their authors or music , movie creators won't give these creative book, song, movie products to any e-music, e-publisher, e-movie merchants to sell from their websites absolutely.

On conclusion, information technology influence any music, publish, movie creative product competitive raising to the traditional paper book publishers, music or movie publishers when many book publishers or music or movie creators choose e-commerce to replace traditional shop visiting sale method. So， it is possible to influence overall publishing and music and movie creative industries will change to e-commence consumption model. Then the traditional book and music and movie visiting stores will disappear and the online websites to these merchants will increase and their price also will reduce in global e-publishing and e-creative product consumption environment. So, information technology will bring some traditional store visiting number decreases and online merchant e-store number increases and consumers can pay less price to buy these creative products from internet.

New trade theory explains IBM and Micro software both compaines cooperative advantages

New trade theory (NTT) suggests that a critical factor in determining international patterns of trade are the very substantial economies of scale and network effects that can occur in key industries.

These economies of scale and network effects can be so significant that they outweigh the more traditional theory of comparative advantage. In some industries, two countries may have no discernible differences in opportunity cost at a particular point in time. But, if one country specialises in a particular industry then it may gain economies of scale and other network benefits from its specialisation.

Another element of new trade theory is that firms who have the advantage of being an early entrant can become a dominant firm in the market. This is because the first firms gain substantial economies of scale meaning that new firms can't compete against the incumbent firms. This means that in these global industries with very large economies of scale, there is likely to be limited competition, with the market dominated by early firms who entered, leading to a form of monopolistic competition.

Monopolistic competition is an important element of New Trade Theory, it suggests that firms are often competing on branding, quality and not just simple price. It explains why countries can both export and import designer clothes. This means that the most lucrative industries are often dominated in capital-intensive countries, who were the first to develop these industries. Therefore, being the first firm to reach industrial maturity gives a very strong competitive advantage. (some may say unfair advantage)

New trade theory also becomes a factor in explaining the growth of globalisation. It means that poorer, developing economies may struggle to ever develop certain industries because they lag too far behind the economies of scale enjoyed in the developed world. This is not due to any intrinsic comparative advantage, but more the economies of scale the developed firms already have.

Examples of New Trade Theory

•Specialisation of IT in Silicon Valley – the US. Hewlett and Packard started their computer business. Success attracted more IT firms to that area. Not because of any particular intrinsic benefit but new firms start to get the network benefits of being around other IT setups.'

•Globalisation has led to increased variety for consumers. The proliferation of brand clothing labels. Firms competing in the model of monopolistic competition and heavy branding. Neither UK or Italy has a particular comparative advantage in producing clothes, but consumers are attracted to brand image of Italian and British fashion labels.

Moral hazard applies to Macrosoft or Microcorp and IBM software cooperational case

Moral hazard is when one party can take risks knowing the other party will bear the consequences. It describes the risk present when two parties don't have the same information about actions that take place after an agreement is in place. The situation creates a temptation to ignore the moral implications of a decision: doing what benefits you most instead of doing what is right.

Example of Moral Hazard in Insurance

Moral hazard is a term that originated in the insurance industry and spread to the financial sphere. To illustrate the concept, imagine you rent a car and opt for the maximum insurance coverage possible. Damaging the vehicle does not have significant negative consequences for you, because the insurance company pays for repairs—or a replacement car—if something happens.

The insurance company uses statistics to estimate how likely the vehicle is to suffer damage, and they price their services accordingly. You pay much less for insurance than it would cost to repair a car because, in most cases, the insurance company won't have to pay for any repairs. But there are times when you might have an unfair information advantage over your insurance company. That's where moral hazard comes in.

You plan to drive into the mountains on rough, narrow roads. So, you get the most generous insurance coverage possible, and you don't worry about bouncing over rocks or scratching the paint in thick brush along the side of the road. You might even have a perfectly good car available at home, but there's no way you're going to drive your vehicle up that road—so you rent a car and buy insurance. The low cost of insurance means you have no incentive to protect the car you rented, but the insurance company doesn't know you're driving it under such conditions.

Moral hazard happens when you have an incentive to take risks that somebody else will pay for. You get to do whatever brings you the greatest potential benefit, and you don't suffer the consequences. In this example, the insurance company bears the risk: the cost of repairing or even replacing the car. The more insulated you are from risk, the more temptation you face.

Examples of Moral Hazard in Lending

Moral hazard became a significant factor during (and after) the financial crisis that began in 2007. The concept can apply to both lenders and borrowers.

Lenders were eager to approve loans before the mortgage crisis. Some mortgage brokers encouraged "subprime" borrowers to lie on loan applications, or they altered documents to make it appear that borrowers were able to afford loans that they really couldn't afford. For example, sometimes they reported inaccurate income numbers or the brokers did not require documentation that would demonstrate a borrower's ability to repay the loan.

Why would lenders hand out money when they don't know if the borrower can afford the payments—especially if they have to commit fraud to get the loans approved? In many cases, the lenders were only originating, or selling, the loans. After approving and funding loans, lenders would sell the loans to investors, who eventually suffered the losses. In other words, the lender took little or no risk. But lenders had an incentive to keep making new loans because that's how originators generate revenue.

When things turned sour, lawmakers and the public got scared. They worried that if major banks collapsed (some of them were loan originators, while others held risky investments), they would bring down the U.S. economy—not to mention the global economy. Because these banks were considered "too big to fail," the U.S. government provided funding to help some of them to weather the economic storm. If those banks suffered significant losses, the government promised to protect deposits (in some cases through the FDIC). Of course, taxpayers fund the U.S. government, so the taxpayers were ultimately bailing out the banks. The moral hazard was the lenders and investment banks taking risks that had consequences not for themselves, but for taxpayers and others.

Borrowers

Moral hazard can occur in almost any agreement, whether it's an informal understanding or a formal contract. If one party has the opportunity to benefit from taking "risks"—while risking almost nothing—moral hazard is at play.

During the financial crisis, as millions of homeowners struggled to pay their mortgages and loan defaults skyrocketed, government programs offered relief. People could avoid foreclosure thanks to money and guarantees from the U.S. government.

The moral hazard in these cases was that borrowers, increasingly underwater on their home loans, would be tempted to walk away from their mortgage rather than repay it. Such an action would put risk back onto the lender. The hazard is that the borrower no longer had an incentive to do the right thing—to pay back the mortgage as agreed.

Hence, such as moral hazard applies to Macrosoft or Microcorp and IBM software cooperational case . If Macrosoft and Microsorp and IBM do not decidc to co-operate to help themselves to expand their software strengths to achieve the aim to improve their software quality and feature and function, then they can not bring any software innovation to let future software users to raise any new softwares invention or improvement useful benefits. Then, global software market can not be improved to let any software users to raise high techological software products choices number. Because they are competitors, they won't hope themselves softwares' quality, feature and function and improvement are worse to compare other softwares companies among them. So, global software users will have moral hazard to enjoy any kinds of new softwares products invention in short time. But, if they can cooperate to buy and sell themselves both shares, then they both will be another softwares owners, they won't hope the another software company loses many software customers because itself new software inventions to attack the another software company. They must hope themselves any new software invention products , they can still attract many new software products customers together. Then, global software users won't have moral hazard to enjoy any new software invention products in short time, because they must cooperate to help themselve to improve their any new softwares ' qualities , features and functions in order to they can have many software customers share in these software market when they are global large software firms.

What are Principal-Agent Problems to Microsoft and IBM both large computer companies cooperation?

For example, a company's stock investors, as part-owners, are principals who rely on the company's chief executive officer (CEO), as their agent, to carry out a strategy in their best interests. That is, they want the stock to increase in price or pay a dividend, or both. If the CEO opts instead to plow all the profits into expansion or pay big bonuses to managers, the principals may feel they have been let down by their agent. There are a number of remedies for the principal-agent problem, and many of them involve clarifying expectations and monitoring results. The principal is generally the only party who can or will correct the problem.

Understanding the Principal-Agent Problem

The principal-agent problem has become a standard factor in political science and economics. The theory was developed in the 1970s by Michael Jensen of Harvard Business School and William Meckling of the University of Rochester. In a paper published in 1976, they outlined a theory of an ownership structure designed to avoid what they defined as agency cost and its cause, which they identified as the separation of ownership and control.The trend has been towards contracts with the agent that link compensation directly to performance measurements set by the principal.

This separation of control occurs when a principal hires an agent, The principal delegates a degree of control and the right to make decisions to the agent. But the principal retains ownership of the assets and the liability for any losses.

Factoring in Agency Costs

Logically, the principal cannot constantly monitor the agent's actions. The risk that the agent will shirk a responsibility, make a poor decision, or otherwise act in a way that is contrary to the principal's best interest, can be defined as agency costs. Additional agency costs can be incurred while dealing with problems that arise from an agent's actions. Agency costs are viewed as a part of transaction costs.

Agency costs may also include the expenses of setting up financial or other incentives to encourage the agent to act in a particular way. Principals are willing to bear these additional costs as long as the expected increase in the return on the investment from hiring the agent is greater than the cost of hiring the agent, including the agency costs.

Examples of the Principal-Agent Problem

The principal-agent problem can crop up in many day-to-day situations beyond the financial world. A client who hires a lawyer may worry that the lawyer will wrack up more billable hours than are necessary. A homeowner may disapprove of the City Council's use of taxpayer funds. A home buyer may suspect that a realtor is more interested in a commission than in the buyer's concerns. In all of these cases, the principal has little choice in the matter. An agent is necessary to get the job done.However, there are ways to resolve the principal-agent problem.

Solutions to the Principal-Agent Problem

The onus is on the principal to create incentives for the agent to act as the principal wants. Consider the first example, the relationship between shareholders and a CEO. The shareholders can take action before and after hiring a manager to overcome some risk. First, they can write the manager's contract in a way that aligns the incentives of the manager with the incentives of the shareholders. The principals can require the agent to regularly report results to them. They can hire outside monitors or auditors to track information. In the worst case, they can replace the manager.

Contract Clauses

In recent years, the trend has been towards employment contracts that connect compensation as closely as possible with performance measurements. For managers of businesses, incentives include performance-based awards of stock or stock options, profit-sharing plans, or directly linking management pay to stock price. At its root, it's the same principle as tipping for good service. Theoretically, tipping aligns the interests of the customer, or the principal, and the agent, or the waiter. Their priorities are now aligned and are focused on good service.

Hence, such as this IBM and microsoft large both companies, if they hope to cooperate , they need to solve which company can have more management authority and which company can have more share owming or investing authory. If IBM can have more management authority to control their both companies, but IBM has less shares number to Microsoft, e.g. IBM has 30 % shares to Microsoft, whether IBM ought earn more profit or less profit to 30% profits from Microsoft, if IBM have more management authory, but IBM can not cooperate to Microsoft to assist it to raise more computer buyers number. So, agent problem will cause IBM and Microsoft cooperation more easily together in nowadays computer market. But, if

IBM can help Microsoft to increase computer buyers number after IBM participates to manage Microsoft's internal organizational management , then IBM can increase Microsoft computer buyers number in long time. Then, their cooperation can be more success, it means that their principle and agent problem will solve between them.

Dependency Theory

● Macrosoft or Microcorp and IBM software cooperational strategy

What is information technologic game strategy? How and why information technological game strategy can influence economic growth? I shall explain as below:

Nowadays, Macrosoft and Microcorp are the global information technological big companies. They own much market share in global information technological industry. Whether what factors influence they can still be global information technological products leaders. Why does computer software consumers still choose their products to compare other software products in preference? I suppose that Macrosoft and Microcorp, their hypothetical any software games have developed a clever new computer game that is certain to be very popular. Although Microcorp have the unique competitive advantage with its own software game engineers and compete against Macrosoft, but it can so it cheaper and better if it can hire any Macrosoft's software game engineers. So, in economic view, it needs to pay high salary (higher cost) to hire Macrosoft's engineers (labor), but Macrosoft's engineers can help Microcorp to invent any new kinds of software games to compete Macrosoft. Although, Microsorp needs to pay higher labor cost, but when it can raise its any software games' design and game playing methods to attract any game players. Then, these new and exciting software games can help it can bring many game entertainment players and then it can sell cheaper price to raise more attractive effort to win its competitor (Macrosoft). So, higher software game designing engineers (skill labor), their game designing effort will be the major factor to influence any one information technological companies in success. If one software designing company can employ one high software game designing effort profession to help it to design any kinds of attractive software games. Although, it may pay high salary (labor cost), but it have much chance to attract many software game buyers to compare that if it pays less salary to employ one poor game software designing profession. Because the poor software game designing profession may need to spend long time to research how to design any kinds of attractive game software to excite game players' playing desires in this playing software game industry market. Long time research to the poor software game designer may be one none any reward to compensate to the software game designing firm when it needs to pay long time salary to employ him. Otherwise, if the software game designing firm can accept to pay higher salary to the higher software game designer, he will have higher chance to help it to design any more attractive software games to influence game players' playing game entertainment desires. So, any software game designing companies their game designers (labor) must be the major factor to influence their business succeeds or fails in this software game entertainment market.

On the employing method hand, Microcorp can choose to include in its contracts with its software engineers that from working for another Macrosoft software company for a certain period of time if they resign from Macrosoft. A move such as this is sometimes called a preeptive move. Its propose is to alter its rivals' payoffs in order to alter their employing strategies. Preemptive moves are usually costly (high slaary), and this one is no exception. In its employment contracts makes Macrosoft a less attractive to let its old game software engineers want to leave their current employer, such as Macrosoft. As a result, Macrosoft must pay its software game designing engineers above the going market salary if it hopes their employment contracts can be continue between Macrosoft and its software gamc cngineers.

Should Macrosoft must need to decide how to react. It can choose to fight Microcorp by aggressively advertising its game, which is costly high, but gives it a larger market share in the game player entertainment market, when Macrosoft had any one profcssion game software engineer(s) leave(s) his company and he/they change(s) to the another Microcorp software game designing company to work, or it can forego the expense of an advertisement campaign and simply share the market 50/50 with its major competitor, Microcorp to be partners.

Their competition has close relationship to influence economic growth because it will have many game players number to be increase if they can cooperate to be partners in success when they can design any new kinds of software game products to satisfy software game players' entertainment feeling. Otherwise, if they can not be one good partners and they only consider their every business benefits and neglect themselves business benefits. Then, their software playing games sale price can either to be reduced in order to attract any software game players when their software games can not be designed to have much new playing methods to attract many game players. Consequently, the GDP income to this software game entertainment market must reduce because any kinds of entertainment software games prices are reduced as well as the game players number is also decreasing. Due to they are the major software entertainment game suppliers in global. Any game players will only choose either Microcorp or Macrosoft to buy their any kinds of entertainment software game products to play majorly. So, their software game manufacturing and sale number must influence global GDP income increases or decreases in macro economy view. It implies that any countries technological software game industry's GDP income will depend on these both Microcorp and Macrosoft software game's cooperation relationship whether they have good or bad cooperation relationship. If their cooperation relationship is good, then they can manufacture high quality and attractive entertainment software games as well as raising sale price and exciting many game players' entertainment desires to achieve the increase to game players number aim more easily.

How to achieve their cooperation relationship more easier. I suppose that, in the software game entertainment industry, over its lifetime, the computer game will generate $500,000 in new income (income minus production cost) for all the firms producing it or its clones. Macrosoft must pay its software engineers an additional $100,000 to get them to agree to accept a contract containing an anticompetition clause. It costs Microcorp $100,000 to develop the software if it can hire Macrosoft's engineers and $200,000 otherwise. Aggressive advertising costs Macrosoft $70,000 and has the effect of giving it a 80% market share if it restricts its engineers' employment and a 72% market share if it does not. So, the fall in total market share is caused by the fact that without some of Macrosoft's advertisements. If however, Macrosoft passively acquiesces to Microcorp's entry and shares the market, then both firms can still achieve a 50% market share fairly. Hence, they must need to achieve 50/50 market share if they hope to achieve the cooperation relationship in success. Otherwise, they will not achieve cooperation relationship in success.

However, the spending advertisement factor will also their cooperation chance in success. For example, it would be more realistic to recast the Software Game as one in which Macrosoft chooses how much to spend on advertising with sales depending continuously on the amount spent. Other examples of continuous cooperation choices may include: the productive capacity of an electrical power plant; the salary to offer a prospective employee; or the insurance premium to charge a prospective policyholder. So, the amount to any of these expenditure factor will influence whether they will decide to cooperate to sell their software games products in global game entertainment market.

How and why Macrosoft and Microcorp's cooperation can influence global economic growth? It is significant that Macrosoft and Microcorp both technological software game designing companies are global the largest firms, they are doing international software game trade business to many countries and they have large market share in the software entertainment game sale market. Aside from trade based on technological gaps and software game product cycles, software game entertainment industry is dynamic in nature or game players' entertainment taste will change any time in completely static in nature. That is, given the nation's game players' playing taste and game entertainment factor, such as game playing designing technological method and game player individual playing game taste both. We proceeded to determine the nation's comparative advantage and the gains from the different kinds of entertainment software game designing supply factor and the game player individual game taste changing factor. So, any nation's software game players number will depend on these both factors to influence whether their number will either increase or decrease in the year in this global software game entertainment market. However, these factors can be changed by time, technology usually can improve any software game playing methods and game player individual playing taste will also change any time. As a result, the nation's comparative advantage also changes over time, such as when the nation has many game players lose their interest to buy any software games to play, then the nation ought not only consider how to develop its software entertainment game in the technological industry, it is right time to research any other new technological industries to develop if it still hopes its GDP income can rise in the technological industry overall aspect. Such as dynamic trade theory is still in its infancy. However, our comparative statics analysis can carry us a long way in analyzing the effect on international trade resulting from changes in factor technology, and tastes over time, such as entertainment software game case.

The growth of factors of production will also influence the software game entertainment industry development, through time, a nation's population usually grows and with its size of its labor force , such as China and India.

Similarly, by utilizing part of its resources to produce capital equipment, e.g. India needs to utilize its technological resources, technological engineers and technological material can need to be used to manufacture either new software game products or computers. But, its technological resources will be shortage (both labor and technological material). So, many technological companies choose to apply more technological material and technological engineers to use much time and money to manufacture any new software game products. Then, these labor and material resources will be reduced to be spent time and material to manufacture any new computer products in the year. In this technological industry case, capital refers to all the man-made means of production, such as machinery, factories, communication and education and training of labor force, all of which greatly enhance the nation's ability to produce either computer products or software game products. So, the national will also continue to assume that it can experiencing economic growth is producing two commodities, such as software game and computer both kinds of technological products under the constant returns to scale. So, if India can not raise the rapid technical process to skill labor and supply technological material supplying number to satisfy to manufacture the enough software game and computer products to supply them to sell to any countries' playing game players and computer users every month. Then, its technological industry will lose many clients, due to it can not supply enough software games and computers number to sell to any countries.

Several empirical studies have indicated that most the increase in real per capita income in technological industrial nations is due to technical progress and much less to capital accumulation. However, the analysis of technical progress is much more complex than the analysis of factor growth because there are several definitions and types of technical progress, and they can take place at different rates in the production of either or both commodities, such as software game and computer.

Technical progress is usually classified into neutral, labor saving , or capital saving. All technical progress , regardless of its types reduces the amount of both labor and capital required to produce any given level of output. So, if India could have good technical progress to raise its technological labor skill and reducing the technological material to be used to manufacture the software games and computers. Then, it will have chance to keep the maximum manufacturing level number to software game and computer products as the same time.

Efficient Market Hypothesis (EMH)

What Is the Efficient Market Hypothesis (EMH)?

The efficient market hypothesis (EMH), alternatively known as the efficient market theory, is a hypothesis that states that share prices reflect all information and consistent alpha generation is impossible. According to the EMH, stocks always trade at their fair value on exchanges, making it impossible for investors to purchase undervalued stocks or sell stocks for inflated prices. Therefore, it should be impossible to outperform the overall market through expert stock selection or market timing, and the only way an investor can obtain higher returns is by purchasing riskier investments.

•The efficient market hypothesis (EMH) or theory states that share prices reflect all information.

•The EMH hypothesizes that stocks trade at their fair market value on exchanges.

•Proponents of EMH posit that investors benefit from investing in a low-cost, passive portfolio.

•Opponents of EMH believe that it is possible to beat the market and that stocks can deviate from their fair market values.

Understanding the Efficient Market Hypothesis

Although it is a cornerstone of modern financial theory, the EMH is highly controversial and often disputed. Believers argue it is pointless to search for undervalued stocks or to try to predict trends in the market through either fundamental or technical analysis. Theoretically, neither technical nor fundamental analysis can produce risk-adjusted excess returns (alpha) consistently, and only inside information can result in outsized risk-adjusted returns. Hence, invetors can gather the company past share price information to evaluate its future market performance more easily.

Fundamental analysis past share value element evaluation method

Fundamental analysis

Fundamental Analysts are concerned with the company that underlies the stock itself. They evaluate a company's past performance as well as the credibility of its accounts. Many performance ratios are created that aid the fundamental analyst with assessing the validity of a stock, such as the P/E ratio.

What fundamental analysis in stock market is trying to achieve, is finding out the true value of a stock, which then can be compared with the value it is being traded with on stock markets and therefore finding out whether the stock on the market is undervalued or not. Finding out the true value can be done by various methods with basically the same principle. The principle being that a company is worth all of its future profits added together. These future profits also have to be discounted to their present value. This principle goes along well with the theory that a business is all about profits and nothing else. Contrary to technical analysis, fundamental analysis is thought of more as a long-term strategy.

Fundamental analysis is built on the belief that human society needs capital to make progress and if a company operates well, it should be rewarded with additional capital and result in a surge in stock price. Fundamental analysis is widely used by fund managers as it is the most reasonable, objective and made from publicly available information like financial statement analysis.

Another meaning of fundamental analysis is beyond bottom-up company analysis, it refers to top-down analysis from first analyzing the global economy, followed by country analysis and then sector analysis, and finally the company level analysis.

The first method is to evaluate the company basic share price , such as stock value, then to predict its future share price whether it's share price will rise up maximum price level or it's share price will fall down maximum price level in order to predict its share price variation level in general.

It has four basic elements of stock value, it can be used to predict share price will rise up or fall down, they include: The Price-to-Book Ratio (P/B) ,
Price-to-Earnings Ratio (P/E) ,The PEG Ratio Dividend Yield and The Bottom Line

Investing has a set of four basic elements that investors use to break down a stock's value. In this article, we will look at four commonly used ratios and what they can tell you about a stock. Financial ratios are powerful tools to help summarize financial statements and the health of a company or enterprise.

•Financial statements can be used by analysts and investors to compute financial ratios that indicate the health or value of a company and its shares.
•P/E, P/B, PEG and dividend yields are four commonly used metrics that can help break down a stock's value and outlook.
•Any single ratio is too narrowly focused to stand alone, so combining these and other financial ratios gives a more complete picture.

(1) The Price-to-Book Ratio (P/B)

Made for glass-half-empty people, the price-to-book (P/B) ratio represents the value of the company if it is torn up and sold today. This is useful to know because many companies in mature industries falter in terms of growth, but can still be a good value based on their assets. The book value usually includes equipment, buildings, land and anything else that can be sold, including stock holdings and bonds. With financial firms, the book value can fluctuate with the market as these stocks tend to have a portfolio of assets that goes up and down in value. Industrial companies tend to have a book value based more in physical assets, which depreciate year over year according to accounting rules. In either case, a low P/B ratio can protect you – but only if it's accurate. This means an investor has to look deeper into the actual assets making up the ratio.

(2) Price-to-Earnings Ratio (P/E)

The price to earnings (P/E) ratio is possibly the most accurate of all the ratios. If sudden increases in a stock's price , then the P/E ratio is the steak. A stock can go up in value without significant earnings increases, but the P/E ratio is what decides if it can stay up. Without earnings to back up the price, a stock will eventually fall back down.

The reason for this is simple: A P/E ratio can be thought of as how long a stock will take to pay back your investment if there is no change in the business. A stock trading at $10 per share with earnings of $5 per share has a P/E ratio of 2, which is sometimes seen as meaning that you'll make your money back in long years if nothing changes.

The reason stocks tend to have high P/E ratios is that investors try to predict which stocks will enjoy progressively larger earnings. An investor may buy a stock with a P/E ratio of 30 if he or she thinks it will double its earnings every year (shortening the payoff period significantly). If this fails to happen, the stock will fall back down to a more reasonable P/E ratio. If the stock does manage to double earnings, then it will likely continue to trade at a high P/E ratio.

(3) The PEG Ratio

Because the P/E ratio isn't enough in and of itself, many investors use the price to earnings growth (PEG) ratio. Instead of merely looking at the price and earnings, the PEG ratio incorporates the historical growth rate of the company's earnings. This ratio also tells you how your stock stacks up against another stock. The PEG ratio is calculated by taking the P/E ratio of a company and dividing it by the year-over-year growth rate of its earnings.

The lower the value of your PEG ratio, the better the deal you're getting for the stock's future estimated earnings.

By comparing two stocks using the PEG, you can see how much you're paying for growth in each case. A PEG of 1 means you're breaking even if growth continues as it has in the past. A PEG of 2 means you're paying twice as much for projected growth when compared to a stock with a PEG of 1. This is speculative because there is no guarantee that growth will continue as it has in the past. The P/E ratio is a snap shot of where a company is and the PEG ratio is a graph plotting where it has been. Armed with this information, an investor has to decide whether it is likely to continue in that direction.

Dividend Yield

It's always nice to have a back-up when a stock's growth . This is why dividend-paying stocks are attractive to many investors – even when prices drop, you get a paycheck. The dividend yield shows how much of a payday you're getting for your money. By dividing the stock's annual dividend by the stock's price, you get a percentage. You can think of that percentage as the interest on your money, with the additional chance at growth through the appreciation of the stock.

Although , there are some things to watch for with the dividend yield. Inconsistent dividends or suspended payments in the past mean that the dividend yield can't be counted on. Whether dividend payments have increased year over year – is essential to making the decision to buy. Dividends also vary by industry, with utilities and some banks typically paying a lot whereas tech firms invest almost all their earnings back into the company to fuel growth.

(4) The Bottom Line

P/E, P/B, PEG and dividend yields are too narrowly focused to stand alone as a single measure of a stock. By combining these methods of valuation, you can get a better view of a stock's worth. Any one of these can be influenced by creative accounting – as can more complex ratios like cash flow. As you add more tools to your valuation methods, discrepancies get easier to spot. These four main ratios may be overshadowed by thousands of customized metrics, but they will always be useful stepping stones for finding out whether a stock is worth buying.

Day traders often find themselves with complex technical indicators, moving averages, and complex algorithms. However, sometimes it helps to step back and get back to the basics. One of those basic indicators is volume (the number of shares bought and sold in any given day). As long as there has been trading, investors have used volume to get a read on where stocks are headed. And unlike most of the tools technical analysts use, this one is easily found on almost any financial Web site or in any daily newspaper with stock tables (usually expressed in thousands of shares).

However, a trader can't be depended by any one indicator. But understanding volume can provide insight into a stock's behavior to help you determine its overall health. The most important rule is this: volume precedes price. Typically, before a stock price moves, volume comes into play. The beauty of this indicator is its flexibility. Changes in volume can be used intra-day to determine short-term price movement or over several days to determine a stock's two to three day trend direction.

Before learning how to interpret volume, you have to know what is calculated. The first step is to identify a stock's typical trading range. Active traders were once relegated to writing down the volumes each day for their favorite stocks and then calculating the averages themselves. The Internet has made such information available to any investor online. Free data is available from hundreds of sites like Yahoo Finance. It will give you the average volume on any stock you choose.

In general, a price change on relatively low volume for a particular stock suggests an aberration, whereas a price change on high volume portends a genuine trend reversal. An active trader looks at volume to determine a price trend and the obvious goal is to trade in the direction of the major price trend. One of the best times to buy is when a stock is going down on low volume (with no news) as compared to recent increases on higher volume. This suggests that the selling is lighter and that the holders of the stock that are going to sell have finished selling and the rest are holding. The sellers of the stocks then may come back into the market when they see the price stabilize. It's also not a bad idea to sell on high volume on the way up (if the volume appears to be tapering off), as this usually creates abnormally high prices that cannot be maintained very long. The basic theory is this: if price and volume are moving in the same direction, the trend of the stock price will continue. If they are running counter to each other, the trend will reverse.

It's also a good sign when a share-price jump is joined by soaring volume or if declines occur on low volume. The idea is that light volume signifies little urgency, so a share-price decline probably wasn't the result of any major bad news. Low volume linked to a share-price increase is also a negative sign, because any lasting upward price movement should be confirmed with increasing volume. The worst-case scenario is high trading volume coupled with a falling share price. Volume should never be used independent of price action to determine buying or selling patterns, but it is an invaluable tool to gain insight into the markets and determine the current price trend. Hence, share buyer can apply the four basic share price elements to attempt to predict share price variation in share purchase and sale market.

Something Behavioral (e.g., Prospect Theory) applies to investor share buying choice

What Is the Prospect Theory?

Prospect theory assumes that losses and gains are valued differently, and thus individuals make decisions based on perceived gains instead of perceived losses. Also known as the "loss-aversion" theory, the general concept is that if two choices are put before an individual, both equal, with one presented in terms of potential gains and the other in terms of possible losses, the former option will be chosen.

How the Prospect Theory Works

Prospect theory belongs to the behavioral economic subgroup, describing how individuals make a choice between probabilistic alternatives where risk is involved and the probability of different outcomes is unknown. This theory was formulated in 1979 and further developed in 1992 by Amos Tversky and Daniel Kahneman, deeming it more psychologically accurate of how decisions are made when compared to the expected utility theory.

The underlying explanation for an individual's behavior, under prospect theory, is that because the choices are independent and singular, the probability of a gain or a loss is reasonably assumed as being 50/50 instead of the probability that is actually presented. Essentially, the probability of a gain is generally perceived as greater. Although there is no difference in the actual gains or losses of a certain product, the prospect theory says investors will choose the product that offers the most perceived gains.

Tversky and Kahneman proposed that losses cause a greater emotional impact on an individual than does an equivalent amount of gain, so given choices presented two ways—with both offering the same result—an individual will pick the option offering perceived gains. For example, assume that the end result is receiving $25. One option is being given the straight $25. The other option is gaining $50 and losing $25. The utility of the $25 is exactly the same in both options. However, individuals are most likely to choose to receive straight cash because a single gain is generally observed as more favorable than initially having more cash and then suffering a loss.

Types of Prospect Theory

According to Tversky and Kahneman, the certainty effect is exhibited when people prefer certain outcomes and underweight outcomes that are only probable. The certainty effect leads to individuals avoiding risk when there is a prospect of a sure gain. It also contributes to individuals seeking risk when one of their options is a sure loss.

The isolation effect occurs when people have presented two options with the same outcome, but different routes to the outcome. In this case, people are likely to cancel out similar information to lighten the cognitive load, and their conclusions will vary depending on how the options are framed.

•The prospect theory says that investors value gains and losses differently, placing more weight on perceived gains versus perceived losses.

•An investor presented with a choice, both equal, will choose the one presented in terms of potential gains.

•The prospect theory is part of behavioral economics, suggesting investors chose perceived gains because losses cause a greater emotional impact.

•The certainty effect says individuals prefer certain outcomes over probable ones, while the isolation effect says individuals cancel out similar information when making a decision.

Prospect Theory Example

Consider an investor is given a pitch for the same mutual fund by two separate financial advisors. One advisor presents the fund to the investor, highlighting that it has an average return of 12% over the past three years. The other advisor tells the investor that the fund has had above-average returns in the past 10 years, but in recent years it has been declining. Prospect theory assumes that though the investor was presented with the exact same mutual fund, he is likely to buy the fund from the first advisor, who expressed the fund's rate of return as an overall gain instead of the advisor presenting the fund as having high returns and losses.

Technical analysis international market competition predicts share price variation

Technical analysis

Technical analysts are not concerned with any of the company's fundamentals. They seek to determine the future price of a stock based solely on the trends of the past price (a form of time series analysis). Technical analysis is rather used for short-term strategies, than the long-term ones. And therefore, it is far more prevalent in commodities and forex markets where traders focus on short-term price movements. There are some basic assumptions used in this analysis, first being that everything significant about a company is already priced into the stock, other being that the price moves in trends and lastly that history (of prices) tends to repeat itself which is mainly because of the market psychology.

● What are the Ways To Predict Market Performance

This widely quoted piece of stock market wisdom warns investors not to get in the way of market trends. The assumption is that the best bet about market movements is that they will continue in the same direction. This concept has is roots in behavioral finance. With so many stocks to choose from, why would investors keep their money in a stock that's falling, as opposed to one that's climbing? It's classic fear and greed. Studies have found that mutual fund inflows are positively correlated with market returns. Momentum plays a part in the decision to invest and when more people invest, the market goes up, encouraging even more people to buy. It's a positive feedback loop.

(1) Reversion

Experienced investors, who have seen many market ups and downs, often take the view that the market will even out, over time. Historically, high market prices often discourage these investors from investing, while historically low prices may represent an opportunity.

The tendency of a variable, such as a stock price, to converge on an average value over time is called mean reversion. The phenomenon has been found in several economic indicators, which are useful to know, including exchange rates, gross domestic product (GDP) growth, interest rates and unemployment. Mean reversion may also be responsible for business cycles. Some studies show mean reversion in some data sets over some periods, but many others do not. A serious obstacle in detecting mean reversion is the absence of reliable long-term series, especially because mean-reversion, if it exists, is thought to be slow and can only be picked up over long horizons." Given that academia has access to at least 80 years of stock market research, this suggests that if the market does have a tendency to mean revert, it is a phenomenon that happens slowly and almost imperceptibly, over many years or even decades.

(2) Martingales

Another possibility is that past returns just don't matter. In 1965, Paul Samuelson studied market returns and found that past pricing trends had no effect on future prices and reasoned that in an efficient market, there should be no such effect. His conclusion was that market prices are martingales.

A martingale is a mathematical series in which the best prediction for the next number is the current number. The concept is used in probability theory, to estimate the results of random motion. For example, suppose that you have $50 and bet it all on a coin toss. How much money will you have after the toss? You may have $100 or more or you may have $0 after the toss, but statistically, the best prediction is $50 -- your original starting position. The prediction of your fortunes after the toss is a martingale.

In stock option pricing, stock market returns could be assumed to be martingales. According to this theory, the valuation of the option does not depend on the past pricing trend, or on any estimate of future price trends. The current price and the estimated volatility are the only stock-specific inputs.

A martingale in which the next number is more likely to be higher is known as a sub-martingale. In popular literature, this motion is known as a random walk with upward drift. This description is consistent with thc more than 80 years of stock market pricing history. Despite many short-term reversals, the overall trend has been consistently higher. If stock returns are essentially random, the best prediction for tomorrow's market price is simply today's price, plus a very small increase. Rather than focusing on past trends and looking for possible momentum or mean reversion, investors should instead concentrate on managing the risk inherent in their volatile investments.

(3) The Search for Value

Value investors purchase stock cheaply and expect to be rewarded later. Their hope is that an inefficient market has underpriced the stock, but that the price will adjust over time. The question is: Does this happen, and why would an inefficient market make this adjustment?

Research suggests this mispricing and readjustment consistently happens, although it presents very little evidence for why it happens. Some share researchers indicate the three-factor model to explain stock market prices. The most significant factor in explaining future price returns was valuation as measured by the price-to-book ratio (P/B). Stocks with low price-to-book ratios delivered significantly better returns than other stocks.

Valuation ratios tend to move results for stocks with low price-earnings (P/E) ratios. Since then, the same effect has been found in many other studies across dozens of markets. However, studies have not explained why the market is consistently mispricing these "value" stocks and then adjusting later. The only conclusion that could be drawn is that these stocks have extra risk, for which investors demand additional compensation for taking extra risk.

Price is the driver of the valuation ratios, therefore, the findings do support the idea of a mean-reverting stock market. As prices climb, the valuation ratios get higher and, as a result, future predicted returns are lower. However, the market P/E ratio has fluctuated widely over time and has never been a consistent buy or sell signal.

(4) The Bottom Line

Even after decades of study by the brightest minds in finance, there are no solid answers. The only conclusion that can be drawn is that there may be some momentum effects, in the short term and a weak mean-reversion effect, in the long term. The current price is a key component of valuation ratios such as P/B and P/E, that have been shown to have some predictive power on the future returns of a stock. However, these ratios should not be viewed as specific buy and sell signals, but as factors that have been shown to play a role in increasing or reducing the expected long-term return.

(5) Initiation Price Changes reflect the company will change share price as soon as possible

Companies are bound to face market situations where they are required to initiate price changes. It means, either they are to cut the prices or increase the present prices to survive, maintain status quo or further growth. Initiating price changes involves two possibilities of price cuts and price increases.

Initiating Price Cuts:

There are good many circumstances where a firm is to resort to price cuts. There are genuine reasons for cutting prices:

First may be existence of excess capacity. In such situation the firm is badly in need of additional business and cannot generate it through increased sales efforts, product improvement or even price rise. It may resort to aggressive pricing, but in initiating price out, the company may trigger a price war. Second reason for initiating price cut is a drive to dominate the market through lower costs, either the company starts with lower costs than its competitors or it initiates price cuts in the hope of gaining the market share and lower costs to price cutting policy involves the following possible reasons:

1. Low-quality reason:
Consumers will assume that quality is low.
2. Fragile-market share reason:
A low price buys market share but not market loyalty. The same customers will shift to any lower- priced firm that comes along.
3. Shallow-pockets reason:
The higher priced competitors may cut their prices and may have longer staying power because of deeper cash resources.

(6) Initiating Price Increases:
Price increase is a source of maximizing the profit or maintaining it if done carefully. Say a company earns 5 percent profit on sales, and one percent price increase will increase profits by 55 per cent if sales volume is not affected.

The factors leading to price increase can be:
1. Increase in cost inflation. That is rising costs unmatched by productivity gains squeeze profit margins and lead companies to regular rounds of price increases. Companies often raise their by more than the cost hike, in anticipation of further inflation or government price controls, in a practice called anticipatory pricing.
2. Over demand can be another cause that leads to price increase. When the company cannot supply all of its customers, it can raise its prices, ration or cut supplies to customers or both.
The price can be increased by at least four ways:
1. Delayed quotation pricing:
Here, the company does not set final price until product is finished or delivered. This pricing is prevalent in industries with long production lead times like construction and heavy industrial equipment.

2. Unbundling:
The company under this plan maintains its price but removes or prices separately one or more elements that were part of the former offer, such as free delivery or installation. Automobile companies, sometimes, add antilock brakes and passenger-side air-bags as supplementary extras to their whiles.

3. Escalator clauses:
Under this, the company asks the customer to pay today's price and all or part of any inflation increase that takes place before delivery. This hike based on specified price index. These escalation clauses are quite common in construction line whether it is a house or industrial project or air-craft and ship building.

4. Reduction of discounts:
The company asks the sales force to offer its normal cash and quantity discounts at reduced rate. To gain four such attempts, the company must avoid looking like a price gouger. Companies also think of who will bear the brunt of the increased prices. It is so because, customer memories are long, and they can turn against the company which is perceived as price variation

(7) Reactions to Price Changes:
Naturally any price change provokes response or reaction from customers, competitors, distributors and suppliers and even the government. Here, we shall touch only the reactions of consumers and competitors.
Customer Reactions:
Consumers are more interested in knowing the cause or causes of price change.
A price cut can be interpreted in several ways:
1. The item or product is about to be replaced by a new model.
2. The item is faulty and it is not selling well.
3. The firm's financial position is badly affected.
4. The price will come down further.
5. The quality has been reduced.

A price may have some positive meanings:
1. The items is 'hot' sale
2. It has a high value because of quality.

Competitor Reactions:
Competitors are most likely to react when the number of firms is few, the product is homogeneous, and buyers are highly informed. Competitor reactions can be a special problem when they have a strong value proposition. The price hike them to take steps based on objectives of such price hike where they will resort to advertising and product improving efforts.
In case of price cuts, they have different interpretations:

1. That the company's trying to steal the market
2. That the company is doing poorly and trying to boost its sales
3. That company wants the whole industry to reduce prices to stimulate total demand.

So technical analysis method is one customer psychological prediction method to evaluate whether the products will be popular to sell to the market in order to predict whether the company share price will rise up or fall down.

What stock prediction techniques
are the most accurate

If you were to run an autocorrelation filter on virtually any security, you will find price movement is not random. In order to exploit these correlations, you can apply techniques used in speech recognition or other dsp applications. The problem is similar: you want to 'predict' an outcome from noisy signals based on past successful outcomes. Wavelet based denoising in conjunction with hidden markov models, fitted with a global optimizer, are a good place to start.

A large shareholder for example,then working as investment banker, I sat on the other side of the table. With a client, who was either angry (pressuring a fire sale) or afraid that a rating would downgrade him and lower the stock. You could tell what he was going to do. It's also a talent as partner .It's because people are predictable.This specifically counts for the small-cap stocks. The real large quant funds some times really fuck the price of large marketcap stocks. I sometimes wonder who is "fucking who", given I've got colleagues sitting in a variety of firms.

There is no single technique which you can say is most accurate but quantitative techniques are becoming popular nowadays because of their accuracy and scalability. The interesting thing about these techniques are that you can work upon them to improve the techniques easily by analyzing the vast data that comes with them along with the power to combine them with other models.

These techniques involve:

1. Simple mathematical techniques and methods of analyzing .
2. Simple Regression models dealing with autocorrelation etc.
3. Pricing models etc.

These techniques also provides you data quantify your risk which gives you much flexible and creative opportunity to work with your risk management

..
I haven't found an AI programs that are

● Recommendation artificial intelligence share price prediction method

We predict future values with technical analysis for wide selection of stocks like Artificial Intelligence Technology Solutions .

What was once thought of as science fiction is now part of our everyday life. Artificial Intelligence and deep learning are topics rarely spoken, artificial intelligence is a sub-field of computer science. The concept of computer system to perform functions using intelligence of a human, such as: visual or audio recognition, computations, decision making, and more. Deep learning is a subfield of machine learning. It is composed of using artificial neural networks consisting of layers to process input data and reach its output result. Such applications are utilized from virtual personal assistants on your phone or computer with Siri, Google Now, or Cortana to fraud detection. And recently, it is being introduced to Amazon first of its kind to offer a shopping experience without the use of cashiers, but instead your phone and visual recognition. By eliminating long lines and reducing labor cost, this could be the future in shopping experience. How did we get here? How is technology continuously finding its use to be applied functionally or in search of answers? Perhaps the biggest question we are asking ourselves is, how can we personally benefit from this?

Investors are constantly in search for strategies and tools to seek consistent or high return on investment given the market's risk. The benefit of utilizing deep learning is its ability to process large amounts of data. It is the challenging for any investor to process such large amounts of data while ignoring the "random noise". The advancement in the use of algorithms and artificial intelligence now accounts for 60-70% of "Buy" and "Sell" orders account of the US equity market volume.

The I Know First self-learning algorithm is used in quantitative trading. This form provides valuable market insight to retail and professional trader alike that is used in conjunction with traditional forms of analysis. Algorithmic traders benefit from this "second opinion" in their decision making process by verifying their own analysis or discovering new market opportunities while still maintaining complete control of their portfolio. These algorithms analyze the structure and the trends in the market, find predictable patterns, and investors trade upon these machine-derived forecasts. This form of trading is very suitable for most investors, retail or professional.

While we cannot speak on every algorithm meant to predict the market, the I Know First market prediction system is based on artificial intelligence (AI), machine learning (ML), as well as utilizes elements of artificial neural networks and genetic algorithms. Machine learning provides an innate acumen to our comprehension of market dynamics and behavior. The algorithm has a built-in general mathematical framework that generates and verifies statistical hypotheses about stock price development. Machine learning tools such as artificial neural networks make this prediction system self-learning, and consistently determined to become more precise. This framework is used to generate initial testing models over a test sample of data. The goal of this phase is to validate the accuracy of the algorithm as well as to fine-tune the fitness function, which represents the actual goal of the algorithm expressed as a mathematical function. When the algorithm finds the global minimum of the fitness function attached to one of the models generated, it fulfills its goal.

Then a learning and prediction cycle is run with the new data included. The algorithm subsequently produces predictions for over 1,400 assets with six time horizons for each. It separates the predictable part from stochastic (random) noise and then creates a model that projects the future trajectory of the given market in the multi-dimensional space of other markets. Thus, I recommend that artificial intelligence (AI) may be the future best tool to help any businesses to predict their share prices whether when they will rise up or fall down in short time to compare other manual share price prediction method.

Lemons Problem influence investor choice

Adverse Selection and the Lemons Problem

What Is the Lemons Problem?

The lemons problem refers to issues that arise regarding the value of an investment or product due to asymmetric information possessed by the buyer and the seller.

Lemons Problem Explained

The lemons problem was put forward in a research paper, "The Market for 'Lemons': Quality Uncertainty and the Market Mechanism," written in the late 1960s by George A. Akerlof, an economist and professor at the University of California, Berkeley. The tag phrase identifying the problem came from the example of used cars Akerlof used to illustrate the concept of asymmetric information, as defective used cars are commonly referred to as lemons.

The lemons problem exists in the marketplace for both consumer and business products, and also in the arena of investing, related to the disparity in the perceived value of an investment between buyers and sellers. The lemons problem is also prevalent in financial sector areas, including insurance and credit markets. For example, in the realm of corporate finance, a lender has asymmetrical and less-than-ideal information regarding the actual creditworthiness of a borrower.

Causes and Consequences of the Lemons Problem

The problem of asymmetrical information arises because buyers and sellers don't have equal amounts of information required to make an informed decision regarding a transaction. The seller or holder of a product or service usually knows its true value, or at least knows whether it is above or below average in quality. Potential buyers, however, typically do not have this knowledge, since they are not privy to all the information the seller has.

How can we be one intelligent investor? I shall indicate some personal psychological and number analytical methods to explain how we can avoid investment lose or risk more easily as below:

On personal psychological hand, we need to know when the inflation will come to influence our investment lose. Inflation have been very much in public's mind in recent years. The shrinkage in the purchasing power of the dollar in the past, and particularly fear (or hope by speculators) of a seriuous further decline in the future, have greatly influenced the share market varies. It is clear that those with a fixed dollar income will suffer when the cost of living advances, and the same applied to a fixed amount of dollar principal.Holders of stocks, on the other hand, have the possibility that a loss of the dollar's purchasing power may be offset by advances in their dividends and the prices of their shares.

ON the basis of these inflation economic environment changing fact, many financial authorities have concluded that: bonds are an undesirable form of investment and

consequently, common stocks are by their very nature more desirable investments than bonds. This is quite a reversal from the earlier ways when trust investments were restricted by law to high-grade bonds (and a few choice preferrable stocks). How inflation influences share price change, for example: What would be the implications of such an advance to influence our living when inflation occurs? It would eat up,in higher living costs, about one-half the income now obtainable on good medium -term tax free bonds (or our assumed after -tax equivalet from high grade corporate bonds). This would be a serious shrinkage, but it should not be exaggerated.

It would not mean that the true value, or the purchasing power, of the investor's fortune need be reduced over the years. If the investor spent half his interest income after taxes
he would maintain this buying power intact, even against a 3% annual inflation.

The another personal psychological factor, is that defensive investor psychological investment factor, the basic characteristics of an investment portfolio are usually determined by the position and characreristics of the owner or owners. At one extreme , we have had savings banks, life insurance companies, and so-called legal trust funds for our saving methods. A generation ago their investments were limited by law in many states to high grade bonds and in some cases, high-grade preferred stocks. At the other extreme we have the well -to-do and experienced businessman, who will include any kind of bond or stock in his security list provided he considered it an attractive purchase.

It has been an old and sound principle that those who can't afford to take risks should be content with a relatively low return on their invested funds. From this there has developed the general notion that the rate of return which the investor should aim for is more or less proportionate to the degree of risk he is ready to run. Our view is different. The rate of return sought should be dependent , rather on the amount of intelligent effort the investor is willing and able to bring to bear on his task. The minimum return goes to our passive investor, who wants both safety and freedom from concern. In many cases, there may be less real risk associated with buying a bargain issue offering the chance of a large profit than with a conventional bond purchase yielding about 4.5% . This statement had more truth in it than we ourselves suspected, since in subsequent years even the best long-term bonds lost a substantial part of their market value because of the rise in interest rates.

The another personal psychological factor is that enterprising investor, by definitionm, will devote a fair amount of his attention and efforts towards obtaining
a better than run-off-the investment result. In our discussion of general investment policy, we has made some suggestions regarding bond investments that are addresses to the enterprising investor as below:

Tax-free new housinng authority bonds effectively guaranteed by the governments, taxable but high-yield new community bonds , also guaranteed by the governments, and tax -free industrial bonds issued by municipalities, but serviced by lease payments made by strong corporations.

On number analytical methods aspect, it may include industry analysis, because the general prospects of the enterprise carry major weight in the establishment of market price, it is natural for the security analyst to devote a great deal of attention to the economic position of the industry and of the individual company in its industry. Studying these companies' past financial position, they are sometimes productive of valuable insights into important factors that will be operative in the future and are insufficiently appreciated by the current market. Where a conclusion of that kind can be drawn with a degree of confidence, it affords a sound basis for investment decisions.

Our own observation, however leads us to minimum somewhat the practical value of most of the industry studies that are made available to investors. The material developed is ordinarily of a kind with which the public is already fairly familiar and that has already considerable influence on market quotations. Rarely does one find a brokerage-house study that points out, with a popular industry is heading for a fall or that an unpopular one is due to prosper. For example, Wall street's view of the longer future is fallible and this necessarily applies to that importanr part of its investigations which is directed towards the forecasting of the course of profits in various industries.

ON predicting growth stock investing style hand, growth companies have above average-growth rates of sales and/or earnings. Growth investors are willing to pay high multiples of earnings for companies with high growth rates, which explains why growth stocks generally have high P/E multiples. For Starbucks office business case example, it has a high P/E multiple of 28 , and the multiple could expand as the company grows at its expected rate. If growth stocks do not sustain their high growth rates, their stock prices are severely punished, as we saw with momentum stock Chipotle Mexican Grill. For Apple computer share example, it is a good example of a growth stock. It has high sustained growth from sales of its iPad, iPhone, and iPod products, which are dominant in tehir respective markets, and they stil have the ability to increase their market shares.

Apple computer has been more innovative than its competitiors, which also underscores its strong management. In addition, Apple paid a 1.57

percent dividend in Sept. 2012, which somewhat a potential fall in the stock price as a result of future disappointing earnings or reduced future estimates of growth. Moreover, in the past record, Apple's stock price for the year from Sept, 2011 to Aug, 2012 shows a BETTER chart pattern than that of Chipotle Mexican Grill , illustrating the risk when momentum stocks fall out of favor. From a value investor's vire, there is more value in Apple stock than in Chipotle Mexican Grill in the futuer. Apple has a strong balance asset in that it has $20 billion in cash and has no long -term debt. Its liquidity is good,

meaning it can easily convert its current assets into cash to pay off its current liabilities (bills) as they come due. Yet despite paying a 1.57 percent dividend yield, it is still very much a growth stock. The company trades at roughly eight times book value and its P/E multiple is around sixteen times its earnings. As long as Apple delivers on its growth in sales and earnings, its stock price will continue to rise. The downside to growth stocks is that should companies fail to grow as rapidly as expected, their stock prices will be punished more severely than value stocks because expectations for growrh stocks are much greater than those for value stocks. So, any investors can seek any companies' past financial performance and stock price to predict their stock price whether it can rises up or falles down in the short times, e.g. one to three months. Because it will have unpredictable environment factors can influence any companies stock sale number effort in long term. So, I mean that predicting long time stock price changes whether either is increasing or decreasing, it is more difficult to compare to predict its' stock price changes in short time.

Finally, any investors can attempt to follow these rewards and risks to stocks' past record to judge whether the company's stock price will rises up or falls down in order to decide investment: ON rewards aspect, is the stock price less than two-thirds of the book value of the stock? Is the stock price less than two -thirds of the net current asset value per share (current assets minus total debt)? On the risks aspect, is the debt-t-o-equity ratio less than one? The total debt of the company should be less than total equity? Is the current ratio equal to rwo or more? The total current assets divided by the total current liabilities should equal two or more? Is the total debt less than twice the net current assets? Is the 10 year average EPS (earning per share) growth rate greater than 7 % ? Were there no more than two years our of the past 10 with earnings declines of greater than 5 %? Moreover, any investors can also analyze how the company's financial performance changed from these information:

Whether the company seeks long term captial appreciation through the growth of the fund's value over a period of time or short term captial appreciation objective? To seek current income through investments that generate dividends and to preserve investors' principal. What are the companies' strategies, e.g. the manager of a stock fund might buy growth or value stocks of companies with a particular size capitalization (small-cap, medium-cap, large-cap stocks). Thusm a value investor looking for a large -cap value fund can comapre the different funds offering these types of securities. Estimating the company's overall performance fund from its' past total return and expenses in order to predict its profit or loss in current year and stock price can be influenced to rise up or fall down in possible.

Thus, in any country stock market, one intelligent investor can attempt to apply personal psychological and number analytical methods to predict any stock price changes more accurately to compare other professionals or friends or families those investing opinions.

How to predict share price

What does stock market prediction mean ? Stock market prediction is the act of trying to determine the future value of a company stock or other financial instrument traded on an exchange. The successful prediction of a stock's future price could yield significant profit. The efficient-market hypothesis suggests that stock prices reflect all currently available information and any price changes that are not based on newly revealed information thus are inherently unpredictable. Others disagree and those with this viewpoint possess myriad methods and technologies which purportedly allow them to gain future price information.

Intrinsic value (true value) is the perceived or calculated value of a company, including tangible and intangible factors, using fundamental analysis. It's also frequently called fundamental value. It is used for comparison with the company's market value and finding out whether the company is undervalued on the stock market or not. When calculating it, the investor looks at both the qualitative and quantitative aspects of the business. It is ordinarily calculated by summing the discounted future income generated by the asset to obtain the present value.

Prediction methodologies fall into three broad categories which can (and often do) overlap. They are fundamental analysis, technical analysis (charting) and technological methods as below:

Fundamental analysis

Fundamental Analysts are concerned with the company that underlies the stock itself. They evaluate a company's past performance as well as the credibility of its accounts. Many performance ratios are created that aid the fundamental analyst with assessing the validity of a stock, such as the P/E ratio. Warren Buffett is perhaps the most famous of all Fundamental Analysts.

What fundamental analysis in stock market is trying to achieve, is finding out the true value of a stock, which then can be compared with the value it is being traded with on stock markets and therefore finding out whether the stock on the market is undervalued or not. Finding out the true value can be done by various methods with basically the same principle. The principle being that a company is worth all of its future profits added together. These future profits also have to be discounted to their present value. This principle goes along well with the theory that a business is all about profits and nothing else. Contrary to technical analysis, fundamental analysis is thought of more as a long-term strategy.

Fundamental analysis is built on the belief that human society needs capital to make progress and if a company operates well, it should be rewarded with additional capital and result in a surge in stock price. Fundamental analysis is widely used by fund managers as it is the most reasonable, objective and made from publicly available information like financial statement analysis.

Another meaning of fundamental analysis is beyond bottom-up company analysis, it refers to top-down analysis from first analyzing the global economy, followed by country analysis and then sector analysis, and finally the company level analysis.

Technical analysis

Technical analysts or chartists are not concerned with any of the company's fundamentals. They seek to determine the future price of a stock based solely on the trends of the past price (a form of time series analysis). Numerous patterns are employed such as the head and shoulders or cup and saucer. Alongside the patterns, techniques are used such as the exponential moving average (EMA), oscillators, support and resistance levels or momentum and volume indicators. Candle stick patterns, believed to have been first developed by Japanese rice merchants, are nowadays widely used by technical analysts. Technical analysis is rather used for short-term strategies, than the long-term ones. And therefore, it is far more prevalent in commodities and forex markets where traders focus on short-term price movements. There are some basic assumptions used in this analysis, first being that everything significant about a company is already priced into the stock, other being that the price moves in trends and lastly that history (of prices) tends to repeat itself which is mainly because of the market psychology.

Machine learning

With the advent of the digital computer, stock market prediction has since moved into the technological realm. The most prominent technique involves the use of artificial neural networks (ANNs) and Genetic Algorithms(GA). Scholars found bacterial chemotaxis optimization method may perform better than GA.[1] ANNs can be thought of as mathematical function approximators. The most common form of ANN in use for stock market prediction is the feed forward network utilizing the backward propagation of errors algorithm to update the network weights. These networks are commonly referred to as Backpropagation networks. For stock prediction with ANNs, there are usually two approaches taken for forecasting different time horizons: independent and joint. The independent approach employs a single ANN for each time horizon, for example, 1-day, 2-day, or 5-day. The advantage of this approach is that network forecasting error for one horizon won't impact the error for another horizon—since each time horizon is typically a unique problem. The joint approach, however, incorporates multiple time horizons together so that they are determined simultaneously. In this approach, forecasting error for one time horizon may share its error with that of another horizon, which can decrease performance. There are also more parameters required for a joint model, which increases the risk of overfitting. Of late, the majority of academic research groups studying ANNs for stock forecasting seem to be using an ensemble of independent ANNs methods more frequently, with greater success. An ensemble of ANNs would use low price and time lags to predict future lows, while another network would use lagged highs to predict future highs. The predicted low and high predictions are then used to form stop prices for buying or selling. Outputs from the individual "low" and "high" networks can also be input into a final network that would also incorporate volume, intermarket data or statistical summaries of prices, leading to a final ensemble output that would trigger buying, selling, or market directional change. A major finding with ANNs and stock prediction is that a classification approach (vs. function approximation) using outputs in the form of buy(y=+1) and sell(y=-1)

results in better predictive reliability than a quantitative output such as low or high price. Since NNs require training and can have a large parameter space; it is useful to optimize the network for optimal predictive ability.
Can share buyer or investor predict the company's share price whether when it will rise or fall ? If any shareholder can predict any firm's share price whether it will rise or fall in the month. Then, he will not lose , even earn share profit more easily. For example, when the shareholder had bought 100 share and every share $1 for the company shares. If he can predict the firm 's shares will rise 50% next month. Although, the firm's share price is falling in this month. Because he predicts the firm's share price will rise 50% next month. So, he won't be influenced to sell his all 100 shares for the firm. He will sell all his shares to earn profit next month. The question is how he can predict the firm's share price when it will rise. I have some recommedation as below:
Predict Market Performance

There are two prices that are critical for any investor to know: the current price of the investment he or she owns or plans to own and its future selling price. Despite this, investors are constantly reviewing past pricing history and using it to influence their future investment decisions. Some investors won't buy a stock or index that has risen too sharply, because they assume it's due for a correction, while other investors avoid a falling stock because they fear it will continue to deteriorate. Does academic evidence support these types of predictions, based on recent pricing? In this article, we'll look at four different views of the market and learn more about the associated academic research that supports each view. The conclusions will help you better understand how the market functions and perhaps eliminate some of your own biases.
This widely quoted piece of stock market wisdom warns investors not to get in the way of market trends. The assumption is that the best bet about market movements is that they will continue in the same direction. This concept has its roots in behavioral finance. With so many stocks to choose from, why would investors keep their money in a stock that's falling, as opposed to one that's climbing? It's classic fear and greed. Studies have found that mutual fund inflows are positively correlated with market returns. Momentum plays a part in the decision to invest and when more people invest, the market goes up, encouraging even more people to buy. It's a positive feedback loop.

Mean Reversion

Experienced investors, who have seen many market ups and downs, often take the view that the market will even out, over time. Historically, high market prices often discourage these investors from investing, while historically low prices may represent an opportunity. The tendency of a variable, such as a stock price, to converge on an average value over time is called mean reversion. The phenomenon has been found in several economic indicators, which are useful to know, including exchange rates, gross domestic product (GDP) growth, interest rates, and unemployment. A mean reversion may also be responsible for business cycles.

The tendency of a variable, such as a stock price, to converge on an average value over time is called mean reversion. The phenomenon has been found in several economic indicators, which are useful to know, including exchange rates, gross domestic product (GDP) growth, interest rates, and unemployment. A mean reversion may also be responsible for business cycles.e jury is still out about whether stock prices revert to the mean. Some studies show mean reversion in some data sets over some periods, but many others do not. For example, in 2000, Ronald Balvers, Yangru Wu and Erik Gilliland found some evidence of mean reversion over long investment horizons, in the relative stock index prices of 18 countries. However, even they weren't completely convinced, as they wrote in their study, "A serious obstacle in detecting mean reversion is the absence of reliable long-term series, especially because mean-reversion, if it exists, is thought to be slow and can only be picked up over long horizons."

Martingales

Another possibility is that past returns just don't matter. In 1965, Paul Samuelson studied market returns and found that past pricing trends had no effect on future prices and reasoned that in an efficient market, there should be no such effect. His conclusion was that market prices are martingales.

A martingale is a mathematical series in which the best prediction for the next number is the current number. The concept is used in probability theory, to estimate the results of random motion. For example, suppose that you have $50 and bet it all on a coin toss. How much money will you have after the toss? You may have $100 or you may have $0 after the toss, but statistically, the best prediction is $50 -- your original starting position. The prediction of your fortunes after the toss is a martingale.

In stock option pricing, stock market returns could be assumed to be martingales. According to this theory, the valuation of the option does not depend on the past pricing trend, or on any estimate of future price trends. The current price and the estimated volatility are the only stock-specific inputs.

A martingale in which the next number is more likely to be higher is known as a sub-martingale. In popular literature, this motion is known as a random walk with upward drift. This description is consistent with more than 80 years of stock market pricing history. Despite many short-term reversals, the overall trend has been consistently higher.

If stock returns are essentially random, the best prediction for tomorrow's market price is simply today's price, plus a very small increase. Rather than focusing on past trends and looking for possible momentum or mean reversion, investors should instead concentrate on managing the risk inherent in their volatile investments.

The Search for Value

Value investors purchase stock cheaply and expect to be rewarded later. Their hope is that an inefficient market has underpriced the stock, but that the price will adjust over time. The question is: Does this happen, and why would an inefficient market make this adjustment?

Research suggests this mispricing and readjustment consistently happens, although it presents very little evidence for why it happens. In 1964, Gene Fama and Ken French studied decades of stock market history and developed the three-factor model to explain stock market prices. The most significant factor in explaining future price returns was valuation as measured by the price-to-book ratio (P/B). Stocks with low price-to-book ratios delivered significantly better returns than other stocks.

Valuation ratios tend to move in the same direction and in 1977, Sanjoy Basu found similar results for stocks with low price-earnings (P/E) ratios. Since then, the same effect has been found in many other studies across dozens of markets. However, studies have not explained why the market is consistently mispricing these "value" stocks and then adjusting later. The only conclusion that could be drawn is that these stocks have extra risk, for which investors demand additional compensation for taking extra risk. Price is the driver of the valuation ratios, therefore, the findings do support the idea of a mean-reverting stock market. As prices climb, the valuation ratios get higher and, as a result, future predicted returns are lower. However, the market P/E ratio has fluctuated widely over time and has never been a consistent buy or sell signal.

The Bottom Line

Even after decades of study by the brightest minds in finance, there are no solid answers. The only conclusion that can be drawn is that there may be some momentum effects, in the short term and a weak mean-reversion effect, in the long term.The current price is a key component of valuation ratios such as P/B and P/E, that have been shown to have some predictive power on the future returns of a stock. However, these ratios should not be viewed as specific buy and sell signals, but as factors that have been shown to play a role in increasing or reducing the expected long-term return.

All of above four kinds of calculation methods can be suitable to attempt to predict any share price variation whether it will rise or fall next month. The another method is that studying the firm's past financial performance. It is one good analysis method to attempt to predict its future share price variation from its past five to ten years performance.

Whether you are looking for good investments or are into stock trading, stock prediction or forecast plays the most crucial role in determining where to put in the money or which stock to be acquired or sold. Market trends often reflect the mood of the market and not essentially the status of a company or the true value of the stocks. It is often that stock prices soar based on external factors and it is not uncommon to find stock traders and investors to base their decisions on current affairs and market trends while trying to forecast the stock of any specific company. Stocks are volatile primarily owing to these reasons since external factors and popular beliefs are almost always based on no solid foundation. Consequentially, the stock prediction goes awry. The two stock forecasting methods any investor or stock trader must use are the Fundamental Research and Stock Forecast Algorithms.

Fundamental Research is a mandatory method for any investor. The method involves meticulous studying of a company's financial health, the value of assets, debts, cash, revenues, expenses, profitability and plans of development. Fundamental Research is a well rounded stock prediction method for all the data that actually matters are taken into consideration while determining the true value of a stock A company may generate healthy revenue but owing to huge expenses, they may not be highly profitable. It is common for a well performing company to sit on a pile of cash and not use it wisely in other investment or diversification avenues. Having all these statistics can be very handy for any investor. Once you have all this information, it is easy to determine if the value of a stock is overhyped or below par. Thus, it is easier to forecast the future of a stock and determine whether to acquire a stock or to sell one. Fundamental Research also helps an investor since it offers insights to dividends the company has been paying over the years and you can have some statistical stock prediction and not just volatility.

But knowing fundamentals is not enough. It is common for stocks to move in waves. Stocks always fluctuate between "oversold" and "overbought" conditions. These terms describe the changing demand or popularity, and are relative to the time frame and to other investment venues. When gold becomes popular, lots of investors get caught in the "Gold Rush" and forget the stock fundamentals and sell stocks to buy gold. They forget that gold does not make anything and just sits there. It's just a trophy, a protection against inflation at best. This is just one example of how different markets interact. Thus knowing the stock fundamentals is not enough. One can buy a good stock at the wrong time and lose money. Sure, eventually it should pay off, but meanwhile, you are in a deficit. Thus you have to be able to predict where the stock is heading.

Stock Forecast Algorithms are aimed at making the best use of the right time, right price and the right quantity of stocks that must be traded. The Algorithm in place helps a trader to forecast the time at which the price would be the most favorable to either buy or sell a stock. The system predicts absolutely on numbers and has not even remotely affected by popular emotions.

Finally, one should not get caught up in the daily trading, and miss out on global trends. This has been a decade of raise of China as the world's strongest growing economy, the fall of Europe and its Euro, and the crisis in the USA. The excesses of fiscal policy, the foolish flight of the US industry into the cheap labor countries, and the expensive wars have ravaged the economy and weakened the US dollar. But all this is behind us, and it seems that these trends have come to the stall. Will they reverse their course? All this requires us to look at the different time ranges of predictions, not only the next week predictions, but also the longer term forecasts. Don't assume that you will be lucky to get out in time. Downward corrections can come rather quickly and be sharper than the upward moves.

What are some mathematical methods which are used to predict stock price movement?

Can mathematical models beat markets? Science is about empirical fact. There is no question that optimistic people think they can beat the market, but they don't do it consistently with mathematical models. No model can consistently predict the future. It can't possibly be.

So what can math predict?

What you can do is predict the risk of a given event. The risk just means the chance that something bad will happen, for example. That you can do with increasing accuracy because we have more and more data. It's like insurance companies: they cannot tell you when you are going to die, but they can predict the risk that you will die given the right information. You can do the same thing with stocks. If you lose less, you get ahead of those who lose more.

Why do economists and "quants"—those who use quantitative analysis to make financial trades—have such faith in their mathematical models then?

If they're just to reduce risk, then they're very valuable. If you're worried, for example, about the segment of the Chinese economy that deals with steel, you make a model of what that whole market is all about and then you see if we did this what would likely happen. They're right some of the time. It's better than nothing. But when they have excessive faith in these models, it's not justified. Math starts with assumptions; the real world does not work that way. Economics, which calls itself a science, too often doesn't start with looking at empirical facts in any great detail. Fifteen years ago even the idea of looking at huge amounts of data did not exist. With a limited amount of data, the chance of a rare event is very low, which gave some economists a false sense of security that long-tail events did not exist.

Why do you argue that financial markets are ruled not by Gaussian functions but by power laws—relations in which the frequency of one event varies as a power of some attribute of that event and are generally more L-shape than bell shape? For anything that is random and fluctuating, like a financial market, a Gaussian function is a wonderful way to make a histogram of the outcome.

The catch is: in a financial market, everything is correlated. The proof of that is that if the stock market were Gaussian, then you'd never have a flash crash. A Gaussian crash would be an event that goes out to maybe five standard deviations [that is, a rarity on par with one part in two million]. In markets, this is simply not true. There are events that are 100 standard deviations. Every economist knows for sure that these rare events occur and cannot be described by a Gaussian function. The question is: What are you going to do about it?

Power math laws are simply way more accurate. If you don't know the risk, you are not going to make the right decision, and the economy is at risk from these big fluctuations. It's no surprise when they come. The only reason you have to wait awhile is because they are rare. Knowing that they will happen forces anyone prudent to have a plan for what to do if it happens. The idea that it would be a power law that describes all the events, the tails and the middle is really a major contribution. It allows one to quantify risk. You can read off a plot of the law the numerical chance for a downturn of any given size. It's very small for something that is 100 standard deviations out but not so small for something that is 10 standard deviations out. In fact, the S&P 500 fluctuations—which if they were Gaussian, would pretty much be constrained to plus or minus five standard deviations—you find, in a 10-year period, the number of events that exceed five standard deviations is not just one, it's 64. And the number that exceeds 10 standard deviations is eight, and there was one event that exceeded 20 standard deviations. It looks like a power law, and that's what it is demonstrated to be when every trade of every stock is analyzed.

Does this understanding of financial markets suggest anything about how to invest, like when to buy or sell? It can't predict the future. The key thing is that it tells you not to listen to those who tell you now is the time to buy or sell if their advice is based on something wrong, as it sometimes is.

Is this all a result of the interlinked global financial system?I believe so. The finances of every country are interlinked to the finances of every other country and, because they are interlinked, if one key players goes down then the other players know things aren't going to be as good. A useful analogy is coupled networks, which are far more susceptible to a cascade of failures than uncoupled networks.

Can anything predict the market? Let me tell you a story: two to the power of 10 is 1,024. One way to predict the market is to call up 1,024 trading places and tell half of them by week's end the market will be up and the other half that the market will be down. At the end of the week, forget about the half that knows you were wrong. Keep doing that for 10 weeks and, at the end, you will have called the market correctly for one person who will think you are a genius. The economy is a very complex system—like the weather—that we understand bits of. You sure as heck can't decide on a Monday whether the weather will be nice on the coming weekend. No one can predict where the market will be at the end of the week.

For math prediction to share price variation example:

The best model we have to predict stock price movements is the Random

Walk model.

R(t+1) = R(t) + e

It basically states that returns on a stock tomorrow can be calculated using the return today plus an error term. An error term is the deviation of reality from your model that cannot be calculated by your model. If it was possible to be calculated, it should have been integrated into your model. This answer tells you nothing except the fact that stock prices are a result of multiple variables, some of which cannot be quantified (sentiment premiums).

Unfortunately, the accuracy of any mathematical model to predict the stock price movement is lower. However, you can use a concept of statistical arbitrage where you predict the relative value of the stock price compared to another stock price. For instance, you can trade on the difference (spread) between prices of two stocks which are cointegrated and use a mathematical model or historical data to predict if the spread is high or low and trade accordingly. An example of a portfolio of possibly cointegrated stocks is the spread between gold ETF (GLD) and gold miners ETF (GDX). The new series "GLD - GDX" forms a stationary portfolio and gives us an opportunity to create a mean-reverting strategy: buy when the spread is low and sell when the spread is high.

Hence, it is very difficult to predict a stock price in the future with more than 10% certainty. Anything above that confidence interval is overestimation of your abilities and pure luck. t seems that investors can attempt to apply math method to predict share price when changes, although it may have wrong chance to estimate the price changes to rise or fall price absolutely. However, it can conclude the minimum price estimation in error to compare the share investor himself/herself personal judgement to the share price.

Comparative advantage

Comparative advantage is when a country produces a good or service for a lower opportunity cost than other countries. Opportunity cost measures a trade-off. A nation with a comparative advantage makes the trade-off worth it. The benefits of buying its good or service outweigh the disadvantages. The country may not be the best at producing something. But the good or service has a low opportunity cost for other countries to import. For example, oil-producing nations have a comparative advantage in chemicals. Their locally-produced oil provides a cheap source of material for the chemicals when compared to countries without it. A lot of the raw ingredients are produced in the oil distillery process. As a result, Saudi Arabia, Kuwait, and Mexico are competitive with U.S. chemical production firms. Their chemicals are inexpensive, making their opportunity cost low. Another example is India's call centers. U.S. companies buy this service because it is cheaper than locating the call center in America. Indian call centers aren't better than U.S. call centers. Their workers don't always speak English very clearly. But they provide the service cheaply enough to make the tradeoff worth it.

In the past, comparative advantages occurred more in goods and rarely in services. That's because products are easier to export. But telecommunication technology like the internet is making services easier to export. Those services include call centers, banking, and entertainment.

The theory of comparative advantage explains why trade protectionism doesn't work in the long run. Political leaders are always under pressure from their local constituents to protect jobs from international competition by raising tariffs. But that's only a temporary fix. In the long run, it hurts the nation's competitiveness. It allows the country to waste resources on unsuccessful industries. It also forces consumers to pay higher prices to buy domestic goods.

David Ricardo started out as a successful stockbroker, making $100 million in today's dollars. After reading Adam Smith's "The Wealth of Nations," he became an economist. He was the first person to point out that significant increases in the money supply create inflation. This theory is known as monetarism. He also developed the law of diminishing marginal returns. That's one of the essential concepts in microeconomics. It states that there is a point in production where the increased output is no longer worth the additional input in raw materials. Investment in human capital is critical to maintaining a comparative advantage in the knowledge-based global economy.

Comparative Advantage Versus Absolute Advantage

Absolute advantage is anything a country does more efficiently than other countries. Nations that are blessed with an abundance of farmland, fresh water, and oil reserves have an absolute advantage in agriculture, gasoline, and petrochemicals. Just because a country has an absolute advantage in an industry doesn't mean that it will be its comparative advantage. That depends on what the trading opportunity costs are. Say its neighbor has no oil but lots of farmland and fresh water. The neighbor is willing to trade a lot of food in exchange for oil. Now the first country has a comparative advantage in oil. It can get more food from its neighbor by trading it for oil than it could produce on its own.

Comparative Advantage Versus Competitive Advantage

Competitive advantage is what a country, business, or individual does that provide a better value to consumers than its competitors. There are three strategies companies use to gain a competitive advantage. First, they could be the low-cost provider. Second, they could offer a better product or service. Third, they could focus on one type of customer.

Competitive advantage applies to e-commerce

Nowadays, many businesses are international trading, due to globalization and opening of markets. E-commerce will be the most popular advertisement and sale method to help any kinds of businesses to promote products to let many clients to know effectively in short time. However, e-ecommerce will bring new organizational structure change to help any organizations to improve performance management, organizational development, and continuous and cumulative process of improvement of multi-national companies, when the organization can have e-commerce sale strategy. I believe that the e-commerce sale strategy can help any organizations to raise sale growth more easily. I shall explain the reasons as below:

On innovation and e-service quality for developing e-retailing mass entrepreneurship aspect, it can bring rapid sale growth advantage to the e-commerce organization, it also needs the business leader has clear vision to create and maintain his learning organization, such as the e-commerce learning organization, e.g. Amazon is a successful e-learning, e-commerce learning organization. It is a e-retailing middleman to help any businesses to sell and delivery their products to clients' homes. When any clients click Amazon website, they can find any kinds of products, e.g. travel bags, computers, books and magazines, movie and music CD, DCD, home, electronic and health etc. products. So, after they paid visa to buy its any its any kinds of products from its website. Then, Amazon will deliver these products to their homes within one week. It can provide rapid product delivery service to let them to feel sale and after sale service satisfactory feeling. Hence, Amazon is a good example of continuous learning in its organizational life, a process helps self understanding, self management and self actualization e-commerce organization. However, Amazon' successful factors can concern on innovation and delivery efficient service, skillful online sale and online management skills are its main successful factors.

Moreover, Amazon can apply psychological knowledge to assist workers to raise industrialized efficiency . It can s managers ought know how help every worker to create talent ability and co-operate to work efficiently in teams during innovation process.

In fact, product technique innovation will be another factor to raise any businesses' competitive effort, e.g. reducing cost benefit aim. So, when the organization can raise new productive technique to help them to reduce manufacturing cost. Then, it will reduce finance burden to the organization for long time. Hence, learning low cost e-service
technique will be one main factor to stable any organizations' existence or alive in long time.

IN business environment, since internet is popular, it can influence customers shopping method to be changed to online purchase channel. So, e-commerce can replace traditional walk-in store purchase channel. Online purchase can bring these benefits to consumers, such as rapid product information search, visa card payment method, safe and quiet home environment purchasing activities, free product delivery and return or refund after sale service conveniently. Moreover, e-commerce or e-retailing business can bring more business activities with more economic growth and supporting technological manufacturing development.

How to attract or encourage consumers' online shopping consumption desires? It is one very important view point, because when one consumer has online shopping desire, then he will have online shopping or buying activity to find the e-retailer's website to click from its website in possible. So, any e-retailers must need to excite their potential online consumers have e-platforms click in their websites to search products desires or needs in preference more than walk in stores to search products method on street. However, I believe that their online product photos whether are attractive or their wirelesses are high or rapid mobile linking speed will influence their online businesses in success. So, online e-service and wireless rapid speed performances will influence every online retailer individual success or fail, instead of product photos whether are clear or information search whether is rapid or enough and sale price whether is low or reasonable and after sale support performance whether is satisfactory factors. So, e-service quality, e-platform, e-product photo and search information performance these will be main factor to influence whether the e-retailer's sale growth. For example, Amazon book company is one famous and successful online e-book publisher among of the similar online e-book publishers, instead of

itself e-middleman product delivery service provision to global buyers. It's success is due to its e-technology is often innovated in product delivery service, such as it has both efficiency after sale service and product delivery departments, of rapid delivery products to any countries' buyers within several days only, e-mail or phone feedback
to every e-buyer's enquiry, such as it organizes different kinds of enquiry questions to let its indicated staffs to answer the kind of indicated enquiry question only. So, its enquiring department staffs can avoid to spend much time to find answers to solve any enquires. In management view, it is " division of labours" concept to be used in Amazon customer service department. Also, it has large warehouse, it applied robotics to help warehouses to find and delivery any kinds of products to the correct delivery positions in order to delivery the product to the client's destination in the short time. So, robotics had help Amazon to reduce warehouse staffs' times and raises efficiencies in warehouses. When the warehouse workers can receive the client name and address and product kind and product purchase number data from its Amazon website e-retail store channel. Then, its warehouse staffs can follow these data to let robotics to know where they need to arrive to find the product(s) and deliver them to the right positions and let the lorry drivers to deliver to either airport (overseas buyers) or local destination (home country buyers). So, e-service quality performance will influence Amazon's product delivery or after sale service performance.

What does e-commerce bring positive or negative impact to traditional publish industry? it seems that e-commerce has an important influence to impact traditional book shop publish industry. Nowadays, due to many publishers begin to choose to apply e-platform to help any publishers themselves to sell their books either e-book format or paper book format. SO, many readers can read e-books from e-book shop or book shops do not need authors to print lot of paper books to put in warehouses before. Because any book shops can apply their e-book store to let readers to choose any topic books from their e-publishing stores , then they can pay visa either to read e-book from their e-book platform or e-library or print the number paper books to be delivered to their homes. So, publishers do not need to print many books for every author before none any readers pay to buy their books from walk-in book stores. It means that the publisher do not need any traditional walk-in book shops to let them to visit, because the reader can click to the publisher's e-platform and he find any book

information to chose which book(s) , he want to buy. He can pay visa to choose either read e-book from its e-platform or e-library or print on demand. So, the warehouse won't have excess book stocks to be kept in warehouses often and the printing costs will decrease as well as
none any old books to need to reduce price to sell because there has none any books stores to be kept in warehouses. So, it can bring waste warehouse places and waste paper printing economic and reducing sale price economic benefits to the e-publisher and readers both, such as Amazon publisher is using this e-service performance method.

E-commerce had changed the young age and female and male sex consumers shopping attitude. Bigne, Enrique (2005) indicated that the main users of online shopping were young men with a high level of income and a university education. This profile is changing. For example, in USA in the early years of internet where were very few women users, but by 2001 year, women were 52.8% of the online population . Socio-cultural pressure has made men generally more independent in their purchase decisions, when women place greater value on personal contact and social relations.
What is the main factor to bring some e-retailers' success. I believe that how to innovate e-service quality, which will be the main successful factor. The reasons may include as below:

There are too many e-retailers sell their products in this e-platform market. So, competition is serious. If one e-retailer could innovate its e-service performance, then its e-service quality will let its online visitors to fell its e-platform or e-store is more unique to compare its similar competitors. It will bring more attractive to raise its competitive ability.

Falk(2005) explained gave these useful opinions for your reference. They may include: The main idea of online shopping is not in having a good looking website that could be listed in a lot of search engines and it is not about the act behind the site ; it also is not only just not disseminating information, because it is all about building relationships and making money; mostly, organizations try to adopt techniques of online shopping without understanding these techniques and/or without a sound business model; rather than supporting the organization's culture and brand name, the website should satisfy customer's expectations; a majority of consumers choose online shopping for faster and more efficient shopping experience; many researchers notify that the uniqueness of the web has dissolved and the need for the design, which will be user centered is very important; companies should always remember that there are certain things, such as

understanding
the customer's wants and needs, living up to promises, never go out of style, because they give reason to come back. All of his opinions concern how to innovate the e-service quality
in order to atract many e-visitors to the e-retailer's website or e-platform or e-store more easily.

As Mc Donaldization theory can be used in terms of online shopping case, because online shopping and Mc Donald restaurant was becoming more popular. Such as Mc Donaldization is one global restaurant business, it has four major principles: efficiency, calculability, predictability and control. So they have similar views, any e-retailers' e-service quality need include: How to predict their e-visitors' online shopping desire absolutely, if they can raise their e-shopping desires, then their sale chance will increase; efficient wireless
speed, after e-sale service provision, efficient warehouse e-client data rapid receipt information for product rapid deliviery service arrangement and avoiding delivery error occurrence;
calculate e-visitor click in website times and controlling they desire to click their websites long time in order to increase shopping transaction occurrence chance and increase visa payment amount and the different kinds of products purchases number.

Why does e-service need to be innovated? Invitation can improve performance, raise productivity, increase yield and output and create growth as well as it can reduce waste, minimize
environment damages. Parasuraman, Zeithaml, and Berry (1988) showed that e-service quality is the strategy that is gaining momentum for online business operators to position themselves
more effectively in the marketplace. Because when any e-visitors click to any e-retailers' websites, they will compare any one e-retailer's website performance, if they feel comfortable
or better emotion to the e-retailer's website. Then, they will be attracted to choose to click the e-retailer's website one more time again, even more times. SO, how to let e-consumers
feel the e-retailer's website is unique or different to other general e-retailers' websites .(differentiates products or services, differentiation comes from the e-retailer's
website name, e.g. http://www.topicecream.com for the ice cream food, unique website design, packaging and delivery service use of wireless speed

technology, unique features , e.g. attracting online shopping process, not complex or simple to research any products informatio from the e-retailer's website, extraordinary customer service, e.g. rapid customer enquiry feedback, take care after e-sale delivery service. All of these are important factors to cause any e-retailers' successes. Hence, it the e-retailer can have unique e-service provision to let any e-visitors to fee. Then, I believe that their product sale price can still keep higher and their customer number will not be influenced to reduce when they choose e-platform to sell their products.

Moreover, the e-retailing website managers need to build good learning insights to predict e-consumer behaviors. Such as consumers' living ways, life style, quality of life, service quality , inspiration, innovation, creativity, curiosity, design thinking, execution. Because when the e-retailer's website managers can have good analysis to judge whether what reasons or factors can influence his e-consumers choose to buy ot not buy his products after they click in whose website store. What reasons cause they change their traditional walk in shops shopping habits. So, how to persuade walk-in consumers to choose to click in the e-retailer's website store. If the e-retailer can persuade them to increase click in whose website times. Then, its online transaction will increase more easily. Hence, it has relationship between click in the e-retailer's website times and the e-service performance innovation.

- Building customer loyalty to online electronic manufacturing services e-commerce industry

Customer loyalty is critical to the success of an electronic manufacturing services. Internet invention can bring electronic manufacturing development. However, electronic manufacturing businessmen need to research these question in order to develop in success: What are the most common factors as well as the critical successful factors affect buyer loyalty ?

In fact, customer loyalty means to relate to consumer buying behaviors, such as electronic manufacturing service industry, if the electronic manufacturing service provider can provide satisfactory electronic manufacturing service to any consumers or it can build good global customer relationship from internet by website advertisement and e-mail communication both channels.

In technological aspect, such as rapid speed internet access, PC household penetration. Hence, when one online client can click the electronic manufacturing company website. Then, he can find many attractive electronic manufacturing product from the internet clear electronic manufacturing product photos. When, he can research any kinds of electronic manufacturing products from the company's website easily and he also feels the photos can show their characteristics or features , e.g. colour, size, price indicated. Then, he can understand every electronic manufacturing product clearly. So, the online bring successful chance will increase, even if the company can provide good enquiry service to him, when he sends email to enquire the individual customer service staff and he can answer his enquiry immediately by the company's email.

In general , because any electronic products are usually small size, to their photos must have large size to let any online visitors to see every electronic parts of every electronic product photo in the e-commerce company website. Every online visitor also needs to know every electronic manufacturing product from every photo, e.g. whether the electronic manufacturing product (laptop or desktop) has discount, how much discount percentage, e.g. 20% and original price and after discount price information from the company website. Hence, every electronic product photo needs to let any online visitors to know all of price information from itself company website clearly. If every can not indicate actual clear price information that will influence their buying decision to be delayed. So, buying transaction will not succeed easily. So, e-ecommerce on electronic manufacturing product industry , it will be more difficult to achieve transaction success from internet channel. If the company can not show its any electronic manufacturing products to let every online visitor to feel understanding clearly.

On conclusion, good quality technological factor will be important to influence electronic manufacturing products e-commerce in success. One repeat online ecommerce electronic manufacturing product buyer who must need to feel much understanding to every electronic product features and characteristics from every firm's website online photos, price issues when he see those photos from the company's website. So, the online electronic manufacturing product buyers' loyalty is built on technological service quality, on time delivery service , past satisfactory or dissatisfactory online search experience to the firm's website, technological and unique website attraction to the firm's website of E-service quality innovation successful factor will influence any e-retailer's success.

New trade theory explains e-commerce influencess China " one belt, one road " strategy comparative advanages

New trade theory (NTT) suggests that a critical factor in determining international patterns of trade are the very substantial economies of scale and network effects that can occur in key industries.

These economies of scale and network effects can be so significant that they outweigh the more traditional theory of comparative advantage. In some industries, two countries may have no discernible differences in opportunity cost at a particular point in time. But, if one country specialises in a particular industry then it may gain economies of scale and other network benefits from its specialisation.

Another element of new trade theory is that firms who have the advantage of being an early entrant can become a dominant firm in the market. This is because the first firms gain substantial economies of scale meaning that new firms can't compete against the incumbent firms. This means that in these global industries with very large economies of scale, there is likely to be limited competition, with the market dominated by early firms who entered, leading to a form of monopolistic competition.

Monopolistic competition is an important element of New Trade Theory, it suggests that firms are often competing on branding, quality and not just simple price. It explains why countries can both export and import designer clothes. This means that the most lucrative industries are often dominated in capital-intensive countries, who were the first to develop these industries. Therefore, being the first firm to reach industrial maturity gives a very strong competitive advantage. (some may say unfair advantage)

New trade theory also becomes a factor in explaining the growth of globalisation. It means that poorer, developing economies may struggle to ever develop certain industries because they lag too far behind the economies of scale enjoyed in the developed world. This is not due to any intrinsic comparative advantage, but more the economies of scale the developed firms already have.

Examples of New Trade Theory

•Specialisation of IT in Silicon Valley – the US. Hewlett and Packard started their computer business. Success attracted more IT firms to that area. Not because of any particular intrinsic benefit but new firms start to get the network benefits of being around other IT setups.'

•Globalisation has led to increased variety for consumers. The proliferation of brand clothing labels. Firms competing in the model of monopolistic competition and heavy branding. Neither UK or Italy has a particular comparative advantage in producing clothes, but consumers are attracted to brand image of Italian and British fashion labels.

Competitive advantage applies to
Globalization e-commerce
Development brings
China " one belt, one road
Strategy" advantages

Globalization can bring China " one belt, one road strategy" global social economic advantages, such as China's 21 St. century " one belt , one road strategy. It aims to bring the different Asia countries, even Western countries' business cooperation more easily after it had built high speed railway to go to different countries which had road transport to link to China on land. So, in long term benefits, China businessmen can cooperate to these participative "one belt, one road strategy businessmen to carry on buying and selling their unique products from road transport conveniently. Even, e-commerce can bring important economic advantages to influence this " one belt, one road strategy " in success. I shall explain the reasons that why e-commerce can bring business advantages to them as below:

China's "one belt, one road strategy " aims to achieve the global world share GNP 55% , as well as global consumer number of 77% and global energy saves 75%. Instead of existing trading investment, China also compromises to provide US one hundred billion dollar of basic facility fund, central Asia one belt, one road strategy fund of forty billion US dollar to invest this "one belt, one road strategy" of long term business development. I believe that it seems that China only hopes to build railway facility and encourage the participative countries to build factories to invest to do businesses between China and these countries as well as create jobs to solve China unemployment ratio, but in fact, I believe that China will apply e-commerce technology to assist its businessmen to do online trading more easily. I shall indicate the reasons to explain that why e-commerce and China 's one belt, one road strategy , they have close economic growth of case and effect relationship.

China will be only one globalization main essential " one belt, one road strategy" country to control all participative countries' businessmen activities and China can help the excess of developing countries' economic development in the same tie. In fact, internet can assist China's future economic development. The reason is that I believe that when China's " one belt, one road strategy " can develop to succeed. It can encourage many " one belt, one road strategy" participative countries businessmen to be persuaded to apply internet technology to do e-commerce in the same time after the railway transport facilities are built to let all of these participative countries businessmen can transport their products to their cities from road transport more easily and rapidly. So, it can being short time product transport advantages when the participative country's consumers buy the product from the online platform as well as the product can be delivered to his home from railway transport rapidly. So, e-commerce and railway transport has close relationship to cause this business activities in success. For example, one Asia "one belt, one road strategy country's participative businessman , he can apply e-commerce technology to sell its products to Western countries , e.g. US, UK online clients in short time rapidly.

The participative countries may include India, Greece, Serbia, Hungary etc. 66 countries. So, these one belt, one road strategy participative countries can cooperate to do e-commerce business to sell themselves unique products to the non-participative "one belt, one road strategy" countries from e-commerce channel. When these non-participative " one belt, one road strategy " countries consumers have none of the kinds products to buy from themselves countries, but they click to these participative " one belt, one road strategy" countries participation businessmen themselves web stores to find the kinds of products which can buy from their web stores. Then, they can apply online to buy the products from these one belt, one road strategy countries' businessmen web stores more easily and conveniently in short time. The important factor is railway transport, when these products can be delivered from railway from China to these participative countries. For example, when one participative country businessman , he has none of this kind of product to sell to the US or US client, but he apply internet channel to click to the China businessman's web store to find the kind of product that he can sell. SO, he can apply internet channel to buy the Chins business's product after he pays visa. The China e-retailer can deliver the kind of product to his store by railway transport rapidly. Railway transport can reduce the transport cost , when the e-retailer (buyer) does not need to pays air freight fee. It is more cheap transport cost. Then, the participative " one belt, one road strategy " e-retailer can deliver the kind of product to the US, or UK buyer by air transport rapidly when he find the kind of product which can be provided from the China e-retailer from online channel immediately. So, railway building and e-commerce channel will influence the " one belt, one road strategy " in success.

The 21 St century sea transport considers different countries consumers' buying need when they feel that they can not buy the kinds of products from themselves countries easily. So, such as the participative " one belt, one road strategy" countries , they can transport their products between China and themselves countries by railway transport, then the sea transport will not be popular to help them to deliver their products because sea transport delivery speed must be slower than railway transport. Any consumers won't hope to receive their products in long transport time. So, railway transport must be one important transport factor to influence China 's "one belt, one road strategy" in success.

Moreover, e-commerce invention can help these participative " one belt, one road strategy" countries e-retailers to apply web stores sale channel to cooperate to sell their unique products between them. When one country e-retailer can buy the another country retailer 's product from web store and it can be delivered to its country by railway transport , then it can still supply the kind of product to the e-consumer , even it has non any of this kind of product stock in its warehouse. Railway transport can help them to deliver their products from road in short time between China and these participative countries. So, they must have geographic advantage to deliver their products rapidly after railway transport facilities are built successfully between China and these countries. Moreover, web store can help them to advertise their products to let the non-participative "one belt, one road strategy" countries consumers to know whether which kinds of products these participative countries e-retailers , they can sell from themselves web stores when they click to their websites to see their product photos immediately.

So, China's " one belt, one road strategy" can influence to achieve global online ecommerce advantage for China and the participative " one belt, one road strategy 66 countries e-retailers and e-commerce can help them to promote their any products to Western countries to let they to know in short time rapidly.

ON currency gain benefit aspect, in fact, e-commerce can help this " one belt, one road strategy" participative countries earn exchange rate transaction more easily because when the non-participative " one belt, one road strategy " countries consumers pay visa to buy their products from their web stores. Usually, they need to pay US dollar to buy their products by visa card for every online transaction. So, when these participative "one belt, one road strategy" online e-retailers receive their US payment by visa. They have more currency earn chance when US dollar needs to exchange high local exchange to their dollar. So, the currency exchange earn will have possible to occur from e-commerce. For example, when one e-US consumer buys one product from the China's online e-retailer , when the e-US consumer pays US currency to buy it by visa. Then, the China E-RETAILER can receive the US currency sale profit and change to Chinese dollar to earn the foreign exchange income when it find decides to change the US currency to Chinese currency in the right time.

So, e-commerce globalization can also raise foreign exchange earn chance between the countries' online consumers and the another e-retailers when they are carrying any e-commerce activities. Hence, e-commerce can assist the China's " one belt, one road strategy" development more success between Asia and Western countries.

However, the internet development can help China's 21 St century " one belt, one road strategy" to achieve these aspects of development, instead of e-commerce development. The five major achievements are such as , 1. Policy coordination, 2. Facilities connectivity, 3. Going out trade, 4. Financial integration, increased economic performance and productivity and 5. Encouraging people to people e-commerce transaction. Because internet development can help any countries consumers to search new products information as well as helping them to cooperate to analyze and achieving the best effective and efficient online shopping activities. So, it may reduce the incentives and opportunities for terrorist movement. Such as Beijing is becoming a top salesman city to promote the China made products and in big discount with some conditions when to achieve the global of made in China e-commerce in " one belt, one road strategy" 2025. ON conclusion, internet invention can help China and the 66 participative one belt, one road strategy" countries to gather any new products information as well as discusses how they can operate do this global e-commerce in success. Nowadays, the world is focus on the China movement on the one belt, one road strategy, how impact of the international financial crisis keeps rapidly, the world economy is recovering slowly, and global development is uneven. So, internet development can encourage the international trade and investment for the participative one belt and one road strategy countries and even these countries still facing big challenges to their e-commerce development. So, internet can assist the one belt, one road strategy cooperative countries' information exchange to achieve success. Internet can help them to bring an economic area through building infrastructure, increasing culture exchange and broadening global e-commerce development. This innovative conceptual strategy will bring China to take a bigger role in global affairs and it is an easy way to let China to export China's reserve products in area of " over production" , such as electrical appliances, steel aluminum , railway equipment and building's material manufacturing between China and the participative countries by railway transport. Internet can help it to apply e-commerce channel to promote its material products to let overseas buyers to know from their web stores in short time. So, internet can bring successful advertisement promotion development to China and the 66 participative one belt, one road countries on overseas online e-commerce sale chance absolutely. Finally, internet can also bring further deepening and expanding beneficial cooperation in such areas as trade, investment, finance, transport and communication aspects to these participative one belt, one road strategy countries. For China example, it is the world's largest producer of gold and also major importer and consumer. It can apply e-commerce trading method to promote its gold products to global gold buyers from the gold sellers' web stores in short time. When the country's one gold buyer research the China's one gold online retailer web store to find its quality and appearance is more attractive to compare his country gold shops. Then, he will pay visa to buy the China gold e-retailer's gold from its web store by visa immediately. So, e-commerce can help China's gold e-retailers to promote their gold products to let global gold buyers to know from their web stores in the short time. Hence, global e-commerce activity can help China to promote products and increase sale chance in short time after its one, belt, one road strategy can implement to achieve successfully.

Reference

Cornelia, B.F. (1999) Rural development news, the North Central Regional Center For Rural Development vol. no 24 , IOWA.

David J. Nowak & Gordon M. Melsler (2016) " Air quality effects of urban trees and parks." National recreation and park association, USA.

De Hollander, A. E. M., J.M. Melse, Elebret & P. G.N. Kramers (1999), " An Aggregate public health indicator to represent the impact of multiple

environmental exposures" Epidemiology: 606-617.
Felce, D. and Perry, J. (1995). Quality of life: A contribution to its definition and measurement,vol. 16, no.1 pp: 51-74.
Los Angeles Country Department Of public Health (2016), Country Health Ranking Model, Retrieved From
www.countryhealthrankgings.org/our-approach. USA.

Melse, J.M. & A.E. M. De Hollander (2001). " Human Health And The Environment", background document for the OECD Environmental Outlook, OECD, Paris.

McGregor, S.L. T., & Goldsmith, E.B. (1998). Expanding our understanding of quality of life, standard of living and well- being. Journal of family and consumer science, 90(2), 2-6, 22.
McMichael, A.J. M. Mckee, J. Shkolnikov and T. Valkanen (2004), " Morality trends and setbacks, global convergence or divergence?", Lancet 363, 1155-1159.

Yale Center For Environmental Law And Policy(2006). Environmental Performance Index. Data available on-line at http://epi.yale.edu

Reference

Cone, J. D. and Hayes, S. C., (1980) Environmental Problems/Behavioral Solutions. Monterey, CA: Brooks/Cole.

Erekson, O.H., Loucks, O.L. Strafford, N.C. 1999.
The context of sustainability . In: Sustainability
perspectives for resources and business
USA, p. 3-21.

Daly, H.E. 1990, Towards some operational
principles of sustainable development,
ecological economics, 2(1), 1-6.

Guerts, M. D. (1986) "The 'bottle bill' effect on grocery stores' costs," International J ournal of Retailing, 1, 12-17.

Kirkby, J; O' Keefe P., Timberlake, L. (eds.) 1995.
The earthscan reader in sustainable development.
Earthscan Publications Ltd., London, 1-14p.

Skinner, B. F. (1953) Science and Human Behavior, NY: Macmillan.

Winkler, R. C. and Winett, R. A. (1982) "Behavioral interventions in resource conservation: a systems approach based on behavioral economics,"

American Psychologist 37: 421-435.

Reference

Sustainable energy for ALL (SE4ALL) initiative, United Nations secretary. http://www.sustainableenergyforall.org

Towards a green economy pathways to sustainable development and poverty eradication. Unites Nations Environment program (UNEP), 2011 http://www.unep.org/greeneconomy

World energy outlook, executive summary, p.7 IEA , 2012

References and Further Reading

Camerer, C., Loewenstein, G., & Prelec, D. (2005) Neuroeconomics: How neuroscience can inform economics. Journal of Economic Literature, 43, 9-64.

Coulter, K. S., & Coulter, R. A. (2005). Size does matter: The effects of magnitude representation congruency on price perceptions and purchase likelihood. Journal of Consumer Psychology, 15(1), 64–76.

Diamond, A. (2013). Executive functions. Annual Review of Psychology, 64, 135-168.

Diclemente, C. C., Marinilli, A. S., Singh, M., & Bellino, L. E., (2001). The role of feedback in the process of health behavior change. American Journal of Health Behavior, 25, 217-227.

Dolan, P., Hallsworth, M., Halpern, D., King, D., & Vlaev, I. (2010). MINDSPACE: Influencing behaviour through public policy. London, UK: Cabinet Office.

Finucane, M. L., Alhakami, A., Slovic, P., & Johnson, S. M. (2000). The affect heuristic in judgments of risks and benefits. Journal of Behavioral Decision Making, 13, 1-17.

Golman, R., Hagmann, D., & Loewenstein, G. (2017). Information avoidance. Journal of Economic Literature, 55(1), 96-135.

Iyengar, S., & Lepper, M. (2000). When choice is demotivating: Can one desire too much of a good thing? Journal of Personality and Social Psychology, 79, 995-1006.

Kahneman, D. (2011). Thinking, fast and slow. London: Allen Lane.

Loewenstein, G. (2000). Emotions in economic theory and economic behavior. The American Economic Review, 90(2), 426-432.

Rick, S. I. (2018). Tightwads and spendthrifts: An interdisciplinary review. Financial Planning Review, 1(1-2), e1010. Retrieved from https://doi.org/10.1002/cfp2.1010.

Schwartz, B. (2004). The paradox of choice: Why more is less. New York:

Ecco.

Sullivan, P. S., Lansky, A., & Drake, A. (2004). Failure to return for HIV test results among persons at high risk for HIV infection: Results from a multistate interview project. JAIDS Journal of Acquired Immune Deficiency Syndromes, 35(5), 511–518.

Thaler, R. H. (1990). Anomalies: Saving, fungibility, and mental accounts. The Journal of Economic Perspectives, 4, 193-205.

Thaler, R. H., & Johnson, E. J. (1990). Gambling with the house money and trying to break even: The effects of prior outcomes on risky choice. Management Science, 36(6), 643-660.

Thorndike, A. N., Sonnenberg, L., Riis, J., Barraclough, S., & Levy, D. E. (2012). A 2- phase labeling and choice architecture intervention to improve healthy food and beverage choices. American Journal of Public Health, 102(3), 527-533.

Tversky, A., & Kahneman, D. (1974). Judgment under uncertainty: Heuristics and biases. Science (New Series), 185, 1124-1131.

Zellermayer, O. (1996). The pain of paying. (Doctoral dissertation). Department of Social and Decision Sciences, Carnegie Mellon University, Pittsburgh, PA.

www.ingramcontent.com/pod-product-compliance
Ingram Content Group UK Ltd.
Pitfield, Milton Keynes, MK11 3LW, UK
UKHW022025190726
13853UKWH00005B/2110

9 798886 060270